NAKED TO MINE ENEMIES

Volume One NAKED TO

CHARLES W. FERGUSON

MINE ENEMIES

The Life of Cardinal Wolsey

With a new introduction
by A. L. Rowse

TIME Reading Program Special Edition
TIME INCORPORATED
NEW YORK

TIME
LIFE
BOOKS

EDITOR *Norman P. Ross*
TEXT DIRECTOR *William Jay Gold*
ART DIRECTOR *Edward A. Hamilton*
CHIEF OF RESEARCH *Beatrice T. Dobie*
ASSISTANT TEXT DIRECTOR *Jerry Korn*

EDITOR, TIME READING PROGRAM *Max Gissen*
RESEARCHER *Ann S. Lang*
DESIGNER *Brigitte Hanf*

PUBLISHER *Rhett Austell*
GENERAL MANAGER *Joseph C. Hazen Jr.*

TIME MAGAZINE
EDITOR *Roy Alexander*
MANAGING EDITOR *Otto Fuerbringer*
PUBLISHER *Bernhard M. Auer*

COVER DESIGN *Louis Di Valentin*

WOLSEY AT ABOUT THE AGE OF FORTY

The original of this drawing, quite possibly by a Flemish artist, was probably painted about the time of Wolsey's visit to Flanders in 1513, two years before he became Cardinal. It bears a contemporary inscription: "Thomas Vulsey Cardinal dyork" and (in a later hand) "autheur du schisme."

Had I but served my God with half the zeal
I served my King, He would not in mine age
Have left me naked to mine enemies.

—SHAKESPEARE
King Henry VIII, Act III, Scene 2

(Based on words spoken by Wolsey
immediately before his death.)

CONTENTS

In which is pictured the early life of Thomas Wolsey and the world of which he was a part; his years at Oxford; his unhappy activities as a young priest; his various employments at Canterbury and Calais; and his acceptance at the court of Henry VII.

Setting forth the rise of Wolsey in the reign of Henry VIII; the stupendous failure and disgrace of his first venture for his King and the amazing accomplishments of his second; his roles as judge, as Church reformer, as educator, as builder of palaces, and as diplomat; the triumph of his policy of friendship with France at the Field of Cloth of Gold.

*CHARLES W.
FERGUSON*

EDITORS' PREFACE

In his own day, Thomas Wolsey was not a well-liked man. Nor have all his biographers been kind to him. Yet his talents were vast and his impress on history enormous. The son of a small-town English butcher, he rose to become a Cardinal of his Church, Lord Chancellor of his nation and mentor to his monarch. While his career was at its zenith, he helped preside over the destruction of the feudal order in England, and his fall marked England's separation from Rome.

By any standards, such a human being and such a career are remarkable. But they were even more remarkable in their time than in ours. For Wolsey was the very model of the self-made man and of the efficient, driving administrator—a type rare 400 years ago, but intimately familiar to the 20th Century. It is primarily in this light that Charles W. Ferguson has told his story, with a wealth of careful and fascinating detail that vividly illuminates the years that formed the link between medieval England and the Elizabethan Age.

Naked to Mine Enemies, which appeared in 1958 to the lavish praise of historians, was Ferguson's fourth book in a writing career that includes titles on such varied subjects as etymology, travel and American social mores. After publishing a novel and a religious work in the late 1920s, Ferguson had put his background as an ordained Methodist minister to use as religious editor for a magazine and later as a book publisher. In 1934 he gravitated into general editing for the *Reader's Digest,* where he has worked ever since.

Ferguson's serious interest in Cardinal Wolsey began when he read, in an encyclopedia account of the prelate's life, the famous statement that Wolsey made just before his death: "If I had served God as diligently as I have done the King, He would not have given me over in my grey hairs"—a remark paraphrased in Shakespeare's *Henry VIII* into the even more famous quotation (see page vii) from which Ferguson took his title. In a sense, this book is a full-scale answer to the challenge of Wolsey's deathbed statement.

Once Ferguson had decided to write Wolsey's life, he plunged into six years of painstaking part-time research. Much of his political information he found in reports of ambassadors to the court of Henry VIII, especially the Spanish and Venetian diplomats. The wealth of personal detail incorporated in the book he drew principally from *The Life of Cardinal Wolsey* by George Cavendish, who was chief usher in the Cardinal's household. After six years' work, Ferguson had accumulated 3,000 pages of notes and produced a text of 450,000 words. On this rough draft he exercised his editorial skills to such good effect that his smooth-flowing narrative never bogged down in the backwaters of historical pedantry. In this book Wolsey stands forth in all his power, complexity and ostentation.

Precisely because Wolsey was a parvenu, he felt a special need to show the outward marks of success. He was a masterful showman who could scarcely leave his home on a commonplace errand without a parade organized down to the last detail of costume and harness. As royalty, the Tudors, too, were upstarts; Henry VIII did not take power for granted but regarded it as an object to be won, increased and displayed. Display was, indeed, an essential part of the exercise of majesty—a visible sign of its strength—and many of Wolsey's exertions on behalf of his monarch were in the organization of pomp. The universally acknowledged English genius for ceremony is not, in fact, indigenous to the race. Just as the pre-eminence of French taste begins with Madame Pompadour, so the English reputation for public ceremonial begins with Wolsey.

Wolsey was not only a showman. He was an architect as well. His accomplishments in this field are also monuments to his administrative energy: while he was working on Cardinal College (now Christ Church) at Oxford, he found time, amid all the affairs of state that occupied him, to negotiate in detail for the shipment of a supply of stone from a

French quarry; through an unceasing flow of letters and messengers, he carried out all the intricate coordinating functions we now call systems engineering.

Education had been the springboard of his own rise, and his hope of advancing education was perhaps his most constructive aim. In addition, it was a motive for some aspects of the program of Church reform he initiated. To obtain the money necessary for the new schools he wanted to build—as well as for the ostentatious routine of the court—Wolsey closed a number of monasteries he considered useless and ordered their property seized. In this action he anticipated the utilitarian standards of a later day, by which it was intolerable that so much potentially valuable property be tied up in prayer and meditation.

Wolsey's campaign against nonproductive Church institutions did not, however, endear him to his contemporaries. The people had long-standing ties of affection to their local religious houses, and they neither shared nor understood Wolsey's standards of efficiency, central direction and progress.

His conduct of the Court of Star Chamber earned him enemies, too—and at a higher social level. The very name of the Star Chamber has, over the years, become a symbol of tyranny, although the precise nature of its abuses is by now obscure. Whatever they may have been, however, one thing seems fairly clear. Like most administrators, Wolsey was impatient with the law's complexities and delays, and he seldom stopped to consider the consequences for the future of any given decision. Ignoring all the principles of consistency and continuity we now include in the phrase "rule of law," he plunged rapidly from case to case dealing out a rough, expedient, *ad hoc* brand of justice. Under Wolsey, the Star Chamber was a kind of seedbed of what the 20th Century knows as "administrative law," the more or less arbitrary employment of broad executive discretion.

As the King's first minister, Wolsey gave much of his time to the conduct of foreign affairs. His record was wildly erratic. He was capable of conceiving intricate diplomatic maneuvers and carrying out their details with greater precision than his rivals in other courts. But as the historian A. L. Rowse points out in his new introduction to this special edition, he repeatedly misjudged the broad tides of international politics. Toward the end of Wolsey's career, it became abundantly clear to men less clever and less subtle than he that the Cardinal's strategic mistakes outweighed the numerous petty triumphs of his tactical skill.

So long as he held the King's approval, however, Wolsey was proof against the envious hostility of the realm. The great issue of the King's divorce was what finished him, and his basic error of judgment in that crisis stemmed directly from the very quality that had brought his success. Wolsey was valuable to a national monarchy rising above feudal and local interests precisely because he realized that the dominant forces of his age were centripetal. And this centralizing bent made him more "papal" than most European churchmen in ecclesiastical affairs—more "papal" indeed than the popes with whom he dealt. Viewed simply as a problem in statecraft, the King's divorce from Catherine of Aragon had to be handled in such a way as to salve the King's conscience and, at the same time, give an adequate color of legitimacy to issue that might emerge from Henry's prospective marriage. The papal divorce that Wolsey sought was one way of achieving those objectives, but it was not the only way. A divorce sanctioned by the English hierarchy, without application to Rome, might have caused a Europe-wide scandal—but scarcely as large a scandal as it became when it was sought *after* the papal decree was refused. The trend of political events in Italy should have made it clear to Wolsey from the outset that the Pope was unlikely to grant the divorce. Yet the Cardinal, an obstinate centralizer, persisted in a policy as unnecessary as it was ruinous to his own career. At no point was the papacy grateful to him for submitting an embarrassing case to it, and the King's rage at Wolsey for his failure was quite predictable. People who make their reputations by "getting things done" are not permitted to fail.

Ferguson's account of the Cardinal's fall and of his last years is especially good. Banished to his see, the huge archdiocese of York, Wolsey for the first time appears to have taken seriously his original vocation, the care of souls. Earlier, he had instigated quarrels; now he became a peacemaker, patching up neighborhood feuds in the North Country. The account of his daylong efforts to arbitrate a dispute between two powerful local figures, Sir Richard Tempest and Mr. Brian Hastings, reads like one of those exercises in labor mediation now performed by Presidents of the United States. The change in Wolsey produced a virtual reversal in the popular attitude toward him. Ferguson quotes a pamphlet of the time: "Who was less beloved in the North than my lord Cardinal before he was amongst them? Who better loved after he had been there awhile? . . . It is a wonder to see how they were turned, how of utter enemies they became his dear friends."

But the change was only local, and it was far too late to do Wolsey's worldly career any good. Wolsey was a sick man when the King's agent arrested him. Keeping an organizer's grip on the scene around his deathbed, he died on his way to the Tower. When his body was prepared for burial, his attendants discovered that he was wearing a hair shirt beneath the robe in which he died.

—THE EDITORS OF TIME

INTRODUCTION

Alfred Leslie Rowse, author of this introduction, is a distinguished English historian and writer, and a fellow of All Souls College, Oxford. His books include *A Cornish Childhood, The Expansion of Elizabethan England, William Shakespeare: a Biography,* and *Christopher Marlowe: a Biography.*

C ardinal Wolsey's career was certainly the most spectacular, and one of the most dramatic, of all English statesmen in history. Briefly, his is the story of the clever son of a not very respectable East Anglian butcher, who rose through the Church to a quasi-papal position in England—Cardinal and legate for life; who accounted himself the equal of kings and emperors—as he was decidedly their superior in gifts and ability; who, after 20 years of nearly absolute power, fell like Lucifer from the firmament, when all that he stood for came crashing in ruins around him. His fall opened the floodgates of the Reformation, with all the consequences it held for English-speaking peoples everywhere.

Such was the power, the vitality of his personality, the impact that it made, that he has never been forgotten. There are, for one thing, the traces that he has left in literature. The most charming English biography is devoted to him; it was written by George Cavendish, his faithful gentleman in attendance. He was the victim of scarifying satires by the Tudor poet John Skelton, who was both mesmerized and repelled by the vainglorious Cardinal—a kind of jealous love-hate complex a good many people experienced when they thought of his intolerable grandeur and his hardly more bearable, because so superior, gifts. He was the subject of highly critical accounts by the chronicler Edward Hall. Lastly, he is viewed with justice of mind, with understanding and with sympathy by no means blind to his faults, in Shakespeare's *Henry VIII,* in which he is the dominant character as he was in fact for the first half of Henry's reign.

In our shoddier age in Britain today his face still looks out at one, bold and brassy under the red Cardinal's cap, advertising woolen underwear from street-hoardings or in the London Underground. More dignified memorials of him still stand in that most splendid of Oxford colleges, Christ Church, which he founded and which was originally called Cardinal College—as a student there I recall the Cardinal's hat on everything, plates and dishes in Hall, washbasins, slop pails, battlements. He built palaces too—Hampton Court, York Place, which Henry VIII took from him to become Whitehall, a residence for subsequent sovereigns, as well as Tittenhanger and The More, sumptuous country houses, which have since disappeared.

Yet this loud, reverberating personality, which acquired so much fame as to remain alive after centuries, is still something of an enigma. Few people know what Wolsey stood for, what he did, what he was like or why he fell with such a resounding crash, bringing so much down with him. His career was really the last throw of the medieval Church in England: with him it gathered all power to itself in the state, and with him it was overthrown.

Wolsey's personality was first and last a political one: politics was the breath of life to him. Though he was a cleric, and the most magnificent example of his order, there was very little of the spiritual about him. Eighteen years older than Henry VIII, he came into the young King's service on the death of Henry VII, made himself indispensable and established an intellectual ascendancy over his monarch which lasted long. Wolsey's administrative abilities were very great; he had immense energy and vitality, was a glutton for work, for power, for building, and—to judge from his figure—for eating and the enjoyment of life. As his authority grew, he began to turn it to political ends. He brought order out of chaos in Henry's first French war (1511-1513) and drew it to a successful conclusion.

At about this time the laity in Parliament began to challenge the immense privileges and abuses of the Church—preliminary mutterings of reform. As a measure of defense Wolsey took as much clerical authority and power as he could into his own hands. Since William Warham, Archbishop of Canterbury, showed no sign of dying—was in fact excessively long-lived—Wolsey had to content himself with the archbishopric of York, with the rich see of Winchester and the wealthy Abbey of St. Albans. He became Cardinal and had himself made legate of the papacy for life. Apparently he really wanted to use his position to reform the Church. He suppressed a number of small superfluous monasteries and used the proceeds to found educational institutions—a fine school at his native Ipswich and his college at Oxford. He worked out plans for turning a dozen of the greater monasteries into more useful bishoprics—a pity that he got no further forward with his scheme. He ended some of the abuses of sanctuary and forwarded the interests of education.

On the secular side, as Lord Chancellor, he showed himself a just and speedy judge, with a sympathy for the poor as against the rich and powerful, the nobles and gentry who hated him. Little enough credit he got for this. People said, in their unkind way, that he was impartial in his administration of justice because he loved nobody, and fell from power because nobody loved him. He was, in his overpowering splendor, a singularly isolated figure. He did what he could to prevent the enclosure of arable lands, by which the peasantry lived, for pasture-enclosure meant only that the well-to-do would profit further. This earned him more hostility from the powerful. But by now he held a complete, an unprecedented, concentration of power in both church and state, and so long as he retained his ascendancy over the King, nobody could touch him.

The trouble was that power had become an end in itself for him; when he had the authority to reform the abuses of the Church, he became its most glaring abuse himself. Insatiable and beyond reason ostentatious, he used his power to accumulate more power and more wealth. He meant, if possible, to make himself pope: his attitude toward Rome, which made the mistake of delegating to him all the power of the Church in England, provides the one consistent thread that runs through his variegated, kaleidoscopic career.

For his immense diplomatic skill and ability enabled him to maneuver his small country into a temporary eminence that its intrinsic resources did not justify. As prince of the Church, he placed himself and Henry on a level with the Emperor Charles V of the Holy Roman Empire and Francis I of France at a time when France had three times the resources of England. This concentration on European politics strained English resources, exhausted the treasury, and necessitated unprecedented taxation and the calling of the one and only Parliament he summoned in all the years of his ascendancy. He involved the country in a second war with France, in alliance with the Emperor, hoping to win the papal election out of it. Charles V twice cheated him of his hopes, and thus made Wolsey a personal enemy. With the Emperor in possession of Rome and with France in defeat, Wolsey switched over to the side of France and, at the same time, encouraged Henry's long-standing doubts as to the validity of his marriage with Catherine of Aragon, the aunt of Charles V.

It was then that Wolsey's European policy collapsed and he found that, with the papacy under the control of Charles V, he could not deliver the goods—divorce from Catherine—to Henry. In the summer of 1529, with the collapse of his schemes in sight, he complained bitterly that the Pope had refused "all the concessions which, relying on him, I had promised the King . . . and that will be my ruin." All along he had relied on Rome and his own power to sway Rome; now both failed him.

His monarch failed him too: Wolsey had finally lost the last foundation of his power—Henry's confidence. With the complete bankruptcy of Wolsey's policy, Henry had to find another way, turn to other men. The King was slowly graduating to power himself, emancipating himself from Wolsey's hold on him—though Wolsey could never quite believe it. Dismissed from office, excluded from power, the fallen minister was still treated with consideration; Henry did no worse than consign him to his long-neglected duties as Archbishop of York.

Wolsey delayed assuming this responsibility for months, hoping for a return to power, and finally switched his allegiance back to Charles V and secretly corresponded with Rome to hold up Henry's divorce. He planned to make his enthronement at York a tremendous demonstration against the new course of Henry's Government. But Henry had been watching him, and at this point the blow fell: the Constable of the Tower of London was sent to fetch him, and the old politician recognized that his schemes had been penetrated—the Tower was the place for those accused of high treason. Hence Wolsey's collapse, his belated repentance, his fatal illness: Wolsey died at Leicester on his way to the Tower.

Shakespeare, as usual, grasped the essence of the historic situation and the personality very justly: after all, he was not far away from the events themselves. Mr. Ferguson takes his title from the famous lines, an adaptation of Wolsey's own words at the end:

> Had I but served my God with half the zeal
> I served my King, He would not in mine age
> Have left me naked to mine enemies.

This actually was unfair to Henry, for Wolsey by his last intrigues brought his fate upon his own head. In that, he was like so many other great figures in history who overreached themselves by their own ambition—Louis XIV, Napoleon and, most recently, Hitler. The moral of Wolsey's career is the classical one of Greek tragedy—that hubris, overweening pride, brings about its own fall, nemesis. The last word on Wolsey as a man was said by Sir Thomas More, the saint who succeeded him as Lord Chancellor: "Glorious was he very far above all measure, and that was great pity; for it did harm and made him abuse many great gifts that God had given him."

Wolsey's place in history has been authoritatively defined by the eminent Tudor historian A. F. Pollard. The value of Mr. Ferguson's biography is that he portrays the great Cardinal with a more modern psychological insight, and perceives that the exhibitionism was perhaps an overcompensation for the lowness of his origins in that Renaissance world. Of course, the Renaissance itself was nothing if not exhibitionist; Wolsey exemplified the pattern, but there may have been an inner insecurity behind the brashness and the overconfidence, the sudden confrontations with reality, the ups and downs of his moods.

History is, in part, histrionics. But Mr. Ferguson knows well that sympathy is a better path to the understanding of the great men of history and the fate they incur in taking exorbitant burdens upon themselves. Wolsey was indubitably one of the grand historic figures; Mr. Ferguson, with his scrupulous and scholarly sympathy, has given us our best account of the man.

He provides us with the vivid and veracious detail in which the truth of history consists, keeping close to the sources. There is no better way of not going wrong, of achieving truth both of fact and of atmosphere: the book has a convincing authenticity. On the one side we have Wolsey as he was, eloquent and plausible, a man of many words, always sanguine; tolerant and not unkindly, certainly not cruel (unlike his master), though easily overbearing; altogether very human. On the other, Mr. Ferguson presents the critical nature of Wolsey's career, the dilemma posed by his ambivalent position between England and Rome, and the crucial turning point it constituted in history.

—A. L. Rowse

THE END AS PROLOGUE

It was Saturday night—the last Saturday night of November in the troubled year of our Lord 1530. A chill mist from the River Soar crept in over the walls surrounding the Abbey of St. Mary of the Meadows, half a mile northward of the town of Leicester, and nestled around its massive hulk, making it look in the gloom of a winter's evening all the more reassuring and hospitable.

Lying near the center of England, known to dukes and beggars alike as a place of certain hospice on the road that led from the north to London, the Abbey would receive to its bounty tonight one who in his person was at once a prince and a pauper—Thomas Cardinal Wolsey, Archbishop of York, returning to London under the King's guard to stand trial for his life.

In the late afternoon a messenger had brought to the Abbot word of the Cardinal's slow progress from Nottingham. Sick with a coldness in his stomach, deterred and weakened by the flux, the Cardinal was said to be scarce able to sit on his mule. He would reach the Abbey grounds near nightfall and enter by the gate that opened off the main traveled road.

In the tower rising high above the Abbey church, a giant bell announced in cadent code to the surrounding countryside the approach of the broken prelate, suspending the stately routine of the black-robed Canons Regular of the Order of St. Augustine and summoning the whole convent to join the Abbot at the gate. Great tapers were lighted. The hounds, which some said were so numerous that they overran the Abbey, caught the itch of excitement and began to dash about and bark their thoughts and inquiries. All through the Abbey expectancy was punctuated by sounds of preparation. Men and beasts both seemed alert to the momentous.

A year before—and for fourteen years before that—Wolsey had ruled England in the name of the King. He had shown Henry VIII what a state was good for and how it could be made to do a man's will better than a man could do it himself. This Ipswich boy had grown up to teach a monarch—and a Tudor monarch at that—the arts and artifices of statecraft. Legend mixed with fact and woven into envy covered him at the height of his glory with vestments richer than the sumptuous robes of his office. He was the most talked-of man in England. Many quaked before his baritone wrath. Few but his servants, and possibly at one time the King, loved him. Not a few hated him lavishly. Yet among all he excited unending curiosity. The pageantry of his living and the shocking power that he wielded at home and among the crowned and mitered heads of Europe combined to leave his contemporaries bewildered. For he was of the people and lowly, yet he consorted with rulers and bent them to his stubborn will and made them seek his favor.

The essence of tragedy is to know the end. The end was now in sight. With Cardinal Wolsey an age was dying, too, and the end could not be casual. The death of one who had lived on such a scale as the Cardinal, and through such thunderous years of change, was not to be treated lightly. And the Cardinal would make an event of it, whether he died before ravenous enemies among the nobility on the Tower green or in the vaulted halls of a great abbey where he could play out the last scenes with inspired eloquence born of courage, for he was now free of the fear cast by the shadow of hope.

His life had been a tumultuous interlude between his christening fifty-nine years before and the moment when, now, broken in health and deprived of all the accouterments of power, he approached the Abbey.

The occasion of his death would be the occasion on which he and those about him relived the days of his years. . . .

—Charles W. Ferguson

BOOK 1

1471-1509 *In which is pictured the early life
of Thomas Wolsey and the world of which he was a part;
his years at Oxford; his unhappy activities as a young priest;
his various employments at Canterbury and Calais;
and his acceptance at the court of Henry VII.*

C H A P T E R

I

Seventy miles northeast of London in the county of Suffolk lies the venerable town of Ipswich. Situated where the River Gipping meets the sea, introduced by a deep and ample estuary, Ipswich in 1471 was a sheltered port through which thousands of fat and sturdy woolsacks passed to the English-held port of Calais on the coast of France. There the wool was sold to merchants on the Continent. And back into Ipswich came the cloth, so that the English had a way of saying that they sold the Flemings a fox for a farthing and bought the tail back for a guilder.

Here in this busy and hospitable port and market town lived a man and his wife by the names of Robert and Joan Wolsey. The name, spelled *Wulcy* until the spelling was modernized, was not uncommon in the region, being Teutonic in origin and signifying an island owned by a man named Wulf or Ulf.

Suffolk was a county made up of many people out of many lands, the beneficiary of many invasions. Evidences of Roman influence were all around. Colchester had been a Roman city of high importance. To the north some fifty miles away stood the indestructible fortress of Burgh Castle, one of the main points in the Roman defense against the savage Saxons. Inside walls built fifteen feet thick of rubble and stone, Roman legions had drilled and farmed and taken to wife women of the countryside until, after A.D. 400, they had suddenly been summoned back to the Eternal City as auxiliary troops to help crush a rebellion there. These legions had never returned, but they had left as an undying reminder of the glory that was Rome their massive fortress on the hills above the sea. And they had left other imperishable and sustaining reminders as well: for the Roman legions were not Roman at all but made up of soldiers from Egypt, Macedonia, and Spain; they were Tartars and Germans and Bohemians; and they had left in Suffolk veins the mixed blood of the known world.[1]

In Saxon times the town had got its name of Gyppeswyk from the small River Gyppes that flowed down from the north. It had enjoyed prosperity even in those days and aroused the covetous interest of the Danes, who made forays and sallies against it across the sea. Twice—in 991 and 1000—Danes had invaded the town, broken down its ramparts, and set it on fire.

To Robert and Joan Wolsey in the year 1471 a son was born. The day of his birth remains uncertain, for there were no parish registers then. Antiquaries who reckon such matters, however, set the month as March, and they believe that St. Thomas of Aquino, whose feast day is celebrated on March 7, may have marked the natal day and given the child his name of Thomas.

There had been harbingers from the sky. Three years before, a blazing star had appeared in the west "and so endured for five or six weeks." The next year there was a second comet, "the flame thereof like a spearhead." In January of 1471 there appeared the most marvelous blazing star that had been seen. It arose in the south "at two of the clock at midnight and continued twelve nights; and it arose easter and easter til it rose full east." It was marked by "white flame of fire fervently burning . . ." Sometimes it would seem quenched out and suddenly it would burn fervently again. In March of 1471 there were "great storms, winds and tempests from the sea."[2]

The year 1471 was a sorry time to bring forth a child. For one thing, the bubonic plague, dubbed the Black Death when in 1349 its clammy hand had claimed nearly half the population of England, returned to waste the land. There was in this year an attack of "the most universal death that ever I wist in England," Sir John Paston wrote to his mother, who resided in a county north of Suffolk. His inquiries of travelers failed to elicit the name of a single town that was not infected.[3]

The disease "took men generally in the head and stomach, appearing first in the groin," says Villani, "or under the armpits, as little knobs and swellings called kernels, boils, blains, pimples or plague-sores; being generally attended with devouring fever, with occasional spitting and vomiting of blood, whence, for the most part, they died presently or in half a day, or within a day or two at the most."[4] One friar tells of seeing penitent and confessor borne together to the same grave.

The unmeasured effects of the Black Death still lingered in 1471. For when the plague tumbled so many of the poor and lowly into swollen graves, it gave a new human worth to those it left. Survivors enjoyed a death benefit. Although of the commonest clay, they took on a strange and unpredictable value. The serf, formerly bound by the thongs of feudalism to the soil, found himself eligible for release. There was no longer an indefinite supply of men whom the lord could make do his bidding. The serf suddenly and unexpectedly became a laborer. And labor, being hard to get, became a commodity. If my lord's bailiff sought to press a serf into compulsory service, the man might desert the manor and flee into the forest. Then later he could emerge on the other side of the forest and find himself hired for good wages. Meanwhile my lord had a field on his hands with none left to till it, and if he were to get aught for it, he would have to find some enterprising fellow who would rent it rather than farm it as a villein.[5]

A spiral of respectability had thus been started by the commotion attending the Black Death. For those who had once been content to be serfs became laborers and forgot their place. It was noised in Parliament that laborers did keep greyhounds and other dogs, "and on the holy days when good Christian people be at church, hearing divine service, they go hunting in parks, warrens and coneyries of lords and others, to the very great destruction of the same."[6]

Land values fell as farms were abandoned by serfs and the gentry confronted demands for higher wages. To meet this frustration there had been enacted by Parliament a series of Statutes of Laborers, fixing in detail the pay of all manner of workmen.

Yet somehow the lower classes would not remain in place, and the spiral could not be halted by the ceiling laws had made. Among those who had been serfs, some had become landless laborers who had sold their brawn; but others had become yeomen farmers, ranking only a little below gentlemen, men with independence and enterprise.

The men of Suffolk in 1471, then, were still at sea regarding the confusion and change wrought by the distant doings of the Black Death. It was a time of growing wealth and strange decay. The wealth came from the backs of sheep, and it settled in the hands of a limited if increasing number of yeomen who had not enjoyed wealth before and who were lusty for it. At the same time, the sheep multiplied out of hand and threatened to overrun and devour the land, upsetting all other types of agriculture. The sheep may have numbered eight million, Bindoff says. If so, this meant that there were three sheep to every human. "The 'golden hoof' turned moss-land into cotton-grass and heather moor into mat grass, and slowly destroyed the oak, the hazel and the birch."[7] And as the number of sheep grew, more and more of the village common lands and farming areas were firmly enclosed in hawthorn hedges to make room for more and more sheep.

"Commons to close and keep; Poor folk for bread to cry and weep; towns pulled down to pasture sheep . . ." ran the lament. Another: "I have heard of an old prophecy that horn and thorn shall make England forlorn."[8]

Robert Wolsey was a man who in his small way rode the crest of the wave of change. He was a grazier who lived off sheep and cattle. A London merchant who visited Ipswich in the summer of 1483 spoke of "the fat cattle he saw feeding on the lands of Maister Wolci." Fetherstone, a learned monk who resided in Ipswich about 1480, told of a squire named Wolci who fattened cattle for butchers on his grass near the town.[9] This squire sold wool to the English market in Calais as well as meat in the market of the town. As merchant and grazier both he was in a fair way to be hated and envied, but he was also in a fair way to accumulate at least some of the tangible rewards and assurances that come from business success.

Under old arrangements a farmer might tend a few sheep and let them graze with the other cattle of the village on the common field. But as the demand for English wool increased abroad and the price rose, and as men of enterprise saw the advantages of sheep farming, the earlier system of open land stretching out from the village would no longer suffice. In order to run large bands of sheep and cattle, which could be cared for almost as cheaply and with as little labor as small ones, vast stretches of land had to be enclosed with hedges.

What happened to the farming villages under the increasing system of enclosure was sad and plain. In one case, Henry Smith, Gentleman, enclosed 640 acres of land, "whereby twelve messuages and four cottages fell to ruin, and eighty persons there inhabiting, being employed about tillage and husbandry, were constrained to depart thence and live miserably. By means whereof, the church grew to such ruin, that it was of no other use than for the shelter of cattle, being with the churchyard wretchedly profaned, to the evil example of others . . ."[10]

From the deserted villages the disinherited wandered about, seeking either work or relief as beggars. Beggars stood in the highway "whom ye be afraid to say nay unto, lest they take it away from you violently."[11] Loiterers lurked in alehouses, of which the towns had an abundance. They would sit "swilling, gulling and carousing all the day long, yea, all the night too . . ."

On the other side of the fence, those who stood to profit from the increasing number of sheepwalks relished and encouraged the transformation of England from a land of small farmers to a land of sheepmen with large holdings. One stapler, grown fat on wool, set in the stained-glass windows of his elegant new house this legend: "I thanke God and ever shall. It is the sheepe hath payed for all."[12]

Even if a wool merchant could not afford stained-glass windows, he might at least afford windows of plain glass. Windows were often covered with oiled linen or thin horn, but the use of glass windows was also becoming common. Sometimes the upper parts of the windows were glazed, while the lower ones were fitted with wooden shutters. Glass was available but the price was high; among fines listed for servants the penalty for "toying with a maid" was fourpence, whereas the fine for breaking a glass was twelvepence.[13]

The growing class of merchants and yeomen were now able to afford chimneys for their houses. Chimneys were looked upon with some scorn and some concern, it being pointed out that in the old days, when the smoke was allowed to escape as best it could, the children suffered from fewer rheums and colds and wheezes.[14] The chimneys and now some of the houses were beginning to be made of brick. At the port towns bricks from Denmark were coming into use. The growing use of brick was only another sign of the prosperity to be had from sheep and of the way men might rise from one class to another on the backs of sheep and cattle.

In the days surrounding 1471, England was bled from the effects of the Hundred Years' War. In this war she had sought to make good her claim to France. There had been moments which carried the promise of success, as at Agincourt, but then England had lost by gradual amputations the territories she had gained in France until only the port of Calais remained as a place for the shipment of her wool to the Continent.

Not only had that dismal war failed in its purpose; its failure had gravely affected the realm. As it staggered to its inglorious end in 1453, more and more soldiers skilled in brutality were loosed upon England, ready to pillage for pay, eager to sell to any lord the only talent they had. Knights and archers, to whom plunder and brawling were a habit, roamed about until they fell into the hands of some shrewd paymaster who would hire them for his lordship's private army and sometimes for his private war. And if they were not hired for some nefarious end by the nobles, they were left with a free lance to fend as best they could, derelict and restless.

With these recruits had begun, fifteen years before Wolsey was born, the bitter and internecine battles known in the poetry of history as the Wars of the Roses. Chivalrously the rival claimants to the Crown accepted as symbols of their bloody contentions the rose—white for the House of York, red for the House of Lancaster. Each thorny faction took unto itself ruffians home from the war in France, ready to wear the rose of any lord for pay; and the gentry that might be drawn into the conflict kept changing their badges as the fortunes of strife brought one or the other contender to the fore.

In the early months of 1471, England was a headless realm. For years her wretched and shadowy King, the sixth Henry, had been held captive in the Tower. Earlier the noble Houses of Lancaster and York had played his image like a card—now in, now out; now dealt, now discarded. Of late the Earl of Warwick, he who was called the Kingmaker, had taken the aging Henry from the Tower, dusted him off, and, after parading him around London on a white charger, had propped him on the throne again.

It was plain, however, that this feeble rulership could not last. For the Yorkist King, Edward IV, who had fled to Europe six months before, was even now preparing to return in force and recover the throne, Warwick and his flabby puppet Henry notwithstanding.

It was a period of suspense in government, when the King's writ ran hardly at all; a period, as it were, between reigns, and it invited riot and civil commotion. Murderers and thieves crept out of sanctuary.

Uneasily the people watched and were right queasy. The English had temporarily deprived of power nearly half the kings who had reigned over them since 1066. The office of king was sacred; the person of any particular king was subject to hazard, often to contempt. It was the idea of king that mattered; his person mattered only if it served the interests of the nobles in power to maintain it. "In the 280 years before Henry VII established the Tudor dynasty, England was ruled by twelve monarchs, beginning with John and ending with Richard III. Of these 12, only three were permitted to reign until death overtook them. Of the remaining nine, seven were stripped of their powers, five lost their lives by violence, two were insane."[15]

The pathetic Henry VI had inherited the throne of England while in his cradle, and at the age of two had been proclaimed King of France as well. He was never in fact King of either country. But all his life he was made ceremoniously to act the role. He had toddled in processions of state at the age of five. At eight he had endured his coronation. At nine he had been carted with pomp and circumstance across the Channel to be crowned in France also.

He was not made to be a king, this Henry; not a ruler, this gentle, feckless, devout fellow. When the times cried for swords and treachery, his pride was to found a school for poor scholars at Eton and the King's College, Cambridge. He wore from his youth square boots like a farmer and a long cloak and hood like a burgess. Nor had he any of the pious cruelty that was common to his day. Once he saw a quarter of a man set over Cripplegate in London and asked what it was. "A traitor false to the King's majesty," was the reply. "Take it away," Henry ordered. "I will not that any Christian man be so cruelly used for me."

In the midst of tumult and change, the sixth Henry remained at inward peace. He gaped not after conquest, took no part in the war abroad, though his countrymen refused to surrender his French claims; those who continued the French war used pretensions made in his behalf to espouse their plunder.

His marriage to a relentless young Frenchwoman, Margaret of Anjou, had done nothing to ease his distracted life. On the contrary, he was constantly harassed by the events which her ambition and quarrelsomeness stirred within the kingdom. After eight fruitless years of marriage, Margaret bore Henry a son and heir. Both the people and the King were astonished, Henry declaring through a glaze of incredulity that the child must have been fathered by the Holy Ghost. Shortly after the birth of his son, Henry lost even the semblance of interest in his office and retreated into amiable madness. There was no violence about him, even when he was deprived of his reason. He merely stared into space, his mind a fugitive for a season from the problems it confronted.

In the pageant of disease, disorder, and mischief, Henry remained an idea, however weak his person. Nobles sought to control him, not to abolish him. He was the national emblem. Weak as a ruler, preoccupied with heavenly matters, impoverished by his own charity, and incapable of rich display, Henry the son of the hero of Agincourt, where the flower of French chivalry had been destroyed, was still the King.

He was still the King, that is, until Edward defeated his troops mercilessly at the battle of Towton, fought on Palm Sunday, 1461, in the north of England, hard by the city of York. Aided by a snowstorm that blinded the Lancastrian archers and a wind that made their arrows fall short, the Yorkists and Edward gained a great slaughter. The Lancastrians were killed as they ran, and the snow all the way to York was colored with blood.[16] Henry had taken refuge in Scotland, then had returned to England, wandering about the west of his whilom Kingdom disguised as a bumpkin (it was not difficult) until agents of Edward found him in a farmer's cottage and brought him to London and lodged him in the Tower. There he remained until, through the maneuvering of Warwick, Edward was forced to flee the kingdom and the ineffectual Henry, he of so many fits and starts and in and outs, was put on England's throne again. It was like a game of musical chairs: when the noise of battle stopped, the player nearest the throne dashed and sat.

Shortly after Thomas Wolsey was born in Ipswich, Edward returned from Europe, where he had fled when Warwick seized the reins of government. He had a few men with him, and he hoped to recruit thousands more as he marched toward London.

A country still suffering from the wastes of a hundred years of costly bloodshed abroad, smitten by the recurrent plague, overrun by thieves and robbers and vagabonds, ruled by a king listless and unhinged, with a foreign harridan for a queen, shaken by the rise of the lower classes to create a new and unexpected class of traders and yeomen farmers and merchants with emerging impudence and arrogance—this distraught land was now to be subjected again to the bloodletting of continued civil war.

During these parlous times the problems that concerned the people of Ipswich were strictly local, and the record of the town's activities showed a sturdy indifference toward matters beyond the walls. With the landing of Edward a gossiped fact, the annals of Ipswich reported only that Ingell Bolton was fined "for nuisance done to the highway at Cole Dunghill, by laying muck therein." Later, with no mention of the fact that meanwhile Edward had defeated the Lancastrians at Barnet, it was solemnly stated: "Such as suffer their hogs to go at large within this Town shall pay for the first offence, for every foot 1d, for the second offence 2d, and for the 3rd offence shall forfeit the hogs so wandering." Whatever happened to kings and princes on blood-soaked fields, what mattered in Ipswich was this: "All the Inhabitants of the Town shall grind their corn at the Town mills under forfeiture of half a bushel of corn ground elsewhere."

Robert Wolsey had come to Ipswich from his native Combes, near Stowmarket, ten miles away. In Ipswich he was therefore an alien, and the plight of the alien there was severe. It was provided "that no stranger being inhabitant in this Towne shall harbor in his house as guests or otherwise any strangers, merchants, mariners or others, under peril of forfeiture of 6s8d for every person so harbored, and imprisoned."[17]

There was a detailed and scrupulous regulation of trade, it being decreed, for example, that "all victuals and fish shall be sold by the owners thereof, and not by retail by the inhabitants of this Town, under peril of seizure." And: "No butcher within this Town or liberties thereof shall sell any flesh of Beasts within this Town, but only in the Butchery, on Mondays, Tuesdays, Thursdays and Saturdays, under forfeiture of 12 pence for each offense."[18]

As an alien from ten miles away, possibly unfamiliar with details of regulations and under ubiquitous suspicion besides, Robert Wolsey was often in trouble with the town authorities. The first notice in the rolls of Edward IV marks his appearance in court for keeping an "hospicium" whereat he sold victuals for excessive gain. Again he was also in the same court, "in company with another Stowmarket butcher, one John Wood, fined for selling bad meat at the Ipswich market and for not exhibiting the skins of beasts which they had slain."

The offenses for which Robert Wolsey was haled before the authorities commenced before the son was born, and by the time his son was nine he was the "greatest offender before the leet. He brewed ale and sold it in illegal measures; he provided horse provender for excessive gain; he did not maintain the street gutter in front of his house in good repair; he permitted his pigs to wander about at large within the borough precincts; and he defiled the highway with filth from his stables instead of placing it within the public pits."[19] Among the charges made against Robert Wolsey was one that he allowed his house to be used for immoral purposes. Precisely what the immoral purposes were is not clear. Under the stern ordinances of the town the charge might have meant that he allowed his house to be used as a place of assignation—or it might have meant that he allowed Dutchmen to stay there.

Preoccupation with local concerns proved sound for Ipswich. By the time the year 1471 was half over, the Kings had settled their affair of honor, and the succession, and the whole realm was to enter upon fourteen warless years. Accompanied by his brother Richard, Duke of Gloucester, Edward had landed at Ravenspur, seventy miles to the north of Ipswich. He had defeated and demolished Warwick's army at Barnet, ten miles north of London. Warwick, unhorsed and unable to flee in his heavy armor, had been killed—a kingmaker dead and turned to clay at the age of forty-four. Weeks later Edward had defeated the Lancastrian forces under Margaret and her eighteen-year-old son in the shambles of the battle of Tewkesbury. It was the lad's first battle and he would not fight another. Overtaken after the battle and cut from his horse, he had his head bashed in like any common knight's. Some said it was Edward's faithful brother Richard who cut him down.

There was no rival heir apparent now. Edward returned to London with Margaret as his prisoner. And the night of his return the unfortunate and bewildered Henry VI found rest at last, murdered in the Tower. History would not impose on him again.

Ipswich could now settle down to the business of shipping wool and to the graver concerns of local government. It made little difference to the citizens in their concerns with wool and hogs and laws that Henry, as Warkworth chronicled, was murdered "on a Tuesday night 21 May between 11 and 12 of the clock." Or that "on the morrow he was chested and brought to St. Paul's, and his face was open that everyone might see him. And in his lying he bled on the pavement there; and afterwards at the Black Friars was brought, and there bled new and fresh; and from thence he was carried to Chertsey Abbey in a boat and buried there in Our Lady's Chapel."[20]

So the sad event stood in the chronicles of the realm, but there is no mention of it in the annals of Ipswich. There we find, in the midst of the stern and stirring events of the day, space given to more immediate local concerns—as, for example: "The Town millers are, at their peril, to take no excessive toll." Apparently a miller was a greater threat than a king, new or old, for the town was in many respects autonomous and must discipline its own, whereas a king could hardly do more than molest the inhabitants occasionally.

Still and all, Edward was back on the throne and he was the King who had said, "Hang the rich by the purse and the others by the neck." It would be well to keep on durable terms with him.

C H A P T E R II It was a period when rulers sought to control restlessness by laws and keep the lower members of society in the proper and ill-fitting uniforms of their class. It had been decided that "because the Commons of this Realm do daily wear excessive and inordinate array to the great displeasure of God," no knight or his wife under a lord's estate might wear cloth of gold or fur of sable.[1] Laced sleeves, stuffed with wool or cotton and known as bolsters, were fashionable among the nobility, and the same statutes marked bolsters as a special privilege of the upper class and forbade any yeoman or person under that degree to wear these full-padded sleeves.

The consignment of certain men and women to certain kinds of labor was construed to be religiously ordained. It was almost mythological in its significance. As one writer depicted it, Mother Eve hid the least favored of her children, "but such as were fair and well made she wisely and cunningly kept with her." God in due course came to call upon her and asked to see her children so that He might promote them in their different degrees. He chose the eldest to be an emperor, the second a king, the third a duke; all the rest he made earls, lords, barons, squires, knights, judges, mayors, and so on down the respectable line. Then Eve produced her other children from their hiding places. They were dirty, rough, and covered with cobwebs, misshapen in stature. God did not conceal His disgust. "None," He said, "can make a vessel of silver out of an earthen pitcher . . . or a bright sword out of a cow's tail." He then went on to pronounce sentence: "You shall all be ploughmen and tillers of the ground, to keep oxen and hogs, to dig and delve, and hedge and dike, and in this wise shall ye live in endless servitude . . . Some of you shall be allowed to dwell in cities . . . butchers, cobblers, tinkers, costardmongers, hostlers or daubers . . ."[2]

The fashion of seeing human history thus cast up in terms of the *status quo* lent a comfortable sense of permanence to the existing order, a species of eternity, as though social distinctions inhered in the very nature of the heavens. Thus interpreted, the spade of Adam was seen to be the first shield in heraldry. Cain was the first churl. Society, in brief, had been ordered from the beginning to remain fixed. It behooved a man to recognize this fact and to stay where he belonged.

In such a society as prevailed at the time of Thomas Wolsey's birth, the lot of children was low. Manifestly the best way to teach a person his place and station in life was to begin with the child. There was in force a statute that any boy or girl who had served at husbandry, at the plow or cart, until the age of twelve "from henceforth shall abide at the same labor without being put to any mystery or handicraft." The only release from this onerous provision lay in the permission of the parent to withdraw the child from labor for schooling. For the statute added: "Provided Always that every Man and Woman, of what Estate or Condition that he be, shall be free to set their Son or Daughter to take learning at any School that pleaseth them within the Realme."[3]

Moreover, a child's work was needed to help win the family bread, or he must be sent elsewhere to make one less mouth to feed. "Poor people," said Thomas Deloney, "whom God lightly blessed with most children, did by meanes of this occupation so order them, that by the time they were come to be six or seven years of age, they were able to get their own bread."[4] In some cases the age might be older, but usually the child was looked upon as a source of revenue, not as a responsibility. Mrs. Green tells us that children came into the towns constantly as young as seven; that they were never older than twelve when they came. And it was said in the letters of the Paston family that "every poor man that hath brought up children to the age of twelve year waiteth then to be holp and profited by his children."[5]

Being important in the economy, children were received with rejoicing and swaddled and coddled in their early years by their parents, just as spring lambs are tenderly cared for by a good sheepman. A child was kept tightly swathed until it was necessary to teach him the use of his limbs. Christina Hole points out that rattles were provided and that there were corals with bells. These helped the baby cut his teeth and were generally believed to have some value in warding off witches and preventing the falling sickness.

Because education was the means by which a child might escape the grim routine society had plotted for him, instruction began early and severely. If a child in his prattle and brightness showed aptitude, he was pushed. If he proved sluggish and inept, he was beaten. In either case he suffered torment along with learning. "Boys and girls alike were frequently beaten for childish faults, and tutors were not only permitted to but expected to underline their instruction with a liberal use of the rod." A parent's word was law and filial piety the chief of infant virtues. Any lapse from prompt obedience or respectful bearing was met with swift punishment, and there were no fancy ideas about self-expression or the danger of inhibitions. "Children addressed their parents as Sir or Madam and stood bareheaded in their presence; on special occasions they knelt before them to ask their blessing."[6] A dictum of the day put the matter plainly: "Never have the rod off a boy's back; specially the daughter should be handled without any cherishing. For cherishing marreth sons, but it utterly destroyeth daughters."[7]

In spite of all the severity and solemnity, there was still time for play. One picture shows a child blowing soap bubbles. The children of rich parents had many toys: whipping tops, dolls, toy windmills, and wooden knights on horseback to play at tilting. The games played by groups of children had the range and vigor of children's games everywhere. In Suffolk, blind man's buff was played as "Blind Hob." Another was a cheery version of "Here Comes One Duke A-Riding." One Ipswich game had the lilt that goes with swinging arms and showed the awareness even at that time of the importance of London town:

> How many miles to London?
> Three score and ten.

Can I get there by candlelight?
Yes, and back again.
Open the gate and let me through,
Here's my black and here's my blue.
Not unless you're black and blue.
Here's my black and here's my blue,
Open the gate and let me through.
Dan, Dan, thread the needle; Dan, Dan, sew.[8]

Sometimes the games were surrounded with a religious atmosphere. One of these had to do with the custom of electing boy bishops and then giving each boy elected wide scope throughout his town and diocese, providing them with all the accouterments of pomp and circumstance.

"After his election, being completely appareled in the episcopal vestments, with a mitre and crozier, he bore the title and state of a bishop and exacted ceremonial obedience from his fellows, who were dressed like priests. Strange as it may appear, they took possession of the church and performed all the ceremonies and offices save Mass."[9]

Clearly the vestments and panoply of the Church afforded children marvelous opportunity for dress and parade, for the kind of matchless play that would, at such times as on St. Nicholas' Day, give their imagination and histrionic bent full scope. The Church was solemn and serious in many aspects, but it prompted play and it aroused the fancy of the child, as these ceremonies surrounding the boy bishops show.

The Ipswich Grammar School had been founded by the burgesses a few years before Thomas Wolsey's birth, and the fee was fixed by the Bishop of Norwich at tenpence a quarter. (One penny would buy that ineluctable luxury, a pound of black soap.) Later the fee was reduced to eightpence. It was reasonable for the students, but it left the master somewhat underpaid, and to supplement his income he was given a monopoly in the town on the sale of quarry stone.

It is recorded in the annals of Ipswich that the master of the grammar school was to have "the government of all scholars within the liberty of this Town (excepting little ones called Apes Eyes) taking such salary as the Bishop of Norwich has appointed." Later it was provided that "every Burgess inhabitant shall pay to the Master of the Grammar School, for a boy 8d per quarter and no more."[10]

The town had begun to awaken, to see the need of contact with the great world beyond. Men wanted to learn to read and write, "to learn the languages used in countries about us, that we might write our minds to them and they to us." Grammar schools had begun to be established by mayors and by merchants. It was specified that masters should teach "all manner of persons, children and other, the Science of Grammar," although the provision wisely added, "as far as lieth in him for to do."[11]

Over and beyond the curriculum of the schools a new educational interest appeared. It was manners. This interest did not make itself felt primarily in the schools for a long while; but it gained currency in the parishes and in the books of the day, and gradually an aim of education came to be the sweetening of life, the cultivation of behavior and civility, the gradual improvement of conduct among the common people.

This was new indeed. In Italy the movement had begun much earlier, and England was coming more and more under the Italian influence. Circumstances in England, too, greatly aided both the wish of those in the upper classes to improve the manners of those in the lower classes and the desire of those in the lower orders to learn the tricks and stratagems of courtesy which were the hallmarks of breeding. As the two orders of society came closer and closer together, and on occasion intermingled, it became important for those to whom manners were formerly a luxury to learn to make them a daily practice. No longer was it convenient for a select few in society to have a monopoly on good behavior. In a word, the movement up from serfdom continued on all fronts, and the etiquette of the lords and ladies was but one further area to be invaded by the poor.

Those who served at the squire's or lord's table often proved to be unruly and rude. Fresh from the barnyard and swilltub, brash and uncouth, they cared little for the elegance of the tables they waited upon; and if they did, they had no training to assure their acting in a seemly manner. Many times they were quarrelsome and corrupt, given to fights and lewd remarks—in general, sloppy and in no regard fitted to the services they were called upon to perform. Particularly was this true as new men rose to wealth and the demand for servants increased.

To meet the new requirements, servants must be trained, not only in the niceties of placing dishes but in the decencies that would keep a household from being corrupted by its servants. One writer said of the servingmen of the period: "Their company, their talk, their over-great experience in mischief, doth easily corrupt the best natures and best brought up wits . . ."

How sore the need for manners was may be seen from some of the early written instructions: "Don't spit or snot at table . . . Don't fire your stern guns or expose your codware . . . Don't pick your teeth with your knife . . . Don't claw your back as if after a flea; or your head as if after a louse . . . Don't pick your nose or let it drip or blow it too loud . . . Don't claw your cods, pick your ears, retch, or spit too far . . . .Don't squirt with your mouth, gape, pout or put your tongue in a dish to pick dust out . . . If you blow your nose, clean your hand. Wipe it with your skirt or put it through your tippet . . . Don't pare your nails at table or pick your teeth with a knife."[12]

Functions of the various officers of a large household appeared in detail in the books of the day, together with pointed and detailed instructions on how the carrying out of these instructions might be improved. The almoner, for example, said grace and put down the alms dish at the beginning of every meal. The carver put the first loaf of bread into it. The almoner had a staff in his hand. He kept the broken food and wine left after the meal for the poor men at the gate, and he was sworn to give it all to them. What was left in the lord's cup went into the alms dish, and in some cases a piece of everything served went into the dish. Also the almoner distributed silver as he rode with his lord or master.[13]

Books prescribed and regulated the management of a house. Fires were to be kept from November 1 to February 2. It was specified, too, that the lord's privy must be kept sweet and clean. "Cover the boards with green cloth, so that no wood showeth at the hole; put a cushion there." Routine smooth and gentle marked giving m'lord a bath: "Hang round the roof sheets full of sweet herbs, have five or six sponges to sit or lean on, and one great sponge to sit on, with a sheet over and a sponge under his feet. Mind the door's shut. With a basin full of hot herbs, wash him with a soft sponge, throw rose water on him . . . Stand him on his foot-sheet, wipe him dry, put his socks and slippers on, take him to bed to cure his troubles."[14]

Deference ran through it all like a refrain, and the arts encouraged and the skills bestowed were all designed to please masters or betters. This rigid insistence upon deference to rank is carried over into the manners of the home. The advice runs: "Don't mock old men . . . Bow to all before you leave . . . Give the wall side to all you meet, and let your better enter first . . . Let your better choose which side of the bed he will lie on . . . Don't go to bed first until he asks you to, and first pull off his hose, shoes. When you're both in bed, lie straight and say 'Good night' when you've done your chat. Next morning wish your fellow 'Good morrow' tho' he's asleep."[15]

There are also household hints now and then, such as the intelligence that cheese is the best cement for broken pots. Occasionally the books go so far as to suggest methods for improving health and the state of mind: "Don't take cream, strawberries or junket unless you eat hard cheese with them. Hard cheese keeps your bowels open."[16] One is advised after dinner to keep standing against a cupboard until the food has had a chance to digest. In sleeping one should have a hole in the top of the nightcap through which the vapors may go out. As for the technique of sleeping: "Shut your windows, lie first on your left side, to sleep grovelling on the belly is bad, on the back upright is worse." Indeed, to "lie upright on the back is to be utterly abhorred."[17]

C H A P T E R

III

As Thomas Wolsey grew up, his father improved in station and came to be a fixture in the community. In 1479 he purchased for eight pounds and a certain amount of land a house just down from the Cornhill, past Rosemary Lane and Dog's Head Street. It was a good address in the heart of things. Nearby rose the massive Church of St. Peter and back of that the Ipswich Grammar School. The house was in the parish of St. Nicholas, and Robert Wolsey was a member of this parish; and in the shadow of the church, which was solid and substantial rather than imposing, Thomas Wolsey lived as a boy. On either side of the door of the church, and at the height of a child's head, were two grimacing griffins, fixed there in stone as if to guard the portals against uglier spirits.

Not far from the Wolsey house stood the town shambles. Here customs made of iron held the merchants to rigid habits. It was an offense to sell the flesh of a bull that had not been baited for at least an hour. The bull was tied to a stake, with its horns guarded, and worried to exhaustion or death by dogs. This savage and noisy practice was said to add to the flavor of the meat, and it provided a daily spectacle as well. If the animal was not dead from mutilation by the end of an hour, it was finished off by the butcher. There was a balcony around the shambles, and the town often used the arena of the shambles as a place for pageants and ceremonies.[1]

In the midst of the pealing of the bells of the fourteen churches of Ipswich and of the bellowing of harried bulls in the town shambles, young Thomas Wolsey played. By the time he was eleven, he had exhausted the local educational facilities. Although Cambridge was in the next shire, he went to Oxford, which was then recovering from the ravages wrought by the heresies of Wycliffe and was still, in spite of the ill repute it had gained, first in the hearts of the countrymen. And a lad so lingual and so intense in application, so eager to advance in learning, deserved the best. The Wolsey boy was set on his way to Oxford a good three years ahead of the age usually chosen in that time for sending boys there.

At Oxford Thomas Wolsey entered the College of St. Mary Magdalen. The College of St. Mary Magdalen was still abuilding when the young Wolsey arrived to take up residence there. It was the handiwork of the pious Bishop William Waynflete and was one of the early efforts to control the rampant students of the day by herding them into sheepcotes called colleges. Up to the time colleges came into being, the students at Oxford had been free to roam the streets, and they could not be compelled to live in any one place. "They might spend their evenings in the tavern and drink as much as they pleased. Drunkenness is rarely treated as a university offense at all."[2]

With the coming of the colleges came discipline, practically unheard of in university circles up to that time. The founding of these colleges marked a change from the period in which students, callow and irresponsible though they were, nonetheless enjoyed treatment as men. The student had been, as Rashdall has called him, a gentleman at large. He came now to be treated in the university as a schoolboy who must be disciplined and held in check. This change had as its accompaniment a new view of the university—as a place of custodial care, not only of the student but of learning, a giant repository or treasury where men must go if they were to enjoy the fruits of education. The university became fixed as a kind of fortress, hard to get into and hard to get out of; a guardian of the realm; a protection in the view of the prelates against the invasion of alien forces.

There had once been a hospital named for St. John the Baptist on the site of Magdalen. The buildings of the hospital were granted by Henry VI to William of Wainfleet with the thought that they be put to educational uses. The foundation stone of the college had been laid only two years after Thomas Wolsey was born, and the first building of the great quadrangle was completed three years before he arrived. Built of heavy stone, the college had a huge door that could be barred against hostile mobs and could hold the student back from the taverns. It was closed at a certain hour, and it stood always as a sign that the Magdalen scholar belonged not to the outside world but to the world within the gates. He was no longer living in a rickety tenement where he could do as he pleased and discipline himself only if he chose. He was no longer free to leave one set of lectures and walk across the street to another set given by a rival lecturer. Rules hard as the stone walls began to curb his impulses. He gradually became accustomed to the birch "at the discretion of the college lecturer for unprepared lessons, playing, laughing or talking in a lecture, making odious comparisons, speaking English, as well as for unpunctuality or non-attendance at chapel."[3]

Statutes enacted at the time Thomas Wolsey entered Oxford forbade swearing, games of chance, "unhonest garrulities," being out after eight in the winter and nine in the summer, entering another man's chamber without his consent, speaking English except at a feast. All were required to attend Mass daily and to hear sermons. Clothes were regulated; inordinate hair was condemned. Card playing was prohibited but chess allowed,[4] being a game in which kings and queens and bishops and knights were maneuvered to advantage.

Poorer students were licensed to beg by the chancellor of the university. There were some known as "battelers" who were required to wait on the others before sitting down to the table. Nor did menial service of this sort constitute any disgrace or set the students apart from their fellows. Rashdall says that there were very few traces of fires in any of the college chambers and that in "the mediaeval lecture room there was no warmth but what was supplied by the straw or rushes upon the floor . . . . The cheerless picture created by the fireless studies is completed by the wooden window-shutters, the clay or tile floors either bare or strewn with straw . . ." The cost of candles put "reading by candlelight beyond the means of the poorest students. This meant disputations and repetitions as evening employments, at which a candle might suffice for the whole company."[5]

The senior enjoyed a bedstead, also certain coverlets and perhaps now and then hanging linen and curtains. The juniors often slept in beds which could be put away under ordinary bedsteads. Each room had a "study," which was movable, being treated as a part of the furniture. Gradually the studies came to have doors and were made into cubicles where a lad might withdraw and concentrate, away from all the commotion that went on outside.

The stern attempt to make angels suddenly out of the medieval students brought in its train a succession of failures. Indeed, it provoked and fostered wild indulgences. On the roads round about "were to be met parties of scholars—many of them expelled or banished for previous transgressions—who had turned highwaymen and now waylaid the more peaceful student approaching the University with his purse equipped for a nine months' residence." Rarely is the report of such a case varied by the statement that the accused was obliged to take sanctuary. "In the majority of cases nothing worse happened to the offender than being compelled to go to Cambridge."[6]

With all the hell-raising, both inside and outside the bounds of the university, a large core of the students applied themselves sedulously to learning. It was clear to the thoughtful that the only careers of distinction which were not in the hands of ecclesiastics were those of the soldier, the lawyer, the physician. The hold of the Church was notable in the line of diplomacy and administration. Thus the young men of Oxford might not always aim at holy orders for holy purposes. They might take the cloth if they were to perform any number of tasks in any number of good administrative positions which might be performed only by those who had been ordained.

The regimen of the colleges was too severe to be endured unless it led to some ultimate surcease. Lectures began at six in the morning, and "often . . . in the dark without artificial light . . ." The first morning lecture might last three hours. As a maximum, the student attended three lectures a day. His schedule during the day and evening was filled near to overflowing, as it was a plan of the authorities that little time should remain either for mischief or the exercise of choice. There was a very early breakfast for some of the more fortunate students, but both the hard and the economical student would omit this meal. Dinner was usually at ten o'clock. This would be followed by a disputation, carried on in impeccable Latin, dealing with matters of ethics or morals. There was some time allowed for relaxation then; but regular schoolwork resumed at noon, and the student either studied or attended other lectures until supper at five.

After supper the student took his postponed pleasure. He was free until eight or nine o'clock. Homemade amusements were encouraged. The disciplinarians of the college allowed storytelling and carol singing or the reading of "poems, chronicles of the realm, or wonders of the world." Assemblies to hear such performances took place around the one fire in the college hall. Much of the recreation was saturated with religion. There are records in the college register during the time Wolsey was in Magdalen of the election of boy bishops. Elections were followed by elaborate ceremonies and processions, so that the elected bishop and his attendants, together with the whole college, had for a day a sense of taking part in the great dignities of the Church.[7]

In 1483, while Thomas Wolsey resided in Magdalen and moved forward to his bachelor's degree, Edward IV died. He died in bed, which was no small feat for an English king. His son, Edward V, was destined not to reign. Instead Richard, Duke of Gloucester, lodged the thirteen-year-old heir and his brother in the Tower (lest a boy king set off again the Wars of the Roses) and had himself proclaimed Richard III.

To extend himself in public favor, Richard chose the device of kings, a royal progress, paying visits at the expense of the people to the several parts of his kingdom and receiving the petitions and obeisance of his subjects. One of Richard's first stops was at Oxford—in July 1483. Magdalen College was required by the statutes of its founding to entertain the kings of England and their eldest sons whenever they came to

Oxford. In line with this requirement, Richard was honorably received there, and Magdalen was his headquarters and the center in Oxford from which the royal radius ran. The visit called for vast preparations, for clearing the halls, for laying in extra food. It provided, too, the chance to observe royalty in action, to note at first hand the customs and practices of the court, the deference accorded the royal person, and the manners proper to those attending upon great stations. Here were the world and the kingdom brought through the great gates and displayed before the eyes of the scholars.

The King for his part entered heartily if briefly into the academic life. The day after his arrival the authorities held for his benefit and possible instruction solemn disputations on moral philosophy and divinity. The brightest scholars were trotted out for the royal pleasure. To those who made orations or engaged brilliantly in the disputes, King Richard scattered his benevolences liberally. Next day he visited several colleges of the university and some of the schools attached to these colleges. In these he listened to more learned disputations.

On the occasion of his visit the two contrasting worlds of nobles and scholars were brought sharply together to the information and benefit of each. A scholar could look at a king; and a king could get, through the disputations and orations, some faint idea of a world he would never know.

In this stirring mixture of worlds, the profligate and the ascetic, the young and impressionable Thomas Wolsey began his career at Oxford, beholding the dramatic pomp of a royal progress and the rewards and royal esteem bestowed upon the glib tongues of those who had mastered the art of philosophical fluency.

Four years were required to attain the degree of Bachelor of Arts at Oxford. According to Wolsey's testimony in later life, he received this degree at the age of fifteen—"a rare thing and seldom seen," the usual age being not less than seventeen. The ceremony by which the degree was attained, known as determination, was both elaborate and hazardous.

The candidate was known as a determiner. Under the supervision of a Master of Arts the determiner took his stand for nine days, fully prepared, he hoped, to demonstrate his learning. For at least seven days he stood at a desk from nine to twelve in the morning and from one to five in the afternoon, ready to defend certain propositions against all comers. As Lyte describes the process, "an ambitious determiner could court attack by raising a knotty point, while conversely an unskilled disputant could almost as surely escape discomfiture by laying down some proposition that could hardly be impugned."[8]

In a word, the successful candidate engaged in the theatrics of learning. His aim was to impress, and the system under which he labored made the occasion of his determination one of vital importance to his future. It was an individual performance, not merely a matter of meeting set requirements. It was the high point of a young man's college career. Unless he took his Bachelor of Arts by determination, he would have to have an extra year beyond the seven required to get the degree of Master of Arts. If he did well in his determination, he might attract students for his future lectures, enlist worthy and wealthy patrons. And he would, of course, gain the plaudits of his classmates and impress himself on the body of the college. So important was the occasion that friends would "stand outside the door and forcibly compel passersby to come in and witness the proceedings."[9] It was an arrangement that encouraged ostentation of mind and put a premium upon a man's resourcefulness under stress and upon his ability to joust with words.

There were, of course, unearned degrees. The Convocation of Canterbury had to deal with this problem in 1486. Boys of ten and twelve might receive a Master's degree after a year's study at Oxford or Cambridge, and, according to one report, they might become venerable archdeacons before they knew how to sing Matins.[10]

That Wolsey was not one of the beneficiaries of this system of indulgence may be seen from the fact that he remained at Oxford for further study and later became a Fellow of Magdalen. He won his degree in the competitive system of the university and became known round about by the sobriquet of the Boy Bachelor. The degree brought to the boy who achieved it a good deal more personal liberty than was accorded the younger boys, and certain privileges; and the accolade bestowed after a dramatic test of wits upon a boy of fifteen singled him out from among the other Bachelors and lifted him to special heights in the college community. Here was a student who, if his health held and his development continued, would sit high in the councils of the godly.

There would be need of strong men in days to come. Times were still unsettled and the people queasy. With all the dignity that attended his station and with all the royal robes draped about him, Richard wore his crown warily. The princes remained in the Tower, and gossip stained the beards of men in the taverns and alehouses and went from ear to ear among the solid womenfolk. Anxiety marked the mood of men, and signs of it showed on every hand. Forces visible and invisible worked behind the pageantry of kings, both at home and on the Continent, and some of these forces took the form of men and some of machines.

William Caxton had brought the printing press to England in 1471. The first book in English had appeared in 1477—*The Dictes and Sayings of the Philosophers,* translated from the French by Lord Rivers. There was no title page, the pages were not numbered, the lines were uneven, and the letters were a close imitation of the handwriting of the period. The sayings which made up the book had been compiled in Latin about 1350 and had been translated into French about 1410. This first book was followed by others, among them Chaucer's *Canterbury Tales.* England became conscious of her language and of its richness. Wandering German printers in other countries had used Latin. England's first printer issued his books in English—in the vernacular. There was now a way by which people could know the language and the ideas of the day without the laborious and tedious business of having scriveners in a monastery copy out the words. Something new had been added, if only barely added, to the blood and mind of a people.

Ideas that once crawled could now walk. In times past, the written word could be speeded in the scriptorium of a monastery only by having one monk dictate from a high stool while scriveners took down his words and turned out identical copies. Now a hundred copies of a page could be printed within a short period. Men's words could speed across the country as fast as roads would permit, and a thousand people might be reading the same words at once, whereas in times but recently past only a few monks could take down what one man said. A thousand men might, so to say, take down what one man said.

But it was too early for the printing press to aid appreciably the circumstances which would quietly alter the face of society, seaming it with new problems men had not even begun to anticipate. Men acted as if they lived in a world immutable, made up entirely of a present formed in the womb of the past. The aristocracy and landed gentry went on cutting each other's throats as if they would enjoy that privilege for years to come.

The system of livery and maintenance still held sway in the days when the lad Wolsey held forth precociously in disputation on subjects of moral philosophy in the walled College of St. Mary Magdalen. A lord had men who were sworn to his service, bound by oath to execute his wishes, however monstrous. These hirelings would terrorize, capture, ransom, beat, or maim upon command. They wore the livery or badge of the noble thug who paid them, and in exchange for their reckless devotion he stood pledged to aid them if they stood trial by jury or fell afoul of the law on any personal matter.

The system kept the land in turmoil and the nobles in a passion and under the illusion of the importance and permanence of their own position. They seemed to be making history as always or as before, yet the formative forces of history were gathering to pass them by. Society appeared still to consist of King and lords, the Church and yeomen and laborers beneath. But, as Gretton puts it, "somewhere hovering on the flanks of these good men is a mysterious, generally dishonest, sly person who stretches cloth or lends money upon usury. He is not regarded as belonging to any class, but appears as a kind of unexplained renegade from uprightness."[11] He is the emerging businessman. In the center of the sound and fury of the old medieval world he goes right on making money and establishing himself firmly in the presence of, and under the stimulus of, confusion—yet he is hardly noticed, save as an annoyance.

Back in Ipswich, Robert Wolsey continued his varied pursuits with vigor while his son was at Oxford. He was able to buy a new house in the south ward of the town. He continued also to fall afoul of the regulations of the town, but apparently they did his progress no great harm. With the grace and help of a substantial income, he achieved an increasing measure of respectability in the parish of St. Nicholas. He was of the new and as yet unnamed class—businessmen—who had no standing by virtue of birth or position but had a larger and larger measure of control because they were able to finance enterprises, including the wars of kings.

Plenty of opportunities for wealth, a lot of them new, showed up close at hand. Chief among these was the manufacture of cloth at home in England and the export of this finished cloth instead of raw wool. And the merchant who had the shrewdness to manage all phases of the manufacture of cloth developed a high degree of business intelligence. It was a new kind of intelligence, that had nothing to do with the succession of kings or with the wars fought to settle that succession. It moved on a different plane entirely, but it would come in handy one day to kings. For it began to be clear that war could no longer be fought casually by independent soldiers but must be organized around the supply and the assembly of all of an army's diverse needs.

To an uneasy King busy with the pageant of royalty, however, imperceptible changes that might one day affect the government did not greatly matter. Richard had much that was immediate and pressing to reckon with, and in his reckonings he made the land as uneasy as himself.

Vague dissatisfaction flared into open rebellion. There was another Henry in the offing, a young man named Henry Tudor. He had been a lad of fourteen when the sixth Henry was restored to the throne for that brief and piteous season in the year of Thomas Wolsey's birth. Then they had brought him up to London from Wales and presented him to the old Henry, who, it was said, being much struck with the boy's "wit and likely towardness," remarked, "Lo, surely, this is he to whom both we and our adversaries shall hereafter give place."[12] For safe keeping, the young man was later sent to France.

The year Thomas Wolsey became a Bachelor of Arts at fifteen, with all the perquisites of privilege attached to that status, this Henry Tudor became King of England at the age of twenty-eight, inheriting the problems of a realm that had been weakened by generations of strife and quarrels, that was without status in the family of nations and without stability, or prospect of stability, at home.

The world of 1485 was like the streets of Oxford, given to quarrels and strife. There was nothing in the affairs of kings to lure a young man who lived in a maze of words. It was a period of dreadful night. The prospect just before Henry became King appeared to be one of endless contention, of continued battles for the succession, though why anyone would want to be king of beasts in a jungle like England was an increasing mystery to the merchants and traders and printers and graziers and all who drew their wealth and prestige from the handling of goods. The vast tournaments of the nobles to decide which man should sit on the throne had become a matter of less and less interest as long as the man who sat there was firm and kept the nobles at peace.

.   The Wars of the Roses, long a tragedy, had become a bore. Even so, Richard could not last. He moved almost constantly about his kingdom. In 1484 when Parliament broke up, he left London early in March and went to Cambridge. He tarried but a while at Cambridge and went on to Stamford and Nottingham. Here he stayed more than a month. It was the center of England, and here he could poise prepared if Henry Tudor landed on England's shores, as he was sure to do, to claim the throne.

It was while he was yet at Nottingham that the King received tidings of the death of his only legitimate son. The news threw him and his queen into the most violent grief, and it removed another of the strands by which he held his hope. There was now no direct heir. He was forced to name a successor, and this act would in itself make the whole matter of the succession fair game. First he named young Edward, Earl of Warwick, but later he changed his mind and nominated John de la Pole, Earl of Lincoln.

Again Richard began to pace about with his throne on his back. He moved to York and then to Durham and then turned south and came to Scarborough; returned to York and was next at Pomfret. During June and July of that year—1484—he moved about from Pomfret to York to Scarborough, and on July 30 he was back at Nottingham, where he remained until August, returning in that month to Westminster. It was at Nottingham that he could best be posted for the invasion. For the news grew bigger with the passing of the months that Henry Tudor would land in England. All along the principal roads, Gairdner tells us, horses were stationed at every twenty miles, "ready to mount and carry messages at a moment's warning. Important news could thus be conveyed by letter transmitted from hand to hand two hundred miles within two days."[13]

But the invasion did not come that summer, and the winter was quiet. In spring and in March, but a year after his son and heir had died, his wife Queen Anne died. She had been visibly declining. On the day of her death there was a great eclipse of the sun. The heavens seemed to be in on the event, and rumor ran that the sun had hid its face because King Richard had poisoned his queen. This rumor was followed by another still more bitter, to wit, that he would now wed Edward's daughter, Elizabeth, his own niece, to make more certain of his throne. Richard did what he could to allay public suspicion. He called a meeting of the mayor and citizens of London at the great hall of the Knights of St.

John at Clerkenwell, "and before them all with a loud voice proclaimed that the design imputed to him was a fiction."[14]

From now on his time would be spent in protest and defense. Toward summer he learned that Henry Tudor had assembled a huge fleet at the mouth of the Seine and was ready to set sail for England. On August 11, Richard heard of the actual landing of his enemies. Yet with all his forethought, he had no proper sense of his real danger. He trusted men who turned against him, who were never really in his camp. He had thought that Sir Walter Hebert and Rhys Ap Thomas would oppose Henry Tudor's march into Wales. The Welsh rebel had landed at Milford Haven. But Richard heard nothing from the system of posts he had put up the year before. Either the sentinels were not provided this year or else they failed him, as did so many others. He knew nothing of the whereabouts of Henry, it appears, until Henry had reached Shrewsbury.

Then Richard sent immediately for the nobles to join him with all their forces. They came. Among them was the Duke of Norfolk, he who had been Sir John Howard of Norfolk, created Duke for his sturdy services to the Yorkist cause. Among the noblemen, too, was Norfolk's son, the Earl of Surrey; also the Earl of Northumberland. Not among them was Lord Stanley, who was joined in marriage to Henry Tudor's mother. His brother, Sir William Stanley, was chamberlain of North Wales, and he had done nothing to stay Henry Tudor's progress toward the center of England. He had already been declared a traitor. Richard held Lord Stanley's son as a hostage, a fact which showed how definitely he suspected this nobleman's loyalty.

Yet whatever Richard thought or suspected, there was nothing he could do but take at once a position where his military skill and experience might turn the tide against an opponent who had never been in battle before. The King moved from Nottingham to Leicester, and on Sunday morning, August 21, he left Leicester with a goodly army, "wearing his crown upon his head that all might see him." A march of about twelve miles westward brought him to the village of Sutton Cheney, two miles south of the town of Market Bosworth. There Richard pitched camp for the night. His scurriers told him that the army of Henry Tudor was but three miles away.

The battle for England was joined the next day. The actual fighting lasted hardly more than an hour.[15] When it was over, Richard was dead and Henry Tudor had been proclaimed upon the field Henry VII. Nobles on whom Richard had counted for support had turned against him at the height of the battle. The battle had not been won. It had been lost. Henry Tudor, an upstart Welshman, who had spent most of his life abroad, had shown no generalship. He displayed no bravery. Treachery and deceit had been his allies. Without the disaffection of the nobles— nobles Henry did not know until the final hour that he could trust to desert Richard—his claim upon the throne would have miscarried.

England was still, as it had been for seventy years, in the hands of powerful houses of lords. There could be no stability in the kingdom until some king became king in fact and put the nobles, outdated by the course of history, in their proper place: subordinate to the Crown.

There seemed little prospect that an untried Welshman, who was now King by the grace of God and the wager of battle, could accomplish this any more than his tragic predecessors. Yet he set to work almost at once to fashion a nation. To make fast his title, Henry summoned Parliament to meet on November 9. He let it be known that he would, as he had promised, marry Elizabeth of York, daughter of Edward IV, and thus bring together in one plant the rival roses of Lancaster and York. But he made it clear that the time of the nuptials must be of his own choosing: if he married her before his coronation and before Parliament had acknowledged his sovereignty, it would appear that he claimed the throne partly in her right.

Next he gave signs that he might unseat nobles as he had unseated a King. At his coronation he bestowed but few honors. He made his uncle Jasper a duke and he acknowledged his debt to Lord Stanley, who had deserted Richard, by making him Earl of Derby. But these honors were as events wagged them, and they had not the disadvantage of loading the nobility with new heads and thus encumbering the kingdom where it already had too much weight. The ends sought were plainly those designed to give strength to the idea of kingship as well as to his person. He appointed a body of yeomen of the guard to secure the King's person —to attend him and all Kings in the future. And the men who made up his Council were in themselves another kind of yeomen, for they were not lords of exalted rank but men who had shown, through law or architecture or some of the other professions, that they knew something about business and administration. He chose those who could use a pen as well as draw a sword.

Having established the character of his reign in these subtle and pointed ways, Henry pressed forward on two other important matters. One was to touch to the quick the pride of the nobles: it dealt openly with the menace of livery and maintenance. All members of the King's household and later the House of Lords and the Commons were made to swear that they would not receive or shelter any known felon, retain any man by indenture or oath, give liveries contrary to the law, or assent to riots or unlawful assemblies. All the lords swore observance, each of the lords spiritual laying his hand upon his breast and each of the lords temporal laying his hand upon the Gospels.

There was much murmuring amongst the lords over the King's exaction, but though they bridled at the thought, they nonetheless took their solemn oath in the presence of the new ruler, and a principle was raised on a standard for all to see.

Not less to the satisfaction of the people was the sound of their own voices and echoes made possible by the meeting of the Parliament. For one of the great pleasures of the people was the pleasure of grievance, the right to petition for the righting of wrongs. Protest was raised against the practice of allowing the royal household to raid the provisions of the citizens of the realm. The Commons pointed out that "food and cattle were constantly requisitioned for the use of the royal household, for which the owners received no adequate compensation." Henry saw the injustice of this casual robbery and devised an arrangement which was accepted. "A sum of £14,000 derived from land and customs dues was to be allocated each year to the king's household and an annual assignment of £2,105 19s. and 11d. was made to the wardrobe."[16] By this settlement of an issue which had nettled the English people for generations the King showed not only a novel sense of justice but an administrative precision which sounded a new note in the music of a monarchy. The new note, almost dissonant in its surprise, was a prudent regard for law.

For all the worth of Henry's measures, Richard's ghost cried out from his grave in the monastery of the Gray Friars in Leicester. Richard still had friends, particularly in the north of England, where he had always been high in the hearts of his countrymen. After Bosworth the corporation of York entered in their records that through the great treason of many who had turned against him Richard had been "piteously slain and murdered to the great heaviness of this city."[17] Soon Henry deemed it wise to forsake the security of London and move out into the northern shires and still the restlessness that lingered against him. It was well that he did. By an admixture of clemency and the threat of force, he quelled a double rebellion in the north and in the west of England. When he returned to London four months later, he had not only shown his royal person and the determination of his countenance to the people on a journey of some five hundred miles, but he had also listened heartily to the people and learned their grievances.

Henry's position as King now appeared tenable if not wholly secure. There had meanwhile been added papal sanction in the form of a bull which threatened with excommunication any who should rebel against Henry. It carried, further, the proviso that in case of Elizabeth's death, his children from any other marriage should still possess unrestricted hereditary right to the crown. This bull was read and proclaimed by the bishops in all the cities. Also Henry had it printed—the first time a king had used the printing press for a proclamation.[18] Everything would be up-to-date in Henry's reign.

In September of 1486, the Queen bore Henry his first child—a son. The boy who seemed destined to be a King was given the name of Arthur, "in honor of the British race." There would be another King Arthur, or so the confident Henry planned in his dreams, perhaps one in whom fact and fable would be incarnate.

Whatever his ultimate fame, the infant son offered Henry immediately a coin with which he could do business abroad and lift his eyes from the pressing problems at home. The young prince was hardly a year old, says Gairdner, when a proposal was made by Henry to Ferdinand and Isabella of Spain and Castile for the marriage of Arthur to their infant daughter Catherine, who was just nine months older. Special envoys came from Spain to consider the matter, and "Henry opened his eyes wide with joy and broke into a *Te Deum Laudamus* when he found that they were armed with powers to conclude the alliance . . . He seemed entirely the servant of the Spanish sovereigns, whose names he never mentioned without taking off his bonnet, with conventional courtesy, in the presence of their representatives."[19]

In the time of these events, Thomas Wolsey remained secure in the citadel of learning. To young men gifted in language and cultivated in casuistry, Oxford was the world and the College of St. Mary Magdalen was a world within. A king might fall; another rise and face revolt. The whole structure of government might change, but Oxford remained intact. Knowledge was endless, at least in the sight of those who were its custodians. There was no use to speed the process of education and face the jolt of a non-Oxford world any sooner than was necessary or customary. There were two places on earth—Oxford and elsewhere. Why hurry?

So the Boy Bachelor settled down and followed his studies diligently and hard. Yet in spite of his burrowing, a mist of occurrences seeped in. A young priest in Oxford had groomed and put forward an impostor who claimed to be the Earl of Warwick, son of the Duke of Clarence, brother to the late King Edward and Richard. The Earl of Warwick at the age of ten had been confined to the Tower by Richard, lest discontented elements gather round him. There were abroad now ugly rumors that Henry had put the young prince to death, Warwick being a likely contender for the throne, his strength of lineage being all the greater for Henry's weakness. Later the rumors changed their character: it was said that the young Earl had escaped from the Tower and was intent upon raising a rebellion.

With these restless rumors the priest, by name Richard Simon, showed a close acquaintance in the scheme he laid. For he craftily found the son of an Oxford artisan, a lad called Lambert Simnel, the same being well mannered and bearing a likely resemblance to the young Earl of Warwick. So it was that the priest, seeing the resemblance and the designs that might be made on it, felt that the Oxford boy might impersonate the Earl, who was well known among Yorkist champions, and do it with such vividness that he might seize the throne.[20]

The better to circumvent any early frustration of his plot, Simon took the impostor to Ireland and played the prologue there, trying out the full effect of his cunning conception on the Irish lords, who were favorable to the Yorkist cause. And as Simnel walked like a well-trained peacock among the Irish and convinced them of the qualities of his person, there grew up and took shape a design that might well put this lad on Henry's throne.

So successful was the plot that Henry had to raise an army to meet the rebels, Henry who only two years before had been a rebel himself. The battle took place at Stoke, three miles from the city of Newark on the Trent. It endured three noisy hours, and when it was over, four thousand lay dead on the soggy meadows round about. As a rebellion, the affair had come to nought and had ended in a bog of blood. But there was more to it than would meet the eye of the historian. The rise and fall of Lambert Simnel had demonstrated an idea before the gaze of the rich and poor, the highborn and the low. One from the artisan class could walk with princes and wear the paraphernalia of royalty and occupy a lofty position, indeed be crowned King of England, if he had a proper tongue and stance. He could, that is, provided his rise and performance were to the advantage and service of his betters.

It was after the decision at Stoke that Henry came on a royal progress to Oxford, accompanied by a right noble train. In the course of the ceremonies attending his reception he was presented with a pair of gloves (costing fourpence) as a token of the esteem in which he was held and possibly with the suggestion that gloves might be needed, seeing all he had to handle.

The College of St. Mary Magdalen entertained him officially by virtue of its charter and the obligation therein to be host to royal persons. There were eight solemn processions among the colleges as the King's train made its way and the King sampled the intellectual wares of the university. There was also another chance in this round of activity for the scholars to mingle with attendants of the court, to see the royal household in operation, and to gather from those stationed with the King an account of this young man, not yet thirty, who held with both hands the crown of his country firmly on his brow and promised to remain steadfast in his claims, albeit there were still rumblings against him and probably new treacheries afoot.

Already he had put to rout two rebellions, one by strategic clemency—this one in the very center of the Yorkist hotbed—and another by force of arms followed by clemency and his favorite practice of exacting fines from the survivors instead of their heads, of drawing their purses instead of their veins. He had a further feather in his cap in that he had exposed to high ridicule an impostor who had fooled not only a vast concourse of Irish, which was easy enough, but also the English who had shown willingness to die for him.

It was an auspicious moment for a visit, a lull between conspiracies, and one could assess with some accuracy and at close range the measure of the man who was now England's ruler. The lads of Oxford could turn from their abstractions and disputations for a holiday in the present.

Yet even at close range they could not be sure of the King, for Henry left men in a quandary. He looked old beyond his years and wore a cowl of gravity which he did not remove even in repose. Yet he was wondrously aware of appearances and of walking always before the gaze of his courtiers and subjects, so that his demeanor when on display was often one of gaiety and cheer; his eyes lighted up when he made speech, and his smile was quick when he engaged in riposte and rejoinder, as was his wont.

No one said he was handsome either of face or body, but he showed that he was supple from riding and hunting and the exercises of the chase; and if his hair was thin and his look quizzical, there was still and all about him the implacable confidence of one born to rule and to serve as father to his countrymen.

In deed and gesture, in proclamation and counsel, he set about to make himself patriarch despite his years. His appearance, which was not distinguished, and his bearing, which was not regal, somehow achieved a combined aspect that was both distinguished and royal: he showed in all that he did that his prime aim was to put the affairs of his house in order and have his national family well in hand before he was through. He was a sovereign, and it is not surprising that in his reign the King of England began to be referred to as His Majesty.

The indulgence Henry showed traitors was as a father pitieth his children. He was a graven image wrought by his own acts and chiseled by his own imagination to serve as father to a people orphaned by the death of many kings and now waiting a steady hand and a solemn face at the head of the table and a firm voice that would bring order and let little men get on with business and commerce. Henry was young, yes, but ages old—old as the Old Testament—in his way with the children of men and with men who were children.

These things were patent and to be seen by one who would see. And to add a cubit to the royal stature, whatever the animadversions and conspiracies raised against him, was the fact that he was a man of many Masses and pious practices, much given to praise and religious observance. He acknowledged with fitting humility the spiritual authority of the Holy Father of Christendom, and he had found it fortunate that some of his decrees had been reinforced with bulls that came without any apparent solicitation from Rome. Whatever the plan of his day, it always left room for God, and no man of the court had more intimate access to the King of England than the priests who served him as chaplains. There was an unction to all his serious acts, and the heady atmosphere of religion which surrounded his person and court made for mystery and enigma and drew a veil across the temple. "On my faith" was Henry's favorite oath.

As the King moved in eight processions around Oxford, news of his accomplishments moved with him. There were many jesters but not many dandies with the court; for the King had seen fit to encourage new men in his train, and these new men were to be judged not so much by family and forebears as by ability to serve their country. Three of these men stood out and lighted signal fires for the rest—Morton, Bray, and Fox. All were men whose loyalty to the King had been tested and burned of dross in past controversies, and none of them had claim to greatness by lineage. They stood on their own recognizance.

John Morton was now Lord Chancellor of England and Archbishop of Canterbury, in which latter position he ranked as head of the Church in the kingdom, and he worthily set about to remedy some of the grossest errors of the clergy. He noted well the laxness of the period and insisted that priests should reside in their own benefices, or, if they had more than one, that they reside in each for a season. He noted with dismay how widely the clergy had grown slack in dress and given up the tonsure. It was his order that they be shorn, and that right early, enough to reveal their ears; and further that no swords or daggers be carried by priests. Only graduates of universities, he ruled, should be allowed fur on their garments.

In the vigor with which he began to prosecute these measures he revealed his devotion to the King's cause and his desire to bring order out of the chaos created by earlier reigns. But what distinguished him, apart from all his specific aims, was an ability that had nothing to do with the cloth he wore: while Bishop of Ely, Morton had proved himself an engineer of high and notable talents, having supervised a great cut, or drain, through the fens from Wisbech to Peterborough. Such a man of practical skill and proven competence in handling tangibles, Henry had made his Lord Chancellor.

The other two of the three most cordially seated in the Council were of a like stripe. Richard Fox, Bishop of Exeter, was the son of a Lancashire yeoman, a priest and a doctor of canon law, versed to the King's liking in secular as well as sacred matters. Sir Reginald Bray was an architect, a diplomatist and a soldier, not a noble either. Bray was Lord Treasurer and his position in the new government was one of yeasty importance. That Henry had bestowed the custody of funds upon one not of the nobility, a plain man who had risen by sheer force of ability and by tasks competently performed, showed the King's firm intent to use men who could aid his hands in the fashioning of a new state and a stable one. There might well be a sprinkling of peers, especially if the King could create new ones to his liking. But there was serious business at hand to be done, and Oxford scholars could note that the King's choice of men to do this work of government would fall on thoughtful and not necessarily noble heads.

The new nobles created tended to be of the rural class, men who had made their wealth and position by the fruits of agriculture and the sale of wool and the produce of herds. They were men of substantial wealth, not merely men who enjoyed suzerainty over great domains through the accident of inheritance. The new nobles had risen out of rather than come down from. Any honest yeoman of good repute and tangible wealth and a knack for management might become a baron— and a useful one at that. The commonalty of men might still be imprisoned in the class and station which God had assigned them by birth. This they demurely knew. But all around now there were signs too unmistakable to miss that men of talent and usefulness could pass from one station to another. They might in a sense serve an apprenticeship to respectability and later be accepted into the guild of the nobility or the higher clergy. Wars and confiscations had plucked many a lord from the ranks of the nobles and left spaces to be filled.

One could note still another reason why new faces appeared at the court. The King was lonely and suffered much from the tortures of suspicion. This Henry, whose garb on occasions of state was adorned with a most rich collar full of great pearls and many other jewels set in four rows, and who in his bonnet wore a pear-shaped pearl—this Henry lived as if in fear of ambush. And well he might, for the times had been out of joint for thirty years. The nation was full of discontent, of unemployed soldiers and turbulent men without livelihood, men ousted from their holdings by the munching encroachment of sheep, ever more menacing.

Even if no other leader arose to foment rebellion among the dissatisfied and the disinherited, there was still plenty to twist the King's head in sidelong glances. "Under the custom of livery and maintenance and the stress of civil war the old judicial and police system of England had broken down," Fisher tells us. "The judges indeed still went on circuit, but the juries were intimidated by the local landlords and could not be relied upon to do their duty. The justices of the peace still held their petty and quarter sessions but they neglected their administrative duties and failed to enforce law and order."[21] Complaint ran that the coroners would in divers places omit to view the body of a slain man, there being no fee or emolument attached to this duty. In these circumstances of negligence a murder might pass unnoticed. And if it were noticed, it might go unpunished. Small wonder that murder was treated as a pastime, following the ravages of a protracted civil war in which the slaying of Englishmen by Englishmen had become a sanctified habit.

By the time of his progress to Oxford Henry had established a new method of dealing with crime and lawlessness. He had turned his Council into a court, a court which met in a room of Westminster Palace known as the Star Chamber. Here was a study indeed for young scholars who would observe the law in action and see it change to meet the iridescent times. For if local authorities would not make the bad behave, the Council would richly see to it that they did. The members of the Court of the Star Chamber were chosen by the King to dispense decisions that others dared not make. Those who still kept large bands of retainers, those who bribed or threatened sheriffs or jurymen, those who took part in riots or upheavals—those who would have escaped scot-free in the days before the sitting of the Court of the Star Chamber—were haled before the King's appointees to give an account of their acts in due season.

These were the cases that were tried without benefit of privilege, and the enormity of their acts was measured against the picture which Henry wanted to paint for his people. The justices of the peace in the shires were in turn urged to refer hard cases to the Star Chamber. In this way the Council and the Court established central control of behavior by forthrightness and by the absence of awkward procedures and safeguards that attended trials in ordinary courts. The justices operating as agents of the Star Chamber enabled this new juridical body to reach out in all directions and fasten on any offender who might think he could with impunity breach the King's peace. Thus not merely such hefty offenses as treason came within the purview of the Court of the Star Chamber but also such offenses as housebreaking, horse stealing, the carrying off of cattle, and assault.

Matters momentous and trifling paraded before the Court of the Star Chamber and there drew a rough and positive justice that by degrees began to get the land on the way to order. With its twenty or thirty men sitting at the hub of affairs, the Court was the busiest and most formidable in the kingdom, what with the six or seven hundred justices throughout the realm supplying grist all the time and the commoners feeling gradually that they had through the King's Council a ready access for their grievances and for airing the injustices they were wont to suffer in humble silence or contentious frustration.

What Henry had fashioned in the room of Westminster Palace decked with stars in the ceiling was in effect a new class—an official class made up of men who gave time daily to the business of governance, whose role it was to spread equity and to regulate from the pivotal point of London the affairs of society on a national scale. Through the justices of the peace this grim arm of the King could reach out into every hamlet and make felt the strength of the central government. The Council was now a place of work, and through its operations the King's eyes peered into every manor and hut to fetch out what was amiss.

CHAPTER IV

For twelve shapeless years there is no record to tell us what Thomas Wolsey did or thought or felt. From the week in 1485 when he held his elders at bay and won his first degree until the day in 1497 when his name adorns the college rolls, only fancy can fill the gap and backward reasoning give us some surmise. We can merely guess how much the shouts of men and the eddy of events touched his growing mind; we can only measure what we know of all else against the youth and man of whom we know nothing.

What affected him? What passed him by? What stirred some sharp incentive to goad him later on? What in this period when the government of England changed before men's eyes and men changed their views, when new forces expanded the mind and sent men out to find new worlds—what if aught of this had its bearing on the Boy Bachelor?

A violence of mind and weather swirled around the walls of Magdalen. Men were on edge, their spirits either restless or defensive, for there came to be an awareness, in spite of walls, of what lay beyond the narrow Thames and even beyond the Channel and the North Sea. The whispers of distant lands came symbolically in a new language. Frowned upon as pagan and of devilish consequence, Greek had suffered for years exclusion from doughty England, where Latin held court and enjoyed obeisance in every school. Then came a man bearing the gift of Greek, William Grocyn by name and a native of Wiltshire, who had traveled in Italy and fallen there to the charms of an ancient literature encased in another language. Thus Greek made its way, smuggled in under the guise of respectability, to Magdalen, bringing with it scents of spices from other climes, as a summer wind carries memories and is laden with traces of treasure from some indefinable country far away.

Greek was more than a language or a new course or an addendum to the curriculum. It was a new culture and a new way of thinking and a new body of literature which might, unbeknownst to those who were steeped in Latin, bring all manner of infectious ideas that could produce vapors, agues, and plagues and might people the atmosphere of a college with apparitions. Why endure the risk? Latin sufficed for all ideas a man could comfortably entertain, and it served a solid and useful purpose besides. It aided the priest, the diplomat, the lawyer, the civil servant, the physician. Like the old Roman roads, Latin led everywhere, and if one wanted his thoughts to travel or the thoughts of others to come to him, Latin was the means. Books on all kinds of subjects were written in Latin; it was the means of communication, real as trade routes, between the scholars of all nations. Besides, it had become firmly entrenched in the schools. Here it was a language required and no other language was allowed. To enforce the use of the language, a spy was paid, the good Trevelyan says, to sneak among his playmates and "report if any of them used an English word in their play."[1]

Manifestly, then, a language so firm in the fortress of education could not regard with equanimity an invader which might usurp its place. Grenadiers of the Latin tongue leaped to battle as the warriors of a reigning king might leap to repel a rebel. Grave doctors preached against the study of Greek. The issue was down, and there were jousts and tilts and, at a later time, trial by street battle. It needed finally a royal edict to quiet the matter. Later in Bishop Fox's College of Corpus Christi the new language found hospice and was "allowed as an alternative to Latin in ordinary talk in hall and chambers and lectures in theology."[2]

Which of these two schools of language that ultimately came to contention with clubs among the scholars had its hold on the mind of the emerging Wolsey? Back of the High Street and the fights, deep in the recesses of the reflective apparatus, lay a war between resistance and awareness. It was more than a language brawl in an intellectual tavern. It was a play, a mystery play, an allegory in which Greek and Latin wore the masks of other forces and men as actors knew inwardly but would not admit the disguise. The question at stake was whether a society furnished with and carpeted by one set of ideas would admit another set of ideas alien and strange of tongue.

Yet the conflict between stability and awareness would not remain a drama of the educational stage to be acted out conveniently in symbols. Men were beginning to sail the roiling seas, and there were signs aplenty of islands and great land masses which might intrude upon the firmly fixed and comfortably known world of England. For in these same days Bartholomew Columbus came before King Henry of the English and with maps and compass persuaded him that the unknown not only might become known but might become England's as well. Bartholomew thought in water, not on land. Men said he was uncouth, but under the gust of his enthusiasm the King's fancy set sail. Let him bring his brother Christophorus, the King ordered, and let an expedition be arranged, that India might be found by sailing north by west. But Bartholomew had fallen among pirates on his journey to England; and he had suffered much delay. Nor had it been easy for an unknown Genoese mariner to arrange an audience with the King. So by the time Bartholomew returned to his brother, he found that Christophorus had already settled with Ferdinand and Isabella. The ships which would launch him on his quest would bear the flag of Spain.

Henry had missed the boats. But his meeting with Bartholomew and his maps, together with the experience Christophorus enjoyed on the crossing, released something like a spring in the practical, matter-of-fact, notebook-carrying Henry. The prospect of gain based on chance touched off the gambler in him. Enormous dice to roll upon the sea, with—who knows?—continents for stakes!

It was common talk that the King looked with longing beyond the rim of the seas and that he was willing to shell out some of the gold that had begun to fatten his coffers if he could find men who would enrich the holdings of England, as the expedition of Christophorus Columbus might have enriched them. It was an odd twist and the subject of much wonder in the realm, this preoccupation of a solemn, precise, and businesslike King (whose favorite gesture was to rub his palms together like a shopkeeper) with distant isles and shores shrouded in the mists of uncertainty. Nothing could so unsettle the mind, especially if it happened to be of a conservative bent and steeped in Latin, as the suspicion that the world was bigger than all its parts and that all parts of it were closer than one had previously thought.

It might be possible to keep Greek out and set the mind and tongue against alien forces. But men could not be chained to the land, particularly if the King encouraged them with his support and sanction and letters patent to wander to and fro upon the waters. Here was a King who by firm measures and stern command had brought a modicum of peace to a shattered society and had put its affairs in order—only to look now beyond the watery borders that kept it safe from molestation and to look, as it were, for new troubles abroad. Better, was it not, to stay at home and improve each shining hour and each shining shilling? Would it be Greek or Latin? New worlds with new problems, or a stable homeland? Europe or the Seven Seas? Where should a young man's mind center if he looked to the future?

To the King, of course; but in this case the royal head looked both ways, one face being grave toward his subjects and the other one light and expectant toward the west. It was plain enough that England now possessed a ruler who possessed the kingdom, a man at its head who, because his claims were dim, meant to make up for any lack of security in lineage by the security of careful government. And the outlook thus became bright for young men of talent and smart operating ability who could adorn routine with energy. But the matter was not as simple and amiable as that, if the resources of England were to be deployed over the whole face of the earth and if the comfort of a self-sufficient and Europe-focused society were to be disturbed by the pulls of distant magnets. This promised for the moment to be the case.

With all his painful problems at home and at the calculating courts of Europe combined, Henry could not keep his eyes off far horizons. He could not forgive himself for the twist of fate that had cheated him from backing Columbus.

So he would back others.

In particular he gave ear to the restless whisperings in Bristol. On his very first royal progress he had paid a visit to this hospitable and enterprising port in the west of England, looking to the wild west of the sea beyond. Bristol was a meeting mart for those who sailed to Iceland and those who came from the warmer climes as well. It was a gossip chamber in which all the tales that stirred men's minds to vast physical speculations were exchanged.

To this port in 1490 came another man of Genoa, by name John

Cabot. In his early manhood he had become a citizen of Venice. Now, after seeking vainly some support from both Spain and Portugal for venturesome voyages he wished to make, he came with his entire family to take up residence in Bristol. And in due course he laid his far-flung hopes and plans before the King, having first inspired other mariners to cast off in search of mythical lands and islands under the financing of Bristol merchants.

To the dreams of John Cabot, fashioned of mist like the rainbow, Henry lent a ready ear. So it came about that John Cabot, together with his three sons, set sail on substantial waters, trusting themselves to the assistance of the sea. They sailed as an adventure, but they carried an adequate ballast of royal approval, for the letters patent granted by the King gave them permission to seek out "regions or provinces of the heathens and infidels which before that time had been unknown to all Christians." It was further the order of the letters that no other English subject might even visit any of the territories discovered by the Cabots without express license and permission of the said John and his sons or their deputies.

The Pope had already divided the new world between the kingdoms of Spain and Portugal, but this stupendous fact Henry piously overlooked under the assumption that the Pope's edict applied only to the south and that Cabot might take a northwest passage and hence find new territory beyond the papal fold. It was odd, all the same, for one who so carefully cultivated the Church and attended her Masses to set Church rulings aside on a matter so important. It simply went to show how strong were the new currents that were passing through the minds of men.

When the Cabots returned in the first week of August in 1497, they brought no myrrh or spices, no tangibles of any kind from their bourn. But they brought further information of the great beyond. They had sailed north and had found land. And though they had not seen inhabitants, they had seen the signs of men; and they had found the waters near the distant shore temperate and heavy with fish, so much so that the fish could be caught up in a weighted basket. In these beneficent waters the Cabots had drifted far to the south, and everything they saw was good. And what they told upon their return refreshed again the imagination of the people who stayed home, and the tidings of these lands stirred the people from the languor of their thinking. There was something of the pull of the tides in these vast new movements of men and ships—and mind was bound to follow.

These tides were a part of the time of the hidden years of Thomas Wolsey, or Master Thomas Wolsey now, whilom Boy Bachelor and by way of becoming a Fellow of Magdalen College and a priest of the Church. There were pulls and tugs on the shores of his mind. Whatever he did in later years, he was now a votary of known wisdom, with Latin as a base, to be sure, but with Greek on his horizons. He pursued his studies of divinity in the cubbyhole of piety, but he could not escape the distractions of discoveries that now sounded loud enough to penetrate the Oxford quiet.

Meanwhile, he was of time and space and a solid citizen of Magdalen, where men of the world and of learning came and went with more frequency than ever and where the elements beat down. Wood tells us that in 1490 the predictions of Thomas Kent and other Oxonian astronomers concerning a great frost and scarcity of grain came to pass. Frost continued until January 29 and "became at length so hard and vehement that carts and horses could pass over the river near Oxford."[3] Game and fish were destroyed in great numbers by the merciless angry weather. Nature, being ever in those days given to violent extremes, as if to set the uncertainty of the times to music, next withdrew her bounty altogether, and the frost was followed by a dearth of rain which endured until the time of the harvest the same year. As a result, wheat and barley were sold in Oxford at a usurious price which brought great grief and trouble to the scholars.

The college, for all its walls, was in these periods of severity becoming an inescapable part of the great outside, and the poor scholars, being without fire, "were fain to walk and run up and down half an hour to get heat in their feet when they went to bed."[4] And the already dismal fare was worsened as the simplest food became dear.

Visitors made for festive occasions, and the ceremony with which they were treated adjourned from time to time the tedium of lectures and the savage pastime of disputations. There had been the royal call paid by Henry shortly after his coronation when he left a characteristically frugal offering on the altar in the chapel. The president of the college, Richard Mayhew, stood high in the royal favor. He had gone to London to attend Henry's coronation. The account books indicate that the president fared well in the disbursements made for various details of administration. In 1484 bed and bedclothes were bought for his lodgings in London and one ell of linen for his shaving cloths. Later a new case was provided "for carrying the college arrows when the president went on progress."[5]

Enough went on to give the College of St. Mary Magdalen touches of convulsive gaiety, but there was always the weather, some grim reminder of the raw. And if it was not tempest or drouth or relentless frost or over-abundant snows or a great water upon the land, there was pestilence. In one instance hardly had the scholars returned to Magdalen after having fled from fear of one disease than they were forced to flee again from another that had seeped into the confines of the College. All activities were suspended when a plague took up residence, and the scholars found refuge in the houses beyond Oxford. Wood tells us that "so frequent were the pestilences in these and after times that they gave a great blow to learning, and caused it much to decrease and lose its vigor . . . It was consulted by great personages of annulling the University."[6]

In this quarrelsome atmosphere of tempest, disease, and insecurity young Master Wolsey pursued his education at Magdalen during the years that the college forgot him. Education went forward somehow and constructive forces worked with steady vitality to keep things in a kind of balance. The physical buildings, the externalization of inward drives, the increase of tangible properties, seemed to be one answer to the confusion and turmoil all around. In one period 139 cart loads of stone were brought in for a wall in the grove. It was in this time that the first cornerstone of the new Tower of Magdalen was laid with fitting ritual by the chancellor of the university. The south cloister was rebuilt and the great gate erected. There were lodgings put up for the president of the college and a school for choristers. Bishop Waynflete, the founder, died and willed all his goods to the college, these being hauled in three fat carts. In one year eighty volumes were given the library by two Fellows, and expenses for chains to hold them were duly noted. In the hall at this time were figures of angels, and in the record there is entered a payment for washing the angels and for saffron for coloring their faces.[7]

There was a policy of progress and upkeep in spite of all difficulties. Gradually the institution grew in substance and tangibles and gave thus some answer to the world and some assurance to its occupants. The Tower of Magdalen rose steadily as if by right and as a symbol that might stand through the centuries. It was evidence in stone of both stability and aspiration. Architecture gathered up and said and amplified what men could not say with words. There might be bloody flux and bubonic plague and the sweat; there might be riot and civil commotion and the intrusion of Greek and foreign bodies of culture. But as long as there were massive edifices abuilding, the university would not be annulled. The tower and the great gate and the cloisters and the new buildings—these were permanence in a world rife with change and uncertainty. If a man would make himself felt, let it be in stone.

Robert Wolsey of Ipswich died respectably in the autumn of 1496. Shortly after his death, the name of Thomas Wolsey began to appear in the records of his college.

In any attempt to reckon the cause and course of events it would be too much to say that the death of the father sired the son or that the interment of the elder signaled the birth of the younger. But by any reckoning it is plain that the son beheld in the father's attainments a sign of what the times required. By the simple acquisition of property, by the ownership of a house and the accumulation of moneys, the elder Wolsey had risen from the rank of an alien butcher to a position of at least moderate local eminence. It was an achievement not to be despised in those days, for the man was not many generations removed from serfdom.

In 1493 Robert Wolsey had become a churchwarden in the parish of St. Nicholas. At his death he was able to bequeath not only funds for the painting of the archangel above the altar of his parish church but other moneys as well to provide that a Mass be sung for him and his friends for the space of one year and at a worthy stipend.

This was the sort of provision that a man of wealth could make. It showed that, whatever the complaints raised against him earlier, he had established himself now in the eyes of the Church. It was a kind of posthumous sanctuary for one who had fled the law, showing in a right convincing way—which is to say, through the hiring of prayers—that the charges of the past were no longer valid.

On every hand now was to be seen the growth of wealth and with it the emergence of new comforts—more, a standard of comfort. Wealth became a criterion, even among the nobles. "The peers were expected to remain as a class the greatest of landowners. Indeed, those who fell below the required standard risked their titles or privileges. In 1477 and again in 1493 a duke was 'demoted' for lack of a sufficiency of land and 'decayed peers' were sometimes not summoned to the House of Lords."[8]

Not only wealth but the appearance of wealth was important. Men of money aimed at splendor, at a conspicuous evidence of wealth, at a display of their possessions. Noble birth had now to be accompanied by signs of commerce. If a man was noble, he had to be wealthy to maintain his nobility—and, by the same token, if a man amassed enough property or fixed upon himself and his heirs and assigns enough wealth, he might even be created a noble. In a word, the measure of a man had begun to change. It had shifted from birth to possessions. Naturally this change affected the whole populace, both in judgments and practices.

In former times the Merchants of the Staple gathered wool and shipped it abroad for refinement and manufacture into cloth. These merchants enjoyed a monopoly of the wool trade and held this monopoly in a grim grip. Then gradually wool began to be sold at home for the manufacture of cloth. "Instead of the 30,000 sacks which they yearly counted in the fourteenth century, they could not at the close of the fifteenth century collect more than 8,624 sacks. England was turned from being a country whose chief business was exporting wool into a country whose chief business was exporting cloth . . ."[9] At the close of the century the English Merchant Adventurers exported 60,000 pieces of cloth yearly."

Under this remarkable change there was a great stirring of trade within the realm, and more and more of the lowly found profitable means of latching on to coin and exchanging their services to advantage. "Great religious corporations and landowners who had once provided on their own estates for local wants recognized the new condition of things and . . . sent every year far and wide across the country to great clothing centers to buy material for their household liveries."

It was upon a world teeming with trade and quickened by the interchange of goods and services, rife with an increasing number of contacts and with people moving hither and yon in the business of buying and selling, that young Thomas Wolsey looked out in 1497. It was a world in which England had discovered how to use her own resources. Bell foundries, cooperworks, brickmaking, the production of glass and stained-glass windows, the brewing of beer and the weaving of linen, the work of lacemakers and ribbon weavers—all contributed to the change in men's habits and men's minds. A man now could step from one class to another on stones of fortune. It was a time of opportunity, of new worlds to conquer close at hand.

The first mention of Thomas Wolsey in the records of the College of St. Mary Magdalen occurs in the year 1497. Then he appears as a Master of Arts and "fourteenth on the list of Fellows." Fellows formed the governing body of the college, members of the inner circle which administratively guided the policies and plans of Magdalen. The honor, it was said, had been conferred upon him for his brilliance and percipience as a scholar. And by now, too, he had had a grounding in the classics and some experience as a teacher.

Indeed, at this stage of his life Thomas Wolsey seemed set and destined for the life of a schoolmaster. The degree of Master of Arts at Oxford disposed him strongly to that career—practically committed him. It was presumed in the very nature of things, and written into the college requirements besides, that a man who learned enough to be a Master would relay his learning to others. The university would "not recognize as a Master anyone who had not already actually undertaken the duties of a teacher in the schools. Great importance was accordingly attached to the occasion on which the licentiate began to teach with authority, or, in technical language, to his 'inception' or 'commencement.' A licentiate who omitted to incept within the year prescribed by his oath was required to pay a heavy fine, and the fine was doubled if he held any lucrative post at the time. His license to teach was also cancelled."[10]

Some reports have it that Thomas Wolsey attained the degree of Master of Arts in two years instead of the seven commonly required. Whatever the speed, he did attain it and with it its dignities. As was befitting the bestowal of a degree so elevated, the ceremony surrounding its completion was a lay ordination, an admission into mysteries and fellowship. The matter was not to be taken lightly and one who entered into the company of Masters had much to remind him of his importance. It was for a young and impressionable man an introduction to the pageantry of superiority.

"On the day of an inception," Lyte tells us, "all lectures and disputations were suspended, in order that members of the different faculties might be present. After the solemn celebration of the mass, every one went to his appointed place in St. Mary's Church, and, at a signal given by one of the Proctors, the proceedings began. First the Father stepping forward delivered a book into the hands of the inceptor, placed a cap—the emblem of magisterial authority—on his head, and greeted him with the kiss of peace . . . Later as he knelt down and placed his hand on a volume of Holy Writ the Proctor, addressing him for the first time as 'Master', made him swear that he would respect the statutes and privileges of the University, that he would not foment discord, that he would not recognize any University in England save Oxford and Cambridge."[11]

In this time-honored, leafy, and almost Druidic manner had the Ipswich boy been inducted into the sacred cult of the learned, the guild of scholars sworn to an institution which, along with Cambridge, enjoyed a monopoly on wisdom. He was by this act, too and likewise, given the crest of authority—to teach other men's minds, to lecture and to pass to lesser men the fruits of his own erudition. He had been vested with authority and clothed with the raiment of learning, he of a sensitive and ambitious nature, in the years that were teeming with new industry and the promise of wealth on every hand, when the severe seventh Henry was putting the nation's house in order and men were in quest of new lands and Oxford was shaken by the invasion of a new language with its threat of a new culture.

From the time Thomas Wolsey's name began to appear in the records of Magdalen, his rise was rapid and conspicuous. His father's will provided that if the son should become a priest within a year of the father's death the son should receive the fee named in the will for the singing of Masses for the father and his friends. Wolsey was not a priest in the prescribed time. He was busy with college affairs. He traveled about on college business, among other things buying cloth for choristers' clothes and developing habits of management and assiduity.[12] He had already gone beyond the academic life. He had become third bursar—one of the treasurers and managers of the property of Magdalen; later he was made second bursar, then chief bursar. And he came for a time to be schoolmaster at the grammar school connected with the college.

In the course of his tutoring and teaching he had under his care three of the sons of Thomas Grey, Marquis of Dorset, a man of parts and wealth who stood in these days close to the throne, even if at the time of the Lambert Simnel affair there had been spread abroad venomous rumors of his disloyalty and Henry had clapped him in the Tower until the rumors—and the rebellion—passed. Since then he had received various tokens of the royal confidence. He had been present at the christening of Arthur, Henry's first-born and heir. In 1492 the Marquis had taken part in an expedition to extricate from one of his perennial difficulties the Emperor Maximilian of the Holy Roman Empire in a bootless foray against the French. In 1497 he held a commission in the forces Henry assembled to suppress an ominous rebellion fomented and formed against the King by the men of Cornwall.

In the stations of the nobility, a young man needed hardly to be reminded, a marquis ranks immediately below a duke. Commonly the favored sons of men of such rank enjoyed release from the college grind, being right well educated by the standards of the day if they learned aptly the manners and trickeries of the chase and if they knew the proper use of courtly manners at the houses of other great and wealthy worthies. Certainly it was not ordinary for the sons of nobles, and especially high nobles, to be among the canaille in colleges.

It stands plainly to reason, then, that the presence of three of the seven sons of the mighty Marquis (he had eight daughters) in the sacred precincts of Magdalen created lusty attention among the young Fellows seeking patrons.

Nor was Wolsey's tutoring and special attention bestowed in vain. For it came about at the glad season of Christmas in 1499 that it pleased the Marquis to summon the schoolmaster to accompany his three sons on their visit home for the holidays and to enjoy with the considerable family there sports and festivities befitting the season.[13]

The family seat of the Greys was a mansion called Bradgate Park, which lay seven miles west of Leicester, not far from the scene of the battle of Bosworth. It was one of the important mansions of the day, pleasantly regarded then and destined to be famous later as the birthplace of the hapless Lady Jane Grey.

The journey to Bradgate Park from Oxford involved a trip of over fifty miles each way—a trip not without hazards, of course, and the presence of a schoolmaster as a guide and guard was a plain convenience to the Marquis. But if it was a convenience to the Marquis it was a joy to the schoolmaster. Here was a chance for a young man of rising dignity —by now he had become chief bursar of Magdalen and responsible for disbursements touching its many activities, including the completion of Magdalen Tower—to meet the family of one of the highest lords of the land in one of the most finely appointed houses of the realm. It was a full-scale chance for the young scholar and university official to get formally and for a convenient season out of the atmosphere—nay, miasma —of Oxford scholasticism. He would visit one of the great houses of the kingdom; but, great though it was, it might prove to be but the gatehouse to something vaster.

There were changes going on in such houses in these days—all in the direction of luxury and privacy. The hall, which at one time was the center and focus of the life of the manor, had become only a passageway. Important members of the household no longer ate with the servants but in rooms withdrawn—some of these rooms having chimneys and other new appointments. Still the hall remained the most spacious apartment in the house, "open to all who were admitted within the precincts." Distinctions in rank and age were apparent and emphasized at every turn. Seats or benches with backs were reserved for "the superior members of the family." In other rooms "one chair . . . was considered enough for a room and was no doubt reserved for the person of most dignity." Fancy cushions "called bankers and dorsers to be placed over the benches and backs of the seats of the better persons at the table were now also in general use."[14]

The movement toward privacy was to be noted in the use of parlors for meals. Cupboards "stood high on long legs and were used to keep bread and cheese or sweetmeats to which you helped yourself between the two main meals of the day." The female members of the family began to use these parlors as sitting rooms, and bedchambers, which in former times had been meeting places, now became much more private. The beds "were large and elaborately upholstered and canopied, and remade as couches by day."[15]

It was an education in itself to see the details of a large and well-managed household. There was an astonishing amount of linen used, much of it woven in England, for underwear, sheets, tablecloths, towels, room hangings. "Torches were made of wood resin and tallow. Flambeaux or iron holders for the flaming wood hung against the stone walls where there was sufficient draught. Candles were made of mutton fat and beeswax with flax, or rarely cotton wicks brought from Sicily."[16] The increase in the use of candles was one of the signs to show how products from many lands were flowing into England to enrich and absorb the new wealth.

Thomas Wolsey was a hearty and talkative young man, full of zest for living and in good fettle with the three sons he had in his charge. In the liveliness of his eloquence he made such good use of his time that the Marquis was delighted with him and with the solid learning he apparently had instilled in the sons.

Here, obviously, was a young man of great talent and promise who deserved a future. And so, obedient to a practice that belongs to no age and an irony that belongs to all ages, the Marquis saw that the schoolmaster must be rewarded for his good teaching by not teaching at all, by being withdrawn from teaching. There was no future in teaching. Education was to fit a man for something else.

The only portal open was the Church. In the Church a man might advance, might get into government, aided by a long English tradition. The priesthood was the ladder, and a man of Thomas Wolsey's promise, having done his work so well and being of an eloquent turn, should get into the priesthood.

It chanced that the Marquis had in his possession a parish church in a town one hundred and fifty miles away—at Limington, near Ilchester in the shire of Somerset. What he had was the right to bestow the income and emoluments of the parish on whom he should choose, the parish being vacant of a rector at that time.

He chose Thomas Wolsey.

A living was a living and not to be despised. If a man named rector of a parish did not relish the idea of ministering there, it was simple for him to use part of the revenues of the place to engage a curé or vicar to say Masses and perform the duties while he went abroad or sought out some other gainful pursuit. Indeed, it was rather expected that the rector would follow this casual course. But whether he stayed or served in absence, the main thing was to have an assured income and get established in the precincts of the Church. For, once this was done, there would, especially in the case of an exceptional fellow, be every chance of advancement.

CHAPTER V The ancient shire of Somerset, which contains the placid village of Limington, is a basin formed on one side by the Bristol Channel and protected on the other three sides by forbidding hills. In the north are the Mendip Hills, penetrated only by deep coombs, among them the Cheddar Gorge.

Partly because of the surrounding hills, Somerset was removed from the main preoccupations of England. It had taken little or no part in the venomous quarrels of the nobility during the Wars of the Roses, and its only sign of real interest in events arose in 1497 when some of its sons championed, to their later remorse, the cause of a pretender to the throne, by name Perkin Warbeck, a fabulous young European who had passed himself off, first in Ireland, of course, and later before the courts of Europe, as the son of Edward IV. The pretender had finally made his bid at arms by trying to seize the city of Exeter in the neighboring county of Devon. His effort failed, and Henry fetched him out of sanctuary and carted him conspicuously back to London.

Otherwise the royal authority seemed vague and distant. Somerset was well contained and sufficient unto itself. Since the eleventh century it had grown grain enough to export, and the quality of its cattle was known then and to be confirmed later when Cheddar came to be celebrated for its cheese. The region had that sort of contentment that comes from isolation. It was a great and well-filled pocket, with plenty of resources in minerals besides the produce of its land.

In a broad valley within the basin, Limington was a village that drew its sustenance from the soil. The village was oddly placed, for it lay only a mile and a half from the ancient Roman town of Ilchester, one of the stations on the old Roman road from Bath to Exeter, the station of Ilchester (the suffix *chester* indicating a walled town or a place where Roman roads crossed) being at a point where the road passed over the River Yeo. It was as if there were little excuse for the town and then, a short distance away, less for the village, save that Limington had been from the time of the Saxons a place where farmers lived and from which they had gone out to work their fertile fields.

Today the houses of the village are strung out like beads on either side of the road. Halfway along among the houses stands the Church of St. Mary. It is a work of the thirteenth century, constructed of sturdy stone, with a nave eighty-seven by twenty-four feet and a chantry on the north. To the west a perpendicular tower rises—a tower big and unwieldy in proportion to the church, which for all its charm looks like a miniature imitation of something vast and important. Although the whole churchyard is encased in ancient cedars, as though they had been grown in the Bible, early pictures indicate that the church stood out above the meadows, and there is a faint suggestion of an alert turtle about it.

To this quiet church in a small rural village in a remote part of the kingdom, Thomas Wolsey came to be instituted as priest on October 10, 1500.[1] It was at first blush an odd choice for a young man who had just wound up his job as bursar of Magdalen. With all the remoteness and the inconveniences and the small scale of the operations at Limington, there had to be reasons for Wolsey's accepting the appointment there. Some of these reasons are not far to seek.

It was a good time to get away from Magdalen. Wolsey had stood well with the president of the college, Richard Mayhew. He had championed the cause of the president while Mayhew was absent from the college and had taken his side against detractors and in a dispute between the Colleges of Magdalen and Morton over the ownership of a mill.[2] But Mayhew's administration had ended in confusion and disorder. There had been controversies; charges and countercharges. There were claims, although they were never supported by evidence, that Wolsey had diverted college funds to the completion of the tower—funds that should have been spent on other causes. Later, after Wolsey and Mayhew left, Magdalen continued in ways unbecoming to the intent of its founder. In 1507 there was a visitation to the college, and some of its members were admonished and told to reform; others suffered penalties for breaches of statutes, especially in respect to card playing. Complaints against members included charges of adultery, of receiving stolen goods, of concealing a thief. One member was charged with having baptized a cat.[3]

Wolsey exchanged the uncertainties and quarrels of Oxford for the patronage of one of the great nobles. Thomas Grey, while he was merely Lord Ferrers of Groby, back in 1471, had been on the Yorkist side. His mother was Elizabeth Woodville, who later, to the consternation of the

Earl of Warwick, who was accustomed to selecting queens as well as kings, married Edward IV. Grey as a stepson of Edward fought with the King at Tewkesbury. Four years later he was created the first Marquis of Dorset, and by family and loyalty he stood high in the royal favor under Edward. Then Edward died, and the Marquis championed the cause of the young King Edward V, his half brother. When Richard III won the throne, the Marquis was suddenly a rebel and attainted. He took vigorous part in the Duke of Buckingham's rebellion against Richard. When this failed, he fled to France and joined the conspiracy formed by Henry Tudor. Of late his honors had been high, and he enjoyed the firmest confidence the King could repose in him—a royal commission to have troops under his command.

Wolsey had been ordained a priest in Lent of 1498.[4] From the moment Bishop Augustine Church (his very name could not escape notice) laid his hands on the young schoolmaster in the parish of St. Peter in Marlborough, the man who had hitherto been ordained a Master in a lesser fraternity of teachers became a vital part of something vast and organized. This sense of belonging to the Church brought the doubly comforting assurance of being a part of the Body of Christ and at the same time on the road to success.

But the ways of the world are wondrous and its caprices hard to calculate. Hardly had young Father Wolsey begun his labors in the parish of Limington than he somehow ran afoul of a custodian of the law. There was in these parts at that year of 1501 a shining and zealous knight by the name of Sir Amias Paulet, a very energetic gentleman who had often been sweaty in good causes. He had been a Lancastrian in the intermittent Wars of the Roses, and after Buckingham's rebellion, at the beginning of the reign of Richard III, Paulet had been attainted by the Yorkists. After the triumph of Henry over the Yorkists at Bosworth, he had been appointed sheriff of both Dorset and Somerset, which meant that his suzerainty extended over an area of 2617 square miles—a territory that should have been adequate even for a man of his nosy talents.

Following the battle of Stoke, Amias Paulet had been knighted, and the scope of his operations given an even more loyal tinge. For now Henry, with an ever-open eye for painless income, sent Sir Amias to levy fines upon those who had dared espouse the cause of Perkin Warbeck.

Revenue gained from Somerset and four adjoining counties equaled an amount sufficient to run the royal household for well over half a year. Thus the rebellion was made to pay in cash. More to the point, however, was the fact that the collections were punitive, and those who might yield moneys for their transgressions in the Warbeck war were hunted down and haled before the King's collectors.

One of the staunchest of those on this errand without mercy was Sir Amias Paulet. He had the run of the King's highways and enjoyed an almost unbearable sense of virtue from prowling the country and poking into the problems of loyalty and ferreting out those who, by any connection with plots against the King, might be susceptible of rough treatment.

In this sort of activity he was busy in the years before Wolsey arrived at Limington. But apparently this activity was not enough to engage all his time or his faculties. His family home was at Hinton St. George, a few miles to the southwest of Limington, and Sir Amias appears to have found time for an interest in local affairs. He and young Father Wolsey clashed head-on. Wolsey, fresh from Oxford, protégé of a marquis and a member of the privileged clergy, was nonetheless seized by the knight-errant and made a public spectacle. He was put in stocks— laid by the heels in a public place for his parishioners and all to gape upon.[5]

What provoked the knight to visit this humiliation upon the priest, no one knows. Rumor still holds that Wolsey was guilty of excessive gaiety; that he grew drunk and disorderly at a country fair and, in the course of his pastimes there, pinched maidenly bottoms. The story, once told, would not down. One hears it to this day in Limington. But in point of fact it gained currency only in later Elizabethan times, and there is no shred of record to support it and little or nothing to lend it plausibility.[6] Rather, the incident of Wolsey's arrest bears all the marks of an officious and vindictive act beyond the line of any duty Sir Amias might have had to perform. The priest was not in the jurisdiction of a secular officer, and the fastening of a man or woman in stocks was a form of punishment meted out to scolds, vagabonds, beggars, petty offenders—persons to be held up to ridicule and scorn.

The Church had full means and procedures for the discipline of the clergy, and the knight had no right to handle a priest. A group of parishes formed a rural deanery. The function of the rural dean "was both administrative and disciplinary. His chief duty seems to have been to report serious cases of clerical or lay incontinence to the bishop's or archdeacon's court. The bishop's consistory court concerned itself with the property, dress and conduct of the clergy from the gravest moral offenses to small breaches of discipline, such as asserting oneself to be as learned as the bishop of London."[7]

In addition to the pain and exposure of public ridicule, then, Wolsey suffered the indignity of having the secular arm reach out and take him from the protective fraternity of which he had recently become an official member. The Church had failed to protect him—and in a quarrel with a lay official associated with the nobility. Possibly the incident showed how the civil authorities were getting out of hand.

In this year and about the time of these sobering events, Thomas Grey, first Marquis of Dorset, died at the age of forty-nine. Plainly it was time for the young priest to shake the dust of Limington off his feet and find another patron.

Although Father Thomas Wolsey departed Limington in the latter part of the year 1501 to become chaplain to Henry Deane, Archbishop of Canterbury and Primate of All England, he did not cut himself off from the revenues of his Limington parish. Indeed, he had already begun that clerical kleptomania which was to mark his career—the sedulous collection of income from appointments which carried emoluments but required no distasteful chores. Already he had influential friends who could recommend him. He obeyed a rewarding custom of his day, but, even in his youth, he obeyed it with unaccustomed zest. While yet at Limington, Father Wolsey had applied for and received permission to hold certain other parishes which he never saw.

The mystery, of course, lies not in the fact that the young priest left his small parish for the immense security of Canterbury but in the fact that, in spite of certain advantages, he had gone to Limington at all. The duties of a parish priest held hardly enough lure to attract a young man of his bounding imagination. A properly organized parish, Gasquet tells us, was a corporation. No lords of the manor or political personages were supposed to have any power or authority over it. In times of change, however, and in local situations, principles long honored were subject to violence, as the clash with Sir Amias Paulet plainly showed. The Church as a massive institution still held sway in theory, but men of the cloth in its outposts might not always be treated with the same deference accorded a prelate. The lords of the Church might be secure, but assaults were often made on unpopular local clergymen.

Added to the vulnerable and exposed position of the parish priest was the soggy tedium of his routine. He preached, and administered the sacraments, as any clergyman must; taught children and adults the Lord's Prayer, Hail Mary, the Ten Commandments; taught people how to cross themselves properly; farmed the glebe and often other land as well; sometimes acted as a tradesman. Also he was expected by the State to act "as a kind of Sunday newspaper and read out from the pulpit official bulletins of victory or other intelligence."[8]

It was no life for a Wolsey. Far better to accept the prevailing rubric of the day—farm the actual work out to a poorly paid priest known as a perpetual vicar and go on to larger fields of service. Under this arrangement the appointed priest would receive the full pay of the rector but leave the duties of the parish in the hands of one who might be known as a chaplain but who would actually be a curate; this unhappy and often wretched mortal would be engaged at the lowest possible wage—from one third to even less of the rector's regular salary—and in some cases he would be sworn not to ask for a larger stipend during his tenure. The scroll in the little Church of St. Mary at Limington proudly displays the name of Wolsey as rector there until 1509, but during the last eight years he held the living he was nowhere near the place.

This arrangement did not make for a contented clergy, but it did provide a smooth and speedy means by which a young man with an eye to the top could get on with his career. For the system had among other things the aim of cultivating the talented, of grooming them for responsible posts which the relatively uneducated and unpromising stipendiaries could not fill. There were classes within the Church as well as within lay society. The Church might offer through its ascending hierarchy the road by which a young man could climb out of his almost destined station; but the ascent of any who did this was based upon the help and work of a whole body of carriers and pack-horse priests who did yeoman service while those of gilded promise and shining eyes went on to the heights. It took a host of yeomen to make a lord, even in the Church. It was in the order of events, then, that Wolsey should go to Canterbury, leaving the custodial care of Limington and his other parishes to lesser men.

Administratively Canterbury ranked supreme. The archiepiscopal province of York contained but three dioceses—York, Durham, and Carlisle. The others—sixteen in all—came under the jurisdiction of the Archbishop of Canterbury. And, as if this were not enough, it had been by long custom appointed that the Archbishop of Canterbury should serve ex officio as Lord Chancellor of England, the Keeper of the Great Seal of England, the man in whose person was summed up both Church and State.

One who served on the staff of such a man in environs rife with ritual and tradition would have every chance to observe the methods by which the business of the Church and the kingdom went forward; and he would be in a position where he must feel, were he sensitive or not, the weight and power of the great institutions of his day. Here he would become, if his mind were alert and open, an apprentice to power.

The occupant of the Archbishop's chair at the time Wolsey was made one of the two chaplains at Canterbury left something to be desired, it is true. Henry Deane was about seventy years of age, and he had grown infirm through a long period of service—distinguished more by its fidelity than its drama. No one was precise about his background, although it was claimed that he was a member of the ancient family of Dene in the Forest of Dean. He was without special flair or assertiveness. Appointed to the archbishopric by Henry VII in 1500, he assumed the office but was never installed, either because he lacked the necessary funds to meet the huge expense or because he accepted the fact that he was not long for this world and thought the elaborate ceremony a waste of labor considering how little time he had to stay. He seemed preoccupied with his own demise and prepared minute stage directions for his funeral, as though resolved that it would be one of the big events of his life. He seemed to prefer it to his installation at Canterbury.

Henry Deane had delighted in building and in repairing. He rebuilt the manor house at Otford, and under his jurisdiction the great bridge at Rochester was put in order again. Whatever he did he did slowly, prudently, and well, and the King rejoiced at so true a man and rewarded him with the highest honors.

At Lambeth Palace, the Archbishop's house near Westminster, he entertained Catherine of Aragon on her way to London after her stormy passage from Spain to marry Prince Arthur. And it was Henry Deane who conducted the marriage ceremony of Catherine and Arthur in November of 1501, thus joining together the royal houses of England and Spain in what Henry had thought to fashion as a shrewd and indestructible alliance.

Where great ceremonies of state were called for, the Archbishop of Canterbury was present. In his person moved the Church. And at the cathedral and monastery of Canterbury, not only could Thomas Wolsey study the chief minister of the Church and the Crown, but he could also feel and experience that long gathering of forces that had made Canterbury more than an administrative post. It was a shrine.

The shrine commemorated the blood and bones of another archbishop, who had been murdered and mutilated in the north transept of the cathedral over three hundred years before. It was the tomb of Thomas Becket, who had defied King Henry II and asserted the supremacy of the Church over secular rulers.

Pilgrims of all classes and quarters came to the shrine in bands. Geoffrey Chaucer, a justice of the peace and commissioner of the riverbank between Greenwich and Woolwich, had watched these pilgrims and celebrated them in a collection of tales. This collection had been among the early books published by William Caxton, and the tales lent interest to the pilgrimages and increased them in the days Wolsey spent at Canterbury. Miraculous cures had been accomplished, and many persons came in great penance and devotion; but not a few came for the ride, and the term *Canterbury gallop,* denoting the leisurely and pleasant pace of the horses of the pilgrims, had begun to take its place in the language, later to be reduced to the word *canter.*[9]

The shrine was one of the sights of the world. An Italian visitor to England noted that the tomb of St. Thomas surpassed all belief. "This, notwithstanding its great size," he wrote, "is entirely covered with plates of pure gold; but the gold is scarcely visible from the variety of precious stones with which it is studded . . . and these beauties of nature are enhanced by human skill, for the gold is carved and engraved in beautiful designs . . ."[10]

What would the shrine signify to a young priest?

Certainly a nimble imagination would see in it a story as rich as the jewels and gold that adorned it, for the tomb held the body of a man who in his life and death and immortality played out the whole drama of the Church and the State, the priest and the king. Here was a man kings and pilgrims alike reckoned with, centuries after his blood and brains had been strewn by assassins around the sacred precincts. In his martyrdom and canonization the person of the priest had been elevated to its highest eminence. One who sought preferment in the Church and advancement in the kingdom would find in him a subject fit for endless reflection.

Once made Archbishop of Canterbury, Becket refused to accept the principles Henry had set forth to curtail rights previously enjoyed by the Church. On Christmas Day, 1170, he lashed his enemies from the pulpit of the cathedral. "When the rights of the Church are violated," he said, "I shall await no man's permission to avenge them." In a voice of thunder he excommunicated from the pulpit in the cathedral men who had offended him and dashed the candle to the pavement in token of the extinction of his enemies.[11]

Four days later Thomas Becket had been done to death, and gruesomely, by courtiers of the King. Few believed that the King was directly responsible for the murder, but that he was indirectly to blame could not be gainsaid. He had declared, it was reported: "What cowards have I brought up in my court, who care nothing for their allegiance to their master! Not one will deliver me from this low-born priest!"[12]

Well, he had been delivered from the Archbishop but into hands of greater evils. The King fell into instant and wide disfavor with his subjects when the report spread that he had laid his hands even indirectly upon the head of the Church in England. At Avranches, France, where he was at the time, Henry swore on the Gospels that he had not ordered or wished the Archbishop's murder.

Still people muttered. Two years later Becket had been canonized, and the kingdom of England was in general revolt. The Scots had crossed the border under their King; Yorkshire had rebelled and the midland counties, too. All hostile movements were fomented and sustained by the belief that Henry had been privy to the murder of the saint.

Penance at Avranches was not enough. The King must come to Canterbury. There followed a scene which history in time would gloss over and forget, aided by the incredible nature of events. But another Thomas at

Canterbury, himself geared for greatness, could not miss or ignore the dramatic humiliation of an English King. Here was the stuff dreams are made of, and cardinals too. If there was any precedent on which a man's thinking might rest when he came to consider the ascendancy of the Church over the State, it was to be found in the story of Henry II at Canterbury.

In the summer of 1174 Henry started from France to England. His passage was marked by a gale that troubled the waters. He landed, however, at Southampton on July 8. "From that moment he began to live on a penitential diet of bread and water. He approached the sacred city of Canterbury on the 12th of July. At the first sight of the Cathedral he leaped from his horse and went on foot to the outskirts of the town. Here at St. Dunstan's Church he paused and stripped his royal robes from him and walked from there on through the city in the guise of a penitent pilgrim. He was barefoot and the rough stones of the streets were marked with blood that started from his feet."

This man was King of England.

Straight to the scene of the murder in the north transept he went. "Here he knelt again and kissed the sacred stone on which the Archbishop had fallen, the prelates standing around to receive his confession. Thence he was conducted to the crypt, where he again knelt, and with groans and tears kissed the tomb and remained long in prayer." The King requested absolution and received the kiss of reconciliation from the prior.

Even now the King had not done with his groveling before the minions of the Church. He removed his clothes, placed his head and shoulders in the tomb, and then received five strokes from each bishop and each abbot who was present, the stroke being laid on with a monastic rod. Then he submitted to three punitive strokes from each of the eighty monks who were there.

It was to be noted that Henry's penance had almost as clear and measurable effect as the murder. For suddenly matters stood better around the land. The Scots were soundly defeated in battle, and the tensions which had laid hold upon the nation subsided. If further proof of the value of the King's acknowledged humiliation had been needed, it could have been found in the favorable turn of national events.[13]

When Thomas Wolsey began his chaplainship in 1501, pilgrims came daily to pay tribute to Thomas Becket, the tribute of memory. And when they came they celebrated the transcendent worth of a prelate backed by the power of the Church and the moral sanction of the ages.

The young priest did not remain long in the most sacred spot of England. The year 1503 was a year when death stalked in high places. Henry's good queen Elizabeth died nine days after the birth of a daughter. She was thirty-seven years of age and had borne Henry seven children, three of whom died in infancy. Her first-born, Arthur, had died the year before and only a few months after his marriage to Catherine of Aragon.

The King was stricken in his grief, and he made up in her funeral and interment for much he had failed to give her when she was alive. All the streets along which the cortege passed were filled with torches. The whole number was hard to reckon, but the chronicler was much impressed with the display and mentioned the two hundred that went with the corpse, adding quaintly, and still impressed, that these were at the King's cost. The bearers of the torches were arrayed in white gowns.

It was a funeral worthy of a queen. But the next week Henry Deane, Archbishop of Canterbury, died; and in ground and water covered his funeral outdid the Queen's. He had seen death ahead and had written a play to go with it. He managed to die in London at Lambeth Palace, which was fitting and proper for the Archbishop, that being his official residence. But it was part of the drama too, for Wolsey and another chaplain had instructions to transport the body by water, in a bedecked and appropriately solemn barge, to Faversham and there to put it in a hearse and convey it to Canterbury, accompanied by thirty-three sailors arrayed in black.[14]

Following hard upon the heels of the Queen's funeral, this one called for surpassing skill in management. Wolsey conducted his part well. Here was a task worthy of his energies and the biblical stretch of his imagination. It called at once for solemnity and for pomp.

CHAPTER

VI

From his Canterbury experience Wolsey got a taste of the tradition and ceremony of the Church. But it was not likely that he would be satisfied with righteousness and ritual. He was meant for government, and he took on now a less pious patron, one to whom he could prove his skill in the handling of the hundred and one details that attended the regulation of men and trade. By this means, seeing that the man to whom he was attached stood well as a servant of the King, Wolsey would be commended to court.

The man who next became his patron was Sir Richard Nanfan, Lord Deputy of the port of Calais. The Deputy of Calais was in a sense the gatekeeper of the kingdom of England, for this seaport of Calais lay twenty-two miles east by south of Dover. Edward III had wrested the old town and the spacious harbor from the French following the battle of Crécy in 1346. The town had fallen after a siege that lasted a year. Being now a possession, an outpost, it was fiercely English; and having been captured and stubbornly held, the port had to be used, whether it was useful or not, and made to seem important. It was a center of business and the point of all coming and going. A man or a shipment was not out of England until past Calais.

No matter was so minor that it could be allowed to escape official attention. The Deputy was ordered in one case to assist the movement of ambassadors to and from England, from France, Spain, and Germany, and at the same time to arrange for two stags and two does to be brought along under diplomatic privileges if the Archduke of Austria might have them to spare. There were remonstrances against tolls levied by the captain of Gravelines on all boats passing from Calais to Flanders and from Flanders to Calais. A close supervision had to be kept over strangers lodging in the town, "the different keepers of lodging houses being sworn to report daily on the number of guests and quality."[1]

Calais was a fortified town. A fort commanded the only road across the "marishes" by which Calais was approached from the south and southwest. It was a fort "possessed of sluice gates to the sea which enabled the holders to flood the surrounding country at will." The gates of the city were closely tended. "The lord deputy himself received the keys every night and gave them to the night-porter at his 'lodge' in the morning, specifying the number of gates he appointed to be opened for the day."[2]

There was plenty of color and pageantry in all the daily doings of Calais. It was a place of movement, a crossroads in water. But back of the pageantry and the official performance was a vast amount of complicated paper work to be done, and it was here that the priest Wolsey came to the aid of the aging Nanfan. For every lordly display of power there were a hundred pieces of paper to be filled out and tucked away. That was the lesson of Calais. Wolsey learned it well and his scrivening diligence did not go unrewarded.

When in 1505 Sir Richard made ready to leave his exacting post and return to England, "intending to live more at quiet," he commended Wolsey for his incessant labor to the special favor of the King. Wolsey was promoted to the King's service and made his chaplain.

So Wolsey came at last to court—and under an arrangement that appeared to have been well worth waiting for. His position, while minor, entitled him to be often in the royal presence. A scrupulous observance of the rituals of the Church had long been the practice of Henry VII. The monarch's health was not good—some said he coughed with every breath—and one might reasonably expect him to show more of a disposition to see his chaplain than his ministers. Wolsey might become on intimate terms with the King.

In one respect, however, the chaplain's arrival at court was marred by disappointment. There was a good deal of severity, if not downright drabness, about the court of the parsimonious Henry. In these days there was little that was gay and less that was convenient to one who had enjoyed the ceremonious living at Calais. The court followed the King, and often there were not adequate sleeping quarters. Wolsey occupied a bed with Lord Darcy of Templehurst, an older man and a Privy Councilor. Darcy wrote Wolsey later to remind him of those grim days, recalling the long hours they had spent revealing their minds and ambitions to each other, talking over their frustrations, each promising to help the other later if he could.[3]

It was hard to know how a resolute and determined man, forward-looking and full of energy, could advance himself in the crowded court of an ailing king who kept everything under his firm control. Wolsey was in the vigor of his middle thirties. The force of his personality may be measured by the fact that he had commended himself to, and had been recommended by, a series of worthy patrons. There is good reason to believe that Sir Reginald Bray, high in the Council of the King, had recommended him to Sir Richard Nanfan; and Nanfan not only had recommended him to Henry VII but had shown further confidence in him by making Wolsey his own executor. His ambition had been encouraged by the Marquis of Dorset and the Archbishop of Canterbury. He impressed the people he dealt with and served. The court was his aim, essential to his fullest success, and he had some justification for thinking, as one biographer reports, that if he could "but set one foot in the court he did not doubt but to obtain anything he could wish for."

Casual accounts of Wolsey's life leave the impression that not much of importance had happened to him before he reached the court of Henry Tudor. Actually he had lived more than half his life, and all the forces that bent and shaped his ambition and oiled his abilities had already worked their effect. In a fixed society he had seen his father change from a rebel to a churchwarden, accepted for his property where he had been rejected as an alien. Thomas Wolsey had proved the power of words when he determined for his degree at Oxford. He had shown his ability for something besides the scholar's life by engaging in the intrigues of the administration of his college. He had run head-on into the civil authorities, and to his sorrow, in his first parish. He had sampled the sweetness of patronage. At Calais he had shown that he knew how to do the world's work.

But what made the arrival of Wolsey at the court of Henry VII significant was the nature of Henry's reign. He was a businessman King who believed in the tidy management of the affairs of the kingdom. There was now a market for competence just as much as there was a market for wool. Henry rated ability higher than nobility. An unusual prince and an extraordinary commoner had met at a given point in history.

At the time of Wolsey's arrival at court, however, Henry was in no mood to make immediate use of the new chaplain's proven abilities. Rather Henry was concerned with the whole question of the succession, of guaranteeing the future of the Tudor line he had established.

Considering the constant threat from dissident elements, the fewness of Henry's executions might be looked upon as a study in Christian forbearance. He had been selective and judicial in his killings. He had even spared Perkin Warbeck as long as he could, although Perkin had dealt him handsome misery for almost ten years. After his capture at Exeter in 1496 Perkin had been brought back to London, fully confessing his perfidy, and had suffered but a token imprisonment, escaping now and then, only to be hauled back each time to genial confinement. It was three years later, after he had been put into the Tower and had been detected in communication with the Earl of Warwick there, that Henry had him disposed of—along with the Earl of Warwick.

Here the case had been legally conclusive. There had been a trial, though there was no record kept of the proceedings. The young Earl had admitted the charges of conspiracy against him. It is true that his wits had been dimmed by fifteen years of close confinement; and the Earl and Perkin had been placed in cells one above the other where they could be caught communicating. But the court adjudged him guilty according to his confession, and he, along with Warbeck, had in November of 1499 been hanged, disemboweled, and quartered.

The execution of the young Earl had not been popular. In the same month a dreadful plague had broken out in London, and the people "on the highway coldly stated that the scourge was sent by heaven for the murder of Warwick."[4] But the disposal of Warwick had been the most necessary execution of all. He was the son of the Duke of Clarence, brother of Edward IV, and as long as he lived there was a living and livid threat to the throne of Henry VII. Warwick was unmistakably of royal blood, and his lineage and claims would stand up under test better than those of Henry Tudor. Henry Tudor, whatever his lineage, had brought peace and unmeasured prosperity to England. It would not do to wreck this peace and squander this prosperity by letting the nation be plunged again into internecine strife.

There was another reason why the hapless young Earl of Warwick could not be allowed to tarnish Tudor claims. This was the Spanish alliance based on the marriage of Catherine of Aragon and the King's son who had been given the name of Arthur after England's king of legendary greatness. Arthur was the hope as well as the son of Henry Tudor. His marriage to Catherine of Aragon had been designed to bring Spain and England indissolubly together; it would be the means of putting the stamp of approval of the most powerful nation of Europe on the validity and soundness of the Tudor dynasty. The Princess Catherine was a descendant of John of Gaunt, and hence of Edward III. Thus she had the royal blood of the Plantagenets. Her descent was "not like the Tudors through a dubious left-hand marriage, but through an undoubted line of royal kings."[5]

The Spanish ambassadors, haggling over the amount of the prospective bride's dowry "did not hesitate to hint at the insecurity of such an upstart dynasty as that of the Tudors. 'Bearing in mind what happens every day to the kings of England,' they declared, 'it is surprising that

Ferdinand and Isabella should dare to give their daughter at all.' "[6]
This remark had been passed when Arthur was only two years old.
But on January 11, 1500, the same ambassadors wrote to their sovereigns: "England has never been so tranquil as at present. There have always been pretenders to the crown of England, but now that Perkin Warbeck and the son of the Duke of Clarence (the Earl of Warwick) have been executed, there does not remain a drop of doubtful royal blood, the only royal blood being the blood of the King, the Queen, and above all, the Prince of Wales."[7]

The wedding had seemed to put the seal of finality on what had been so devoutly hoped for. Yet the marriage, so full of promise, had not endured. Its failure and the events that followed made it seem that there might be some curse of blood upon it. For Arthur had sickened and died at Ludlow five months after the ceremony, leaving the young Catherine in widow's weeds and in a strange land. For Arthur, death was a sleep and a forgetting; for Henry VII, the loss of his son was an awakening from a dream. The death of the Prince, proud hope of a new England, threatened the very structure of the future. The solidity of the Tudor dynasty, to which Henry had given such devious thought and persistent energy, rested on the marriage. Catherine must not be allowed to return to Spain. Not only would her return weaken claims which the fruits of her marriage would make secure; there was the possibility also that the first instalment of her dowry, duly paid by Ferdinand and Isabella, might return with her.

Henry faced a predicament which he could not hack his way out of with the executioner's axe. Yet he must move at once to save both the dynasty and the dowry. There was still his second son, five years younger than Catherine, but a sturdy lad and tall and full of the seeds of promise. Catherine had never herself been well in drafty, damp, and gloomy England; but if she survived, it might be possible to get the consent of her bargaining parents for her marriage to young Henry. Then it would be necessary to solicit a dispensation from the Pope. The

Pope alone could grant permission for a man—even a prince—to marry his brother's widow, seeing that the Levitical code expressly forbade such a marriage.

Appropriate petitions were addressed to the Pope, but Alexander VI died inconsiderately while the matter was before him. His successor, Pius III, died a month later—in the summer of 1503. Julius II was not elected until November of that year, but he made it his early business to entertain the singular request from England, and on November 26, 1503, a bull was issued allowing the young Henry to marry his brother's widow, provided he himself agreed to the arrangement when he reached the canonical age of consent.

It had been a period of suspense and waiting. Henry VII waited ten months after Arthur's death before he named his younger son Prince of Wales; by then it was decently obvious that there would be no issue from the marriage of Catherine and Arthur. The King waited another four months before he allowed the younger Henry to enter into a contract to marry his brother's widow. When the younger Henry reached the age of thirteen, the same being the canonical age of consent, he immediately renounced the contract. And the elder Henry, having by now developed chilly qualms about the marriage, gave his royal sanction to the renunciation. Catherine meanwhile remained in England, her status undecided, her life a coin in the hands of kings, her comfort neglected. There was some talk that the bald, widowed, and aging Henry might marry her himself, rather than let the dowry and alliance go; but the rumor probably arose from Spanish sources, and if it was more than a rumor Isabella put a prompt end to it when the matter came to her shocked attention.

With all his royal prerogatives, Henry VII could not decide Catherine's fate alone: it was endlessly hashed over in his Council. And if Wolsey found the King preoccupied in his devotions and worries and little inclined to notice him, the Council proved to be a place where his talents as a talker could command an audience. Cardinal Morton was dead, likewise Reginald Bray. And there were those who said that the character of the King had changed with the passing of these men and the death of his wife, Elizabeth of York. He was more severe, less tempered in his judgments. But there were others who remained near him and were staunch and were able to influence him.

One of these was Richard Fox, now Bishop of Winchester, and to him Wolsey commended and attached himself. Fox enjoyed the full confidence of his royal master, and through him rather than through contact at the altar did Wolsey make his approach to Henry.

Instead of idling his time or spending it on books and scrivening, Wolsey at this period sought the company of men who would be seen by other men, following the path of advancement by association. If the King would not notice him, he would impress his presence upon men whom the King would notice.

In this way it came about that, when the King wanted a mission accomplished, there were those who could recommend Wolsey for his ability to talk and to act as a negotiator. To Henry there was nothing more important than negotiation. He had been busy all his royal life with embassies. Following the death of the Queen in 1503, Henry's mind turned to marriage schemes. Hardly more than a year after Elizabeth of York was laid away he thought of marrying the young Queen of Naples, a widow. To find out whether she might prove a suitable match for him he sent three gentlemen from his court on a confidential mission.

There were twenty-four items to be investigated. Item sixteen required that they "mark her breasts or paps, whether they be big or small." The ambassadors reported: "The said queen's breasts be somewhat great and full, and inasmuch as they are trussed somewhat high, after the manner of the country, the which causeth her grace to seem much fuller and her neck to be shorter." Item 24 was decisive: "The said King's servants, by the wisest ways that they can use, shall make inquisition and ensearch what land or livelihood the said Queen hath or shall have after the decease of her mother." There was, alas, no satisfactory answer to this question. The embassy ended in failure. Henry would not make overtures to a person if she could not contribute visibly to his coffers.[8]

Besides, there were other queens in the pack. There was Margaret of Angoulême, a creature to toy with in his multifarious negotiations, just to keep notice before Europe that Henry was in the market for a bride and the competition was sprightly. The person he really had his beady eye upon was Margaret of Savoy, regent of the Netherlands, daughter of Maximilian of Austria, impecunious and evasive Emperor of the Holy Roman Empire. She was likewise the sister of Philip, Archduke of Flanders, and in 1506 the Archduke, having been driven upon English shores by an adverse wind while he was seeking passage to Spain, found that he could not escape his polite confinement unless he signed a treaty with the King of England. This treaty was full of provisions, many of them concerned with trade and allowing English goods to be imported advantageously into the Netherlands. It also provided that the hand of Philip's sister Margaret of Savoy would be given in marriage to the King of England, and a marriage portion of 300,000 crowns was fixed, each crown to be worth four shillings.

It was a neat arrangement on paper, but the lady Margaret had a will of her own. She had also had two husbands before and she was in no hurry to take on the ailing Henry VII. Some pressure would be needed to bring the marriage off, and in the spring of 1508 it was found that the Emperor Maximilian lay in the Netherlands for a season and an embassy should be sent to urge him that he might expedite the marriage. The man needed to perform the task must be eloquent, persuasive, and able to impress the wily Emperor with the advantages of pushing the marriage forward.

Richard Fox and Sir Thomas Lovell, trusted advisers to the King, hit upon the idea of sending Wolsey. They went straight to the King with the matter, and he consented to see the priest and to render judgment as to his fitness. Having separate eyes and compartments for his religion and for his policy, he had paid no heed to Wolsey as a chaplain; but he looked upon him with favor as a messenger, seeing that he was so highly recommended to his attention and finding him smooth and personable in his discourse.

Accordingly it was settled that one of the King's chaplains should set off on the King's business to the Low Countries. Cautious arrangements would have to be made, of course, and there would be many meetings of the Council to discuss odd ends of the mission. Meanwhile the King, never too sure of anything, felt it expedient to trust Wolsey with a lesser mission to Scotland. Henry had complained to James IV of Scotland that Scotsmen, "among them men of high rank, traveled through England in disguise and without passports, and even took with them the envoys of foreign powers." Wolsey went to Scotland to protest, but he confessed to Henry that, "according to the information he had gathered, the offenses of Englishmen were to those of Scotsmen as four to one."[9] Wolsey had thus shown that he could make an honest report even if it involved telling the King facts he did not expect to encounter. He also had a constructive suggestion to make, not content merely to be an errand runner. He suggested that the Kings of England and Scotland meet and talk matters over between them. The idea seems to have found favor with James, but there was no enthusiasm for it among his Council.

In his mission to Scotland Wolsey demonstrated his diplomatic skill and confirmed the prophecies and recommendations of his friends. Men said that the peace of the two kingdoms was assured by his mission. He should now go to the Netherlands and to the Emperor. During the time the letter was being prepared and he was receiving instructions from the King, commending himself to the royal presence with every appearance, Wolsey had obviously prepared a plan for the speedy execution of his mission. He knew the King and had taken his measure; he understood the importance of carrying out the assignment with dexterity and singleness of mind. It was not a job for a courtier but a runner. It was business;

and a plain chaplain, if he put his tempered mind to it, could do it better than a prince given to ceremony and dawdling politeness.

Wolsey had his final audience of leave with the King at four in the afternoon at Richmond. He took a barge immediately for Gravesend, having seen to it that the barge was ready for immediate departure. By virtue of the time of departure he had the aid of the wind and especially of the tide on the Thames, and he reached Gravesend in hardly more than three hours. Post horses had been arranged at Gravesend for the passage to Dover, where he would take ship for the Continent. With such planning and with more post horses prepared in relay, he reached Dover the next morning at the very moment when the packet across the Channel got under way. By noon he was at Calais, and by late afternoon, riding hard, he was at the residence of the Emperor.

When the Emperor heard that a messenger from Henry had arrived, he gave orders that the man be brought at once to his imperial closet, for, as he explained, "his affection to the king of England was such, that he was glad of any opportunitie to doe him a curtesie." Wolsey stated his mission and his requests promptly and asked the Emperor for a decision within the briefest compass consistent with his royal pleasure. Evidently he did his job well, for he had his answers early the next morning—all of them favorable. Whether the Emperor meant Yes or would do what he said was not a part of Wolsey's responsibility, and he need not tarry in meditation on this point. Rather he left immediately for Calais, accompanied by a splendid train of nobles from the Emperor's court to do him honor. From Calais he took packet after an uneventful night's rest and was back at Dover by ten the next morning. That night he was at Richmond. The whole mission had taken less than seventy hours.

Wolsey was up at daybreak—ahead of the King. He stood outside the royal bedchamber as the King left for early Mass. Seeing him there and thinking him remiss in his embassy, the King said, "Why have you not passed on your journey?"

To which Wolsey replied, "Sire, if it may stand with your Highness's pleasure, I have already been with the Emperor and dispatched your affairs, I trust to your Grace's liking."

Then the King inquired about a messenger he had sent after Wolsey with further instructions. "I encountered him, Sire," said Wolsey. "And I made bold, your Grace, upon my own discretion, to despatch the same. And for as much as I have exceeded your Grace's commission, I most humbly crave your gracious remission and pardon."

To this Henry blinked and replied, "We do not only pardon you thereof, but also give you our princely thanks, and also for your good and speedy exploit."[10]

The story of the mission comes from Wolsey's own recollections of it years later. It may not be true or accurate in every detail, but it could be true; and whatever the detail, it bears the test of history, for from the moment of the visit to Maximilian dates Wolsey's favor with Henry VII. He had proved himself able and fast, and that he could gird his priestly robes about him when the occasion demanded. Such a man the King needed.

Of course a good man must needs be rewarded in some coin that betokens the true measure of his worth, and here again the King's cunning found the energetic Wolsey to his satisfaction. This eager fellow ranked only as a humble priest, one of a stable of royal chaplains: it would not be necessary to give him a slice of the King's lands or to dole out to him precious and husbanded funds from the royal coffers.

Rome could pay his wages, and England could enjoy his talents.

It was an honored custom that the man who wore the crown could appoint his royal servants to posts in the Church and have his actions sanctioned by the man who wore the tiara. Henry had taken Richard Mayhew, he who had been President of Magdalen College, and, in exchange for his counsel and services as Almoner, had named him Bishop of Hereford in 1504. It was logical, then, that he should take this other

Magdalen product, the priest who had proved himself such a swift harbinger on his mission to Maximilian, and make him Dean of Lincoln.

The system had its conveniences all around. It reduced government
costs, a matter of importance to the acquisitive Henry; and it gave the
Church a host of men habitually at court and close to the King's presence. It was a highly dignified way in which the King and the Pope could
scratch each other's backs across the intervening miles between London
and Rome.

At this moment the circumstances required, however, that Wolsey
should have income and offices consonant with his high position at
court. There must be badges and honors appropriate to his station.
One could not expect a man who was privy to the King to continue living
off such parishes as Limington and the few others that had been doled
out to him. He still held Limington in his grasp, nor would he let go of it
until he had full assurance of other honors. These came thick and fast.
Not only was he made Dean of Lincoln on February 3, 1508, but a few
days later he was presented with a prebend in the same cathedral, which
too he held until he managed to exchange it for one more valuable in another cathedral. It was not contemplated that he should actually serve
Lincoln. He was installed by proxy and did not take possession, and then
only formally, until two years later. He was also given the Vicarage of
Lydd in Kent by the Cistercian Abbot of Tintern. And to cap his honors
in the Church, he next achieved sufficient status at court to be made
Royal Almoner—on November 3, 1508. Through his rise in the Church
he now had enough stature to occupy a dignified position in the royal
household. Now he was willing to hand over the rectorship of Limington
to another priest. This he did some time before July 2, 1509.[11]

Around the court it was plainly understood that Wolsey had high
honors in his destiny. He was under the care and tutelage of Richard
Fox, who, along with William Warham, Archbishop of Canterbury in
succession to Henry Deane, represented the Church at court and stood

for its honors and influence there. Henry's piety and genuflections gave the churchmen some ascendancy, but there were remnants of the old nobility still around the edges, and it was just as well to keep these remnants in their place. Their spokesman was Thomas Howard, Earl of Surrey, Lord High Treasurer of England, and the fact that he was there at all served notice upon all who attended the King that Henry would place his stamp on loyalty and ability and not weight his Council to the full with any single element of the realm.

Howard's father, the first Duke of Norfolk, had been killed with Richard at Bosworth. The title had been attainted and the son deprived of his lands and his freedom and confined to the Tower of London after the battle. A year later, however, he was pardoned and given an honorable office in the north of England. After a steadfast performance there, he had been brought back to court and restored to the earldom of Surrey.

Thomas Howard was in the best tradition of the English nobility. His loyalty was not to be questioned, and Henry knew it. When Henry talked with him after Bosworth, Howard made it plain that he had fought for his King, and that he would have died willingly if Henry had been his King. Henry liked the mettle of that. He liked also the sense of identification with the great of the past, a kind of connection between the nobility and his own throne. The nobles were to be kept in their place and not allowed to thrash the land again with their wars. But they were not to be eliminated. Rather they were to be represented; for they were one of the priceless ingredients in English life, and Henry knew it.

Fox as a churchman could be expected to have different ideas. To stand against the old nobility and the great landowners who remained, he thought it well to groom Wolsey and see that he had the King's favor. With rumbles of anticlericalism abroad in the land and signs to be seen at every turn of hostility toward the wealth of the Church, and with threats to deprive the clergy of their privileges, the first order of business ought to be to see that the Church had a friend at court—preferably a young friend who would grow up with the government, whose power would increase within the Church and the State at one and the same time.

For this ultimate purpose a priest who came inconspicuously to the service of the King, and grew through royal favor, was ideal. Especially if he showed that he had the kind of managerial ability that the reign of Henry VII placed approval on. Government had ceased to be a matter of conduct in wars and had become a very high order of humdrum, of keeping accounts, of administering justice, of collecting revenues, of maintaining peace on the King's highway, of promoting trade, of rolling up revenues and guarantees against adversity. The King had become a housekeeper, and for all the details connected with this kind of national housekeeping, he needed worthy assistants.

Continuity was all the more urgent as the health of the King worsened and a new and more vigorous reign impended. Catherine was still in the kingdom and the Council still meditated her status, but Henry VII in his fits of conscience still forbade the young Prince, now taller than his father, to marry the Princess.

But Henry's preoccupation with his own marriage was intense. As Bacon put it later, if he "had been young, a man would have judged him to be amorous." One could see in all his moves in the midst of threats and disease and his own decline an incurable desire to perpetuate himself, to stake out many claims of blood against adverse fortune, to trust the future of the present he had created to no single reed.

Again in October of 1508, Wolsey was sent off to the Netherlands to hasten the marriage with Margaret. On his first mission he had succeeded, at least as far as one could succeed in dealing with the Emperor Maximilian and his kin. For early in October Margaret had executed the marriage treaty and agreed to fines that should be paid if the marriage did not take place. On the same mission Wolsey had been able to advance the proposed marriage between Archduke Charles and the daughter of the King, the Princess Mary. Thus Henry had the prospect of another conquest by marriage. Even if the young Henry did not go through with his marriage to Catherine of Aragon, his sister Mary was now pledged to Charles, who upon the death of Ferdinand would rule Spain.

Still and all, Henry the elder must marry Margaret. In doing it he would wed the Netherlands, rich in trade. Wolsey stayed on the Continent from the beginning of October into November, trying to straighten out details to Henry's satisfaction—and Margaret's in particular. Henry tried to move Margaret by a letter addressed directly to her. There was a grand embassy headed by the Earl of Surrey. Yet the marriage was delayed. Events gradually closed in around Henry, while Margaret dallied with the idea of decision and the execution of her earlier decision. Henry's last cause became a lost cause.

His health, which would have killed a less determined man years before, now grew sharply worse under his frustrations. The doctors had long said that he ought to rest less and sleep more. He began to be troubled with gout, an irony considering the proper and diligent life he led.

In the spring of 1509 rumors of the King's illness spread all over Europe. Thomas Wolsey became less the priest who served as diplomatic messenger and more the King's Almoner, in charge of Henry's increasing charities—in charge, that is, as far as anybody could be in charge of anything touching Henry. The King gave daily alms to the poor and needy. He sent money for ten thousand Masses to be recited in his behalf. He had built the Savoy Hospital, near Charing Cross, in London, to afford shelter for one hundred poor persons; "and in the last year of his life he determined to erect at Bath a large hospital on the model of the one in Paris."[12] To accomplish this—and both Wolsey and the younger Henry might well have noted the act—he appropriated the revenues of ecclesiastical houses that were falling into decay. These houses were to be closed and their money spent for more useful purposes.

Henry could amply afford the lavish gifts he laid upon the altar of appeasement at the end of his life, whether out of remorse or zeal. His life had been a study in acquisitive thrift, and if it proved one thing above all things visible it was that a man in high position could lay up treasures on earth and still serve the general good. One need only think primarily in terms of money, not war.

Early in his reign there had been a threat of war with France. Say rather a prospect of it. Henry could ill afford not to press English claims in France, so long standing were these claims. Accordingly he assembled Parliament and laid the matter before their deliberations. They readily granted funds for an invasion of France, and now Henry was under the necessity of making warlike moves. His elaborate and conspicuous preparations impressed both England and France. At last the King "actually crossed the Channel to take command of the army of invasion; and sat down before Boulogne. Then on a sudden the air cleared." It appeared that the French King did not want a war any more than Henry VII. But he must make a settlement to get rid of the English army. The settlement Henry gladly accepted and withdrew. Thus he "secured Peace with Honour and a solid cash equivalent for his expenditure."[13]

This was but an instance of the principle he had established: that any enterprise worth undertaking at all should be made to pay a handsome profit for the good of the realm. And in all cases he took the money personally and kept it in hiding under his own lock and key at his beloved Palace of Richmond. He would hold the purse and handle the coffers and dole out to his Almoner and Lord High Treasurer only what he decided should be given away or spent.

With all his charities, the King's conscience would not rest. It was as if he would make peace with his Maker as he had made peace with France—by a cash settlement, but in reverse. He gave abundantly, and in his last days he gave lenience—this time lavishly and on a wide scale and with no view to reward this side of heaven: he granted a general pardon to those who had offended against the King's laws, and the prisons and jails were emptied, and pilgrimages were organized among the wealthy and the dispossessed to pray for his recovery.

Nothing helped. On April 21, 1509, he died at Richmond. On May 10 he was buried. As the casket with his wasted remains was placed in the vault at Westminster by the side of the body of Elizabeth of York, "the heralds took their tabards from their shoulders, hung them on the railing round the catafalque, and cried out in French the lamentation, 'The noble King Henry VII is dead!' Then they put their tabards on again, and with loud voices uttered the joyful cry, 'Long live the noble King Henry VIII!'"

He who mounted the throne as the eighth Henry to reign over the English was not yet eighteen years of age.

Thomas Wolsey, firm in the Council and ascendant in the Church, was twenty years his senior.

BOOK 2

1509-1520 *Setting forth the rise of Wolsey
in the reign of Henry VIII; the stupendous failure
and disgrace
of his first venture for his King
and the amazing accomplishments
of his second; his roles as judge,
as Church reformer, as educator, as builder of palaces,
and as diplomat;
the triumph of his policy of friendship
with France
at the Field of Cloth of Gold.*

CHAPTER

Thomas Wolsey had lost another patron.

In this case, however, he was fortunately circumstanced. He knew the lie of the royal household, and he held a position of responsibility, flanked by appointments within the Church, that gave him status. And since the young man who came to the throne was unversed in the day-to-day business of the court, Wolsey could become a patron himself, for his increasing command of court detail might enable the Almoner to shepherd the King through tasks for which the monarch was unprepared.

Apart from talks, often wearisome, occasionally stimulating, with men who populated his father's household, young Henry had had little contact with the world beyond the confines of a parsimonious court except in jousts and competitive games. He was a master at archery and could contend with the best when he drew the bow—long or short. Likewise in other sports. Giustiniani, the Venetian ambassador, wrote: "He is extremely fond of tennis, at which game it is the prettiest thing in the world to see him play, his fair skin glowing through a shirt of the finest texture."[1]

Too, young Henry had a proven skill at music. Even when Duke of York, he had had a band of minstrels apart from those of his father and his brother. "He became an expert performer on the lute, the organ and the harpsichord and all the cares of State could not divert him from practising these instruments both day and night."[2] In the years that formed him, when by his brother's seniority and his father's sternness he had been isolated from his times, he had grown fond of his mind. In music the spirit was free and eternal and richly above the humdrum of shallow courtiers and toothy men flitting busily about the court with airs of solemnity. Music belonged to religion, to the Mass, and it belonged to Maypoles, strolling minstrels, and the limbo where men withdraw from chores and exactions.

Upon the head of this versatile lad, brilliantly trained in many arts and pastimes but not in the art of governance, was placed the scratchy crown of his father, and into his good right hand was thrust the rusty scepter. A magic moment in an ancient ceremony attended by the mitered and caparisoned dignitaries of Church and State was supposed to turn this impetuous boy, this tennis player, this performer on the lute, instantly into a king. It was an old English custom to expect it, and often it worked: the metaphysics of change might touch with some wand the latent greatness of all men and give it special force in one man. But coronation was at best a magnificent experiment, a venture in confidence; and, on a plain and practical level, men of wisdom, whether in court or tavern, were never sure that the miracle would work.

In the case of the accession of young Henry VIII hopes were unfeignedly high, for the news of the passing of the old King had occasioned undisguised satisfaction. It was time for a change. The moment had struck when one could hear the swish of history as it turned a corner. An almost national sigh seemed to signal that a long period of boredom had come to an end. The joy was not only prompted by the comely and stalwart person of the young King; it also sprang from incurable expectations, from the feeling that, whatever happened, here would at least be a contrast and hence welcome.

The old King had left a fortune of £1,800,000. He had applied himself almost endlessly to the business of being King. He had not played upon the virginals. In all he did he wrapped the whole mantle of government firmly and securely about himself. It was therefore plain upon the accession of young Henry, with his love of music and sport and his addiction to personal pleasures, that someone would have to do, or see that the young King did, all the work that the old King had done. This was an item of great concern to the Council. The lad now on the throne might be very fit for a king in public and remain a dilettante in private, a lute player with a mountain of wearisome documents to be handled.

This serious question could be suspended in the first days of the new regime, for there were certain ceremonies that with the English must take precedence over all matters of state. The pageantry of kingship must be preserved. In this the Council could not have found a better actor. Henry's first royal decision was clear and unequivocal: he would marry Catherine of Aragon, put an end to the uncertainty of her status, keep the dowry beyond question, and seal the alliance with Spain.

On the wisdom of the marriage, the Council had been divided. William Warham, Archbishop of Canterbury and Primate of All England, had grave ecclesiastical doubts about the validity of the bull from Julius II. It had been slow in coming; its delivery had been postponed from time to time; and when the bull and the documents with it arrived, it evidently had not been satisfactory, for immediately thereafter the young Henry "on the eve of his fourteenth birthday made secret but formal protest against the validity of his marriage to Catherine." It was known that the old Henry, with all his eagerness for the alliance and the dowry, could not then bring his aching conscience to urge the marriage.

And even if the bull had been explicit and had satisfied lay and ecclesiastical minds, it did not take an archbishop to see that in the laws of the ancient Hebrews the Lord had spoken unto Moses, saying: "And if a man shall take his brother's wife, it is an unclean thing: he hath uncovered his brother's nakedness; they shall be childless."[3] The same law which forbade men to lie sexually with animals or other men forbade even a king to lie with his brother's wife. Nay, in the case of a king the matter was worse; for the law of the Lord said he would be childless.

The decision taken was momentous; and it was taken in part because Richard Fox—himself an ecclesiastic even more than Warham, for Warham had been a lawyer and had simply been given an ecclesiastical post—saw the marriage of Henry and Catherine as a practical matter, an affair of state. Besides, there was clearly no evidence that Catherine and the sickly Arthur had lived together as man and wife. Young Henry had imbibed piety from his father; he was alert to the laws of the Church and a dutiful son of the Church, for with all his many interests and affairs of culture he still found time for three Masses every day. His own reckoning of the law, therefore, and the beck of his own conscience, should be respected. If there had not been union between Arthur and Catherine, she had not been in fact but only in name and outward appearance his brother's wife.

Other considerations were put forward by the party in the Council headed by Wolsey's sponsor. Henry VII in his death agony had besought his son to carry out the marriage with Catherine. In his final insecurity he had seen the importance of the alliance. Moreover, the bride's father, Ferdinand, upon hearing of Henry's impending death, had sent forward representations to the English court that France and the other powers of Europe would endeavor to prevent the marriage and break off the alliance with Spain. To Catherine, Ferdinand wrote bluntly that she would get no other husband.

Fox, and by proxy Wolsey, prevailed. So in the excitement of the new reign Henry and Catherine were joined together in almost unseemly haste—scarcely six weeks after the death of Henry VII. As Burke puts it, the news was suddenly announced to the Council "that the King and Princess had gone early on a June morning to the chapel of the Observant Friars at Greenwich and 'had a private marriage,' and were 'determined with God's assistance to abide by that contract to the death.' "[4]

Catherine of Aragon was at last, and with all her embarrassment, wed to a king. And it was to be noted that at the ceremony she had been conspicuously and pointedly dressed in white to show her virginity. Three weeks later, the coronation of the royal pair took place at Westminster, and Archbishop Warham placed the crowns upon their heads. Again Catherine appeared as a virgin. Londoners first saw her as Queen while she was borne from the Tower to Westminster, "sitting in a litter of cloth of gold slung between white palfreys, clad, herself, all in white satin, the costume of a virgin bride, with her gleaming hair 'hanging down her back, of a very great length, beautiful and goodly to behold.' "[5]

There would, at the outset of the new regime, continue to be a touch of sobriety and severity in the court of England. Not for long. The beginning of any reign is, in some respects, bound to be an interregnum in which the royal advisers square off to tilt for power; a period in which the King himself accustoms himself to the business of being king and decides which of a hundred white horses he will ride.

Wolsey kept his presence at court, which was the important thing for a man whose strength and power lay chiefly in the impressiveness of his personality. He aided in the disposition of the effects of the dead King. When after four months he was appointed Almoner to the new King, he began to operate on a more lavish scale, for there was a dash and color about the new regime lacking in the old. The kingship came out of hiding. Henry VIII made it a point to be seen on every occasion. He was given to display, and yet he felt himself at all times keenly identified with the people of the country he ruled. The affairs and ceremonies of his court, as a consequence, took on some of the thrust and zest of his person. The realm had endured penurious prosperity long enough. It would now enjoy a pageant.

In his moderate habits and dress Henry VII had tried to serve as a sober model for his people. With his furred gown and square cap, he had sought to make simplicity stylish. The nobility, however, being curtailed in many particulars, had stood regulation ill in matters of dress; extravagance would flare up among them on such occasions as funerals, and it had become necessary to control the expenditures allowed for mourning. Yet with all the rebellious outbursts of color there had been a tendency toward moderation. When Henry VII died, men of all classes "were wearing long hose or tights called stocks, low round-neck shirts, short jerkins or doublets and a longer gown or cloak for warmth. The doublet was usually like a waistcoat, with or without sleeves and reaching to the waist, and the stocks were tied to this garment with a sort of bootlace called 'points' . . . The hair was often worn long or just to the shoulders." There were ways, of course, by which even this somber attire could be made conspicuous. "Small hats or caps decorated with a feather gave a jaunty air to the young gallant. Excess of fashion was displayed by the tightness of the nether garments and the extreme brevity of the jerkins which in some cases finished with a frill at the waist. The more sober-minded covered their thighs."[6]

When His Grace young Henry VIII came to the throne and to wide public gaze, dress blossomed, both because the desire had been pent up and because the treaties engaged in by his father had made goods available. Formerly the cloth needed for a fashionable jerkin had been only two yards. Now it was seven or eight. Other signs announced the assertive change. Garments were slashed "to show a contrasting undergarment of lining," so that by this token observers might behold layers of wealth beyond what first met the eye. "Sleeves, both for men and for women, were now separate articles of dress, and were of different colors and materials from the rest of the body-clothing. They were trussed at the shoulders by points." The hood, worn for so long a time, disappeared, "and the flat hats were cut and slashed, and edged or laden with feathers . . . The small, flat, round bonnet continued in general use; it lingered long with the apprentices, and was spoken of as 'the city flat cap.'"[7]

For all the change toward gaiety and extravagance, Henry VIII served as a new model, brandishing his love of dress wherever he went. He came to be known as "the best dressed sovereign in the world, for he put on new clothes every holy day." He could be seen in a black-and-gold-embroidered shirt of slashed velvet. His stocks or tights might be one color and his hose another, for stocks and hose had now become separate garments. Both descended into slashed, broad-toed shoes.

The whole emphasis on dress announced that parsimony had ceased to be a national standard; the vogue was now for the consumption of goods. Even the dressing of horses was made an art. Henry made dress and the display of goods a policy, a sign of the richness of the kingdom, a model for prelates and all of the upper classes. Clothes were assets, both in terms of station and of actual wealth, for there was little besides clothes and houses on which money could be spent. Indeed the right to dress in costly attire was, by being confined to the upper classes, made an incentive to wealth, and it became necessary to renew again the laws which confined sumptuous apparel to those of rank. In the first Parliament Henry called, it was enacted that no man under the rank of duke should wear any cloth of gold; "not any under the rank of an earl should wear any sables . . ."[8] The King, on the other hand, might wear what he pleased, and he had the right to license the wearing of special apparel among those who deserved the royal favor. The clothes of the class above might be a reward or a perquisite.

While the office of almoner in the royal household carried no great prestige, it could be executed with competitive aplomb if the man who occupied it put his mind to the task and calculated with proper histrionics what effect the bestowal of gifts could make. It was an honorable and customary office in all grand houses, secular and religious—a part of the courtly condescension of the rich and mighty to the poor and needy. At the Abbey of St. Augustine at Canterbury and at Westminster Abbey "twice a week the Almoner distributed food to all the poor who came to the dole house . . ." No one went away without a share. "It was the duty of the Almoner to find out the sick and the poor in the neighborhood, to visit them with his servants and to take them food and drink."[9]

There were more lofty offices in the staff of a great house and in the court, but the office of almoner brought with it the privilege of contact with the outside world. The Almoner represented the King's graciousness and wealth in public; if he doled well, he extended the King's public relations and burrowed into the hearts of the people. The way he passed out alms afforded one of those vast intangibles by which the royal person became manifest and vivid.

Wolsey showed himself a good and faithful servant in the few things early entrusted to him. Less than seven months after Henry VIII came to the throne, Wolsey received a notable mark of the royal favor which showed that his labors and learnings would not go without reward: he was given a grant of one of the houses forfeited by the attainder of Sir Richard Empson. The house lay at Bridewell. In a grant dated January 10, 1510, it was called "La Maison curiale, with twelve gardens and orchards between the Thames and St. Bride's gardens in Fleetstreet." Here Wolsey lived in a "noncanonical" marriage with a woman called Joan Larke. The edict that priests, regardless of their functions or the character of their work, should remain celibate had not been wholeheartedly accepted in England. Hence the rule of celibacy was not uncommonly honored in the breach and the offense forgiven by regular fines, which, in some places, constituted a source of episcopal revenues. "There were many ecclesiastics, from the popes downward, who had wives . . . Warham is said by Erasmus to have had a wife who was not secluded from the knowledge and society of his friends."[10]

Wolsey's views of marriage may not have been exemplary in his chosen profession, but they were forthright, open, and strenuously aired, a circumstance shown by the fact that he later made himself responsible (in the Parliament of 1523) for an act which relieved six clerical priests employed as clerks in Chancery from taking vows of celibacy. A vast number of clergy in England were engaged in clerical work, the term "clerical" deriving from the fact that many of the services of society were under the hand of the Church. It did not seem essential that such men, engaged in secular work, be asked to avoid marriage.

There is no indication that Wolsey was married but once. Although records are obscure, the woman he married appears to have been the daughter of one Peter Larke, "gentleman of Huntingdonshire." In 1463, members of a Larke family were associated with the town of Thetford, not far from Ipswich, and a man named Peter Larke was twice mayor of that town. He is described as a farmer and a grazier and as the grandfather of Joan Larke. A kinsman of Joan's father was Thomas Larke, who became "surveyor of the King's works" and later was Wolsey's confessor. Erasmus said that of all the men he had known in England, Larke was the most cultured and sincere; and the Latin secretary to the King wrote that he was "omnipotent with the Cardinal."[11]

Obviously the connections of the marriage were good, and the union was in its odd way respectable. Wolsey seems to have remained faithful to his wife and later to have given her in marriage as a father might— even fixing upon her a dowry—when she was wed publicly and formally to George Legh of Adlington, a wealthy landowner in the county of Cheshire.[12] Wolsey continued his friendship with the Larke family and gave tokens of it from time to time: Joan's brother Thomas was instituted by him to the rich living of Winwick in Lancashire and was entrusted with the education of the future Earl of Derby; likewise he remained on close family terms with George Legh after the marriage of his noncanonical wife to that young gentleman.

Two children were born from Wolsey's marriage with Joan Larke. One, a daughter named Dorothy, was later consigned to a nunnery in the fashion of the day; but the son was given all the emoluments of affection any lavish and preoccupied father might bestow upon his heir in lieu of companionship. He was known as Thomas Wynter; and he was spoken of sometimes by his father and by others as Wolsey's son, "sometimes, according to the euphemism of the time, as his nephew." He was "brought up carefully as a wealthy man's son and educated by private tutors in England and at the universities of Louvain, Padua, and Paris." When the boy was scarcely ten years old he was given the revenues of a parish. The scandalous way in which Wolsey managed to make the Church provide this comfortable, if not ruinous, allowance afforded his enemies with some of their best reasons for their final vituperative attack. As a father, Wolsey made the mistakes of other fathers, all growing out of overstuffed privilege and a lack of close personal relationship with his son.

With his house and his family and all the accouterments of respectability, Wolsey was now part of the ruling fraternity in terms of property as well as status. This time he had been rewarded out of the royal coffers, directly and well, and not simply with another benefice in the Church. He did not relinquish his religious honors or permit himself to be identified wholly with the throne. The King ruled the homeland, but Rome ruled the world. There was no need for one to surrender the larger scope of the Church, especially if this scope could be turned to good account in the homeland. One might be a lawgiver but still remain a prophet.

The new King summoned Parliament to meet on January 10, 1510—the first time it had met in six years. Members of the Commons—squires and burgesses all—came reluctantly. Parliament was a bore. The scant wages of the members of the lower House were paid by local constituencies, and a man lost touch with his private business and his family when he came to London and spent forty or sixty days sitting around drafty halls, hearing wise men talk as if they were wiser, and carrying out the haughty instructions of the Lords. Most of the bills originated with the Lords and were often written in the Council. The Commons felt that its chief business was to ratify the labors of its betters, though occasionally there were conferences designed to compromise moot matters.

This Parliament lasted only twenty-nine days. Its achievements were not weighty, but the fact that it had met and that the Commons had asserted themselves showed the ripple of a trend which men with a proper sense of society might well mark.

But Wolsey was too busy with the King and the Council to see much of anything. By 1511, while still officially only the Royal Almoner, he was engaged in circumventing the normal procedures of the King's officers and expressing himself freely and cozily on affairs of the court. One of his earliest private letters extant was written on September 30, 1511, to tell Fox that Thomas Howard, Earl of Surrey and the chief of the nobility around the King, had met with a cool reception at court and had gone home the next day. Wolsey then proceeded to observe "that with a little help he might be 'utterly excluded' therefrom, 'whereof in my poor judgment no little good should ensue.' "[13] It was big talk from the son of an Ipswich commoner, whose native county had long stood cap in hand to the Howards of Norfolk. But the Ipswich boy had been transformed by his closeness to the King.

Already he enjoyed the confidence of the young King to an astonishing extent, and he showed that he was resolved to use this confidence to the full. A few months earlier he had side-stepped and by-passed all official procedure. There was an established method of giving legal effect to the royal will. The King would sign a bill or petition presented to him and pass it to his secretary. The secretary would in turn write a letter under the King's signet to the Lord Privy Seal, keeping the bill signed by the King. The Lord Privy Seal would then write under that seal to the Lord Chancellor as Keeper of the Great Seal, holding the secretary's letter as his warrant; and the Lord Chancellor would issue paper orders. On May 26, 1511, "Wolsey produced for the chancellor a signed bill which had gone through none of this official routine; and the chancellor acted without his proper warrant, safeguarding himself by the singular entry on his record that he had expedited the matter because Wolsey had given him the letters by the king's command, *ut asseruit dictus dominus Wulcy*."[14] To trespass thus on prerogatives, ignoring all channels of procedure, was a highhanded act for a lowborn cleric. And the fact that the Lord Chancellor of England accepted the act without question showed how close the Almoner stood to the King.

He stood close on religious as well as secular grounds. Wolsey wrote to Fox about the illness of Pope Julius II, who was said to be dead or dying. He reported to Fox that the day before at Mass he "brake with the King in this matter and showed unto his grace how much honour and also furtherance of all his affairs in time to come should issue to him if that by his commendation some Cardinal might attain to be Pope."[15]

But any report that Julius II was dead left a wholly false impression. He was much alive and full of schemes, "this swarthy and pugnacious Genoese," who let it be known that he had pulled a galley oar in his youth and who conducted the office of pontiff as if he were a sailor on leave. Julius II saw the world about him as one of conflict. He had a sharp sense of the physical, and he aggressively believed that the Pope, being the ruler of Christendom's spirit, should have a fair possession of Christendom's territory, a series of buffer and protective states so that the Holy Father would not be molested in his duties by quarreling kings.

To this estimable end he had in 1510 invited the Most Christian King of France (kings of France were so designated by a pontiff in the previous century) to put the Republic of Venice in its proper place. The Most Christian King, in this case Louis XII, had done the job better than the Pope bargained for. At the battle of Agnadello the French won a crushing victory. "In one day," wrote Machiavelli, "the Venetians lost all they had acquired during eight hundred years of strenuous effort."[16] The Most Christian King loomed now as a bulky threat to the Pope's peace of mind: he had advanced too far and too powerfully for comfort. More practically, an ally of the Most Christian King, the Duke of Ferrara, had begun with shocking impiety to produce salt at Commachio, "to the detriment of the papal monopoly at Cervia."[17]

The situation manifestly called for a realignment, and Julius, disregarding the treaty by which the Most Christian King had come to his aid, formed now a league to expel Louis from Italy. Julius made a treaty with the Swiss, who agreed to supply him with 6000 troops at a good export price. He absolved the Venetians and brought them back into the papal camp against Louis. Then the Pope took the field in person and with warlike mien led a combination of troops to two victories in the north of Italy. He enlisted also the aid of Ferdinand and called the coalition he had formed against France the Holy League.

When the Holy Father became warlike, the Most Christian King, as seems appropriate, became theological. Louis XII assembled the French clergy and secured from them a declaration that a general council of the Church should be held. From Milan on May 16, 1511, half a dozen dissident cardinals called for a council to be held at Pisa in September. They summoned the Pope to attend. Julius retorted by calling for a Lateran Council to be held in April 1512, excommunicated the cardinals who had rebelled against his authority, and created eight new ones, just to be on the safe side. One of those he named was Christopher Bainbridge, Archbishop of York, whom Henry VIII had sent as his ambassador to the Holy See. Bainbridge had actually gone to protest the investiture of Venice, which Henry had deplored. Knowing the English addiction to Venice, Julius had made it appear that he had forgiven the Venetians at Henry's behest. And as a token of his appreciation of Henry's splendid interference he sent the King of England on April 10, 1511, a golden rose. There was a not unreasonable hope nestled in the canny mind of Julius that the impetuous young King of England, son-in-law of the King of Spain, advised by a brilliant priest who had risen to strength through the good offices of the Church, might join the Holy League against the Most Christian King, who had compounded his offense against the Holy See by outrageously daring to call a council of the Church without the Pope's consent.

CHAPTER 11

This is the way matters stood in distant Rome when Wolsey became a member of the King's Council and began to transact the King's business without recourse to the petty nonsense of protocol. With a persuasive tongue long trained in eloquent conversation, a commanding figure with the grace of quick movements, a manner attentive and deferential to those who rated his deference, he moved about the court earnestly and diligently. Accustomed to advancement through the simple and unfailing expedient of pleasing his superiors by doing their work, he made a perfect companion for the young King. And it was natural that for a time as king Henry VIII should follow the practices in which he had been reared and be satisfied to have servitors following after him, tidying up, while he changed his attire and showed himself like a jewel. Members of the Council urged that he attend the deliberations in which important decisions were made; but by the testimony of some Wolsey gave the opposite advice, saying, according to Godwin, that the King should "hawk and hunt and not intermeddle with old men's cares."[1]

His gentleman-usher testifies that older advisers of the young King would persuade him to spend some time at the Council table, but this pleased the King not at all: "he loved nothing worse than to be constrained to do anything contrary to his royal will and pleasure." This Wolsey understood, says Cavendish, "and so fast as the other counsellors advised the king to leave his pleasure, and to attend to the affairs of his realm, so busily did the almoner persuade him to the contrary; which delighted him much, and caused him to have the greater affection to the almoner."[2]

But if the bustling Wolsey protected the lute-player from the distractions and tedium of governing a people, he could do little but admire the King in his jousts and tilts and games. These jousts were not to be taken lightly; the aggressive side of Henry's nature must find an outlet, as it had in childhood, and it was plain that to him the sport of fighting was more than a commodity for home consumption. After all, war was hardly more than a tourney on a large scale. Early in his career Henry VIII showed that he was not likely to follow the cautious and plodding footsteps of his progenitor, who had settled for cash the only war he undertook.

The new reign would be a new regime in more ways than one. The elder Henry had even made peace with the Scots, though the act was considered unnatural for an English King. Now young Henry would set a fiercer face to the north, and he began by refusing to hand over to Margaret the jewels bequeathed to her, as wife of the Scottish King, by her father. Border incidents increased. Then Sir Edward Howard in the summer of 1511 killed Andrew Barton in a body of water known as The

Downs and captured his ships. Barton was a favorite of the Scottish King, James IV. He had in the past committed depredations on English ships, but there was no evidence that he had attacked the Howards before the slaughter in The Downs. Henry was pledged by treaty to consider Scottish grievances, but in this case he replied to the protest haughtily that "kings do not concern themselves with the affairs of pirates."[3] By this supercilious act he broke with a spit of contempt the alliance which his father had so methodically put together.

The temperament of the young Henry had begun to reveal itself. He would make himself felt beyond his borders. He would have trial by wager of battle and not by the dullness of jury. He would have some part in the world of affairs—but it would be the known world, the world he could tilt at and ride horseback on, the visible world near at hand. His father had shown a keen interest in the world to the west beyond the seas, where rewards might be ultimate and rich. Spain had already shrewdly won an empire there. Even Portugal, not fit for the better quarrels of Europe, had established itself in India. There were those in the Council who pointed enviously to these achievements and felt that the energies of the nation should be directed to the west. They suggested that "when we enlarge ourselves, let it be in that way we can and to which it seems the eternal providence hath destined us, which is by the sea."[4]

But Henry turned his back on the willowy worlds that might one day develop across the seas and entered the lists of Europe with a comfortable horse under him and a trusty sword in his youthful hand. The decision was his, and it expressed his nature. But the credit for it went, in the judgment of the day, to Thomas Wolsey of Ipswich, still the King's Almoner. Because the war that followed was known as Wolsey's War; and for the fiasco that ended the first phase of it—a fiasco unparalleled in the annals of English history—the upstart from Ipswich got the blame. By encouraging the ambitions of a boy-king, by relying on a nation untrained in the arts and cruelties of war and unprepared for foreign enterprise, and by depending on an ally who had no intention of keeping his solemn word, the priest brought disgrace on England and made his sovereign the laughingstock of Europe.

Wolsey's venture of 1512 was a case of ingenious theory applied to slippery facts. The theory was to aid the Pope against his savage enemy, the Most Christian King, who was at once a menace to the peace of the world and an offender against the Holy See in the schismatic scheme for a council at Pisa. To this end on November 13, 1511, Henry joined the Holy League the Pope had formed. Ferdinand had joined it in October. Four days after Henry joined the League, he made a solemn treaty with Ferdinand to attack France before April 1512. That Henry had renewed the treaty of peace his father had made with France did not seem to matter greatly; this treaty would simply serve the better to disguise his preparations. The theory further held that Ferdinand and Henry would attack France together, Ferdinand through his own borders and Henry across the Channel.

Ferdinand's solemn treaty promise to Henry, his son-in-law, provided the fulcrum on which the whole plan rested. It was a noble plan and satisfied the aspirations of all concerned, providing Henry with an early chance to assert the manly qualities of his reign and of his countrymen and affording the Dean of Lincoln a chance to show the Pope where England and its ministers stood on matters touching the Church. It also afforded Ferdinand some proper notion of the fact that the marriage alliance would be an alliance in fact.

In England there was every good reason to believe that Ferdinand would behave according to plan. Certainly the man seemed harmless and amiable enough. And to give further assurance, his daughter, the wife of the King of England, was his ambassador. She had been the means of a close and informal contact between the two sovereigns. On November 1, 1509, Henry had informed Ferdinand that Catherine was pregnant and that the child had quickened. On January 31, 1510, after days of labor, she had given birth to a daughter, but the child was stillborn. In the May following she wrote to her father to say that the stillbirth had been considered an evil omen in England "but that Henry took it cheerfully and she thanked God for having given her such a husband." On January 1, 1511, she had been delivered of her first-born son. "A tourney was held to celebrate the joyous event and the heralds received a handsome largesse at the christening. The child was named Henry, styled Prince of Wales . . . Three days later he was dead; he was buried at the cost of some ten thousand pounds in Westminster Abbey."[5] He had lived but seven weeks.

At the death of his son, Henry had been so grief-stricken that "ambassadors dared not even offer their condolences."[6] But he had recovered with that resilience which was in him, and in spite of haunting prospects suggested by the Levitical code, he continued demonstrative toward Catherine. He was heard frequently to say, "This will please the Queen," or, "The Queen must hear this."[7]

With Catherine cozy to the King of England and at the same time representing her father's interests, it was possible to make the impending war seem like a family affair as well as a crusade against the enemy of the Pope. All three of the principals in England—Catherine, Henry, and Wolsey—had strong motives, diverse but easily unified. Henry was spoiling to show his manliness on a stage bigger than the tourney field; Catherine was a dutiful daughter and devout in her father's cause; Wolsey knew the importance of the Pope as the arbiter of Christendom and his value in future moves that England might make on the Continent.

Thus the decision gathered force. There was little opposition. Only William Warham, forlorn Archbishop of Canterbury, held out. When Parliament was assembled on February 4, 1511, to consider ways and means of financing the war against the Most Christian King, Warham opened it with an address on the theme, "Justice and peace have kissed."[8] He reminded the assembled lawgivers sternly that God permitted war only because of the sins of princes and peoples.

But Parliament paid the solemn voice of the prelate scant heed. The Archbishop of Canterbury was the Primate of All England, but he was less than Pope. A papal brief in English translation was read to Lords and communicated to Commons. It recounted the "wrongs done to the Holy See by the impiety of the French king." The Parliament was also told of the Scottish outrages and of the threat of invasion from France. It was said that Bretons knew every landing place in Cornwall and that the whole area from Plymouth to Land's End would have to be fortified. "A statute was passed to promote the use of the long-bow and to enforce the acts against unlawful games which were supposed to compete with the practise of archery . . . Justices, mayors and constables in the maritime counties were empowered to impress labor for the construction of fortresses."[9]

Evidently the King thought the best defense was to attack France while the fortifications were being built. England made no declaration of war, but the plan of attack was worked out in handsome detail and showed the beginning of Wolsey's easy-chair strategy in the affairs of Europe. The command of the invading army was placed under the second Marquis of Dorset, son of Wolsey's first patron.

Why the King and his Almoner chose to put the young Marquis in charge of a far-flung operation involving the navy as well as the army is not clear. During the older Henry's life the Marquis had fallen under royal suspicion, and in 1508 he had been imprisoned in the Tower and later sent to Calais. But he was dear to the heart of the new King because he was a great jouster, and Henry could not rid himself of the notion that if a man had unseated his opponents on the field of play he might surely unseat the enemy on the field of battle. For this reason, if for no other, a courtier of thirty-five, with no more administrative experience than the King himself, was chosen to command an expedition involving the transport and care of the largest English army an English king had ever set across the Channel.

The whole strategy of the attack was conceived in the crafty mind of Ferdinand and accepted by Henry. Dorset "was to land at Feunterrabia, a town on the southern border of Guienne, with a force of 10,000 men; there he would be met by an equal force provided by the King of Aragon, one half of which was to be mounted."[10]

Only a small part of the operation went according to plan. While the young Marquis and his ships tarried at Southampton for a fair wind, news came that the papal forces in Italy had been soundly defeated at Ravenna, a town near the sea east of Bologna. Undaunted by the news, Henry sent forward the attack. The Marquis set out with his expedition, landing June 7 at St. Sebastián on the coast of Spain, where the English army would take up its position for the attack on Guienne. It advanced twelve miles to Feunterrabia, and there waited for the promised transport and reinforcements. The English continued to wait throughout the summer. Ferdinand never came; nor did he make a move of his royal muscles toward aiding the English. He left them without cavalry or transport. To the protestations of the Marquis he answered with excuses for delay. To John Stile, Henry's ambassador to Ferdinand, he said, according to Stile's report, that he would yet "perform everything unto your grace, and that all the delays of time hath been for the best advantage for your enterprize of Guienne, that Navarre should be first put in a surety." And Stile concluded: "It is evidently seen and known, by his policy and long drifts he attaineth many things to other men's pains."[11]

It took the English three unendurable months of inaction and demoralization in the Spanish sun to believe that Ferdinand had no intention of carrying out his part of the agreement. Gradually it became clear that he had merely used the English force to guard his flank while he busied himself with the conquest of Navarre, adding this landlocked and petty kingdom to his possessions while the Marquis of Dorset and ten thousand men lay sweltering without transport on the shore of Spain in the pious hope that he would join them in their attack on France.

The treachery, so successfully executed, was a damaging enough blow to the King of England. It revealed the stark innocence of this boy who occupied the throne of his country and fancied himself a warrior worthy of a decisive role in the military intrigues of an old Continent where kings survived only by a brutal respect for their own advantage. Yet the unfolding perfidy, so familiar to all the other crowned heads and yet so shocking to the beardless Henry, was not the worst of the damage done. For to complete the disgrace to the King and his Almoner who fashioned this war, the English troops, at least those who survived the pestilential summer, revolted against the plan, mutinied against their officers, defied the King's command, and sailed for home.

The priest had reckoned without the flesh. Men do not behave on paper but on earth. The troops sent with the young Marquis, while impressive in number, were shire levies, which meant that they were country bumpkins without any training in the automatic responses of military discipline, hastily assembled at the King's command, and sent, much against the inclination of their home-loving bowels, to fight on foreign soil for a cause that was as vague as Rome was distant.

Even so, they might have stayed in line and acquitted themselves with honor if there had been a staunch and visible enemy. There was nothing to fight but the Spanish weather. It was a season of almost incessant rains, and the troops were without proper tents. There were no musters or drills to maintain the appearance of army order. Worse still, and disastrous, was the want of beer—the allowance for an English fighting man being a gallon a day. The men drank Spanish wine instead, which made their "blood to boil in their bellies that 3000 of them fell ill of the flux and thereof 1800 died." Lacking proper provisions, they raided the commissariat, and, being bored and idle and hungry, found that their money would not serve their needs. So they struck for more pay—eightpence instead of sixpence a day.[12]

All of this was duly and disgracefully reported to Wolsey. All the correspondence from Spain was addressed to him. As summer wore on, conditions grew steadily more alarming in the ranks. Without a proper enemy, the character of the English yeoman soldier, a farmer with a bow, asserted itself; what seemed to the court at Westminster rank indiscipline became a form of discipline characteristically English—a twitch toward self-government. Officers as well as men formed a council of war and planned a campaign of their own: its object was to return to England the last of September, and they announced that they would abide in Spain after Michaelmas "for no man."

A letter to Wolsey from Dr. Knight told of the council of war and of the plans to return. A herald was sent to tell the whole army they must winter in Spain. This advertisement of the King's orders met with shouts of defiance. The men "crowded round their leaders, crying 'Home! Home!'"[13] The Marquis of Dorset, with scant choice, acceded to the demands of his officers and troops. By the time the news reached the court, the recalcitrant army had provisioned its ships and, early in October, baked its biscuit for the voyage home. Ferdinand, all indignation, protested the move, and Henry showed his royal temper and kingly fury. He wrote Ferdinand to stop the return of the army and to cut every man's throat who refused obedience. But this request of an English king to a foreign monarch to cut the throats of English troops, futile and rhetorical anyway, came too late. The bedraggled and defiant army was already on the sea.

In this humiliating manner ended Henry's first foray into the maze of Europe. The expedition had wasted two hundred thousand ducats and it had lost nearly two thousand English lives, without striking a single organized military blow. Its failure confirmed indelibly every low impression the old heads of the Continent had of this upstart young King who would dare to take an honorable part in their experienced quarrels. And it made plain, too—this failure of Homeric proportions— that the King of England was in the toils of bad advice. There were no secrets kept in Europe. In England the resentment was concentrated on "this Ipswich fellow" who was deemed to be the author of all the mischief. By an extension of the arm of blame, Wolsey was held responsible not only for the war but for the outcome and for the triumphant treachery of Ferdinand, who had outfoxed his English ally and killed his own prey while the English masked the French for him.

In his first effort beyond the comfortable confines of the court, where he could use his eloquence and his favor to silence opposition, Wolsey had failed. His failure had been lavish in scale, shameless in detail. As a priest who enjoyed no higher rank than Almoner, he had arrogated to himself the role of chief councilor and executive. He had been the means, through the lack of thoroughness with which the Spanish campaign was planned, of bringing disgrace upon his King and country. And the country which had suffered knew his intimate part in the affair.

What could be the future of such a priest?

It was part of the temperament of Thomas Wolsey that he met failure by a magnificent scheme for success. The mistakes of the Spanish campaign were plain for all to see, and in their remedy might well lie the secret of victory where defeat had followed before. Obviously the best arrangement would be to invade France again, this time thoroughly prepared in all particulars, especially beer, and with the person of the King as the commander who could hold the troops to their course.

Such an invasion was, in fact, a national necessity. There was no other way in which to escape the disgrace which the Spanish fiasco had fastened on the throne of England. Wolsey may have taken the blame at home for this failure, but the King knew that he himself shared it. Among kings and rulers Henry and not the priest would be the object of laughter and scorn. He was thus in the odd position of having to rescue Wolsey from the low esteem into which his minister had fallen.

There were other reasons, of course, and other forces steadily at work. The best way to cover the embarrassment of a mutiny was to plan another war. Henry had wanted to bring the Marquis of Dorset to trial, along with his subordinates. But it was generally reasoned in the Council that it would be hard to fix degrees of blame where all were responsible for the withdrawal of the army. So the disaffection was treated quietly, and as the voices of the other kings and rulers of Europe reached the English court, Henry instructed his ambassadors formally to state that he and Ferdinand had mutually agreed "upon the return of the troops in consequence of the rainy weather."[14] It was a charitable statement and it covered a multitude of sins.

As early as November, after the return of the recalcitrant army in October, it was reported in London that the King and Queen were bent on continuing the war. At first the Council demurred. The patent reasons which led to the launching of the attack the year before had disappeared. The Most Christian King could not longer be adjudged a threat to Christendom. By one of those curious reversals of fortune, and with no thanks to the sterling efforts of the King of England, France had suddenly fallen into weakness. She had been driven out of Lombardy only a few months after her victory at Ravenna. Moreover, the threat to the spiritual rights of the Holy See as forecast in the Council of Pisa had failed to materialize, and the schismatic cardinals had come to terms with the Pope. There was no reason to argue or believe that the palladium of the Church suffered threat any longer from France or her king, whose fortunes had sadly ebbed and who was now depressed, aging, and gouty besides.

Yet the war must go on, even if the reason for it had changed. Ferdinand professed himself to be outraged at English perfidy and was loud in his comment on the weakness of his son-in-law for letting his troops desert en masse. Catherine was his dutiful and devout daughter. Most of all, an impression had to be corrected. This impression, which shook and riled the soul of the young Henry, was best expressed by Margaret, who told the English ambassador that Englishmen had "so long abstained from war, they lack experience from disuse, and, as it is reported, they now be almost weary of it."[15] Henry had no choice, if he were not to retire from being a respectable and competitive monarch, but to redeem the failure of 1512. The war changed from a crusade to a demonstration of national might and preparations for it were undertaken accordingly so that no man could henceforth taunt Henry.

In January 1513 the bellicose Julius II, whose trumpet of war had first aroused the nations against France, died and was succeeded by Cardinal Giovanni de' Medici, who took the title of Leo X. He was a man of artistic rather than military or political concerns, but he had enough stamina and interest to continue the Holy League against the Most Christian King. After due and proper negotiations among its members this League, now slightly changed in its membership, drew up a covenant to attack France. It was signed on April 3, 1513, by envoys representing Leo, Ferdinand, Margaret of Burgundy, and Henry. Four days before the agreement was signed, Ferdinand had signed a year's truce with France.

If the war now afforded an opportunity for the English King to redeem himself in the eyes of Europe, it afforded no less of an opportunity for Thomas Wolsey to redeem himself in the eyes of his master. For the entire burden of equipping and victualing an army of 40,000 men and transporting it across the Channel for the invasion of France was placed firmly and exclusively upon the shoulders of the Royal Almoner. No English army remotely comparable in numbers or arms had been sent to foreign shores before. There being no precedent for it, there was likewise no organization, no departments of government, to carry out the project. The King and his Almoner were the high command and the whole command. The two were identified again, this time in a colossal enterprise. On its success, in their estimation, would the future of England depend. If England succeeded, she must be reckoned with by all the nations of her world. If Wolsey succeeded, he would prove himself indispensable to the King.

The stubborn confidence of Henry VIII in the lowborn Thomas Wolsey, a confidence which endured for fifteen years in the face of all outcries and criticisms and astonished the diplomats of Europe and the upper classes of English society, dates from this feat in preparing for the invasion of France during the early months of 1513. Henry found in Wolsey a servitor who not only would but could do anything he was told. The priest wrought with the energy of a demon. No plan was too large and no detail too small to engage his fanatically patient attention.

He was forty-two years old at the time, still in abundant health, and he needed every bit of it for the long, solid days and infinite number of nights spent haggling over prices, scurrying for provisions, corresponding with ambassadors and purveyors and admirals and lords. Since the disaffection and ill-content of the English soldiers in Spain had been due to lack of beer, this item was made of first order of importance. The English soldier's habits and hankerings must be respected; there was no use taking any chances with human nature. If beer was to be stored on the transports in good supply, there must be casks for the beer—called foists. Of these, pursers on board the ships of the King's navy were very careless, and Wolsey was forced to write in protest that he could not properly provision the ships if foists continued to be burned or broken. Fox declared that the pursers deserved hanging for their carelessness with the King's equipment. And Wolsey warned the Admiral, Sir Edward Howard, that if the wasting and burning of foists did not stop the King's whole enterprise would be endangered. "Orders should at once be given," said the Almoner to the Admiral, "that the offenders be punished."[16]

Every single phase of his task led sooner or later to a firmament thick with detail that came like stars out of the darkness. For once the casks for beer were secured, and at as fair a price as the purveyors could be brought to offer in view of the demand, he had to have assurance that they were sound and firm and that the beer would not go bad once it was on board, or stored at Calais for use in the campaign. It was one thing to see that the standard allowance of a gallon a day was met on paper and another to follow through and see that the purveyors did not cheat on their casks. There must not be another mutiny for lack of beer.

The same thoroughness, the same capacity for seeing a transaction entire and looking to the King's economy, was to be noted in his pur-chase of victuals. He ordered the slaughter of 25,000 oxen, and when he contracted for "oxen for salting, he would have only the finest beasts from Lincolnshire and Holland; and he insisted on securing rebates for the hides and the tallow. The prices of flitches of bacon are also submit-ted to him, likewise those of biscuits, cheese, dry cod, ling, beef; also of cauldrons to seethe meat in."[17]

There had never been an enterprise like this in the history of any man living. First it was calculated that 30,000 men would be set across the Channel. Then the number was raised to 40,000, these troops to be joined there by an additional 10,000 mercenaries from Germany. The full movement of these troops must be allowed for, and their supply must be reckoned sagely at every turn. But Wolsey went further. He even allowed and made definite plans for the return of the King's forces, and his calculations included schemes for meeting any contingency that might arise if the return of the army should be delayed by adverse winds even a few days beyond the time set provisionally for its return.

Nothing must be overlooked, least of all those things which in the test of battle and conflict would add to the striking power of the good right arm of the King. Henry must have not only men and provisions but arms—great arms, new weapons. Up to now England had relied on for-eign countries for such cannon as it employed. Now it would make these in its own bailiwick. The attaché of the Venetian embassy, much im-pressed with the preoccupying preparations he saw on every hand, wrote: "These English go a good pace, I can tell you . . . Night and day and on all festivals the cannon founders are at work."[18] Heavy guns were coming into use for the first time, and Henry would outstrip his rivals in their manufacture and use. Besides, he would make great use of them as a threat, and he let gossip of the monsters be spread abroad by his ambas-sadors. The feature of his arsenal for the attack on France was to be a collection of a dozen great guns "bigger than any ever cast before, each named after one of the Apostles and furnished with an effigy of the Saint;

so that throughout Europe was bruited the fame of the King of England's 'Twelve Apostles,' who were to preach in tones of thunder and with tongues of fire, Henry's new crusade in defense of the Church of God and the Christian faith."[19]

But with the recollections of the Spanish campaign fresh upon the royal mind, the main scurrying of the King's Almoner turned to day and night supplies for the soldiers who would represent the kingdom abroad. Soldiers must be well cared for by the government, so drastically had times changed since the days when a man went to battle under the aegis of his lord or squire. For this enterprise carried with it the name of England; performance must be above reproach. Thus item by item the Almoner checked his list, and in checking it he came to tents. The lack of tents, what with men ill clad and undernourished, sleeping under bushes or the open sky, exposed to rains and a merciless sun, had been one of the bitterest complaints that had led to the return of the mutinous army from Spain. Wolsey set as his standard that all of the 40,000 men the King took to France would be under canvas. There was at least a department of the government for this undertaking; but the supply was short, and it was necessary for workers to mend old tents as well as fashion new ones. The supervision of this department alone was enough work for a dozen sturdy men in high places, but Wolsey studiously kept all control and responsibility in his hands, being accountable only to the King.

His fierce sense of responsibility had advantages, which his calculating eye well saw. If he succeeded, the King succeeded. That was meat and drink for the morrow and honors heaped beyond even his own febrile imagining. But it also had its drawbacks, for murmurs and complaints among the people, strained by so huge an enterprise, would be directed toward him. Prices rose. As stores poured into Calais during January, February, and March, including such items as 1000 lambs to supplement the diet promised by the slaughter of the 25,000 oxen, the price of meat more than doubled. The price of bread rose, too. There was a public clamor inevitably, and it was the Almoner who got the blame. Merchants from abroad complained that business was at a standstill, that the English had no use for goods that did not help the King's immediate cause. The Venetians were bitter, and their letters are full of the lament that England in these days was no longer a market.

More serious and painful than the discontent over the rising prices of meat and bread were the prospect of financing a gigantic war and the criticism voiced of the King's Almoner because of the mounting national budget. During the first three years of the young Henry's reign, crown expenditures did not exceed £65,000 a year. At this pace the resources Henry VII had husbanded—the fortune of £1,800,000 which he is reckoned to have left—would have run the regime comfortably for years on end, and taxgatherers would not have needed to molest the land. But in 1512, the year of Henry's decision to rescue the Pope from the Most Christian King, crown expenditures bounded to £270,000. And as the people paled before this figure, the King's Almoner, busy with foists and fodder, beef and bacon and bread and beer, totaled up the costs of the war and reckoned that the invasion of France on the scale contemplated would come to £64,000 a year; and this was above and beyond the amount the lords of the manors and those in high places would be expected to spend in the care and maintenance of their own retinues. An obedient Parliament, still under the spell of the King's bidding, granted the amount in theory; but £64,000 was easier to say than to raise, and the process of separating it from the fists of nobles and clergy and farmers and artisans had many of the aspects of wholesale amputations, with nothing but the heat of indignation against Wolsey to cauterize the wounds.

Wolsey wangled the best prices he could, and his Ipswich eye scrutinized all values. He investigated "the wages of the servitors on board his Majesty's ships; the cost of masters' and pilots' coats . . . the cost of anchors and cables for the fleet." There is in the Record Office a letter telling how he had bargained for the carrying of the King's two great siege guns with twenty-eight mares at tenpence a day for each mare. The son of

Suffolk, academician though he was in the days of his training, knew the cost of everything; and the bursar who had been in charge at Magdalen when the Tower was completed came now to apply bursaring on a stupendous scale.

Yet with all his shopping and bargaining and shrewd handling of a per diem for mares, the total costs of the impending war rose like a great wind, and the people were aware of it and of the man who, at the King's behest, sat in the countinghouse and counted out the money. Assessments were levied on the basis of a man's wealth, and the King's commissioners visited victims with searching inquiries. They examined a man's property, his books and records, talked with his neighbors and servants, fingered his coins, pawed at his tapestries and clothing, nosed about his house, ran appraising eyes over his stock and lands. These roving commissioners were empowered to evaluate on the spot and to make assessments at once. No man of any means or property escaped. There was no way to assure passover, for the King's men were everywhere. Empson and Dudley had been publicly disposed of and a lesson made of them, and the new Henry was precisely legal and most orderly in his depredations. The levies hurt just the same, and the gossip that went with them told on every estate and in every hamlet of the new priest at the court who was sitting on the money bags.

Wolsey still had no rank beyond the smile of the King's countenance. He was still officially the Royal Almoner. He had accumulated offices within the Church, but only gradually and always at the King's hand or the hands of the King's councilors. On January 16, 1512, he had been made a prebendary in York Cathedral. This had been at the instigation of Christopher Bainbridge, Archbishop of York, whom Henry had sent as his ambassador to the Holy See; the Pope had seen it wise to make Bainbridge a cardinal and Bainbridge, knowing through his whispering agents the importance of Wolsey in the King's practical plans, had recommended the York appointment. A year later, and in the midst of the confusing purchases and preparations for the defeat of France, Wolsey had been made Dean of York. He was a man of growing stature, yes, but still he was no tower within the Church, and the work of the assessors in the King's enterprise fell upon the clergy as well as upon the laity: the same humiliation of inspection of means and the same crushing assessments for the King's war, with the money going straight into the hands of a man who was not even a bishop.

With all the grumbling at prices and taxes, the work of readying the army and the navy went forward like an unfolding drama before the incredulous eyes of the nation. The King meant business, and he had a style and an imagination made to the scale of his enterprise. He had learned his lesson. War was not a casual affair, at least not on foreign soil. It might be a tourney, but the setting and the arrangements had to be complete before it started. This he knew, and he had in Wolsey a manager of detail who would let nothing amiss come to pass.

So it seemed. So much stress and emphasis had been put on intense preparedness that the King and his Almoner were ill prepared for the blow that struck them when the actual fighting began; being prepared had seemed to offer a guarantee, to provide a kind of charm for success. But the navy, in which the King took as much personal pride as he did in the Twelve Apostles, met with disaster when it made its first sally at the coast of France. It returned to port mutinous and disheartened, having lost its doughty Admiral, its failure due, of all things, to lack of victuals. Impatience was the real enemy in this case, and there was no occasion save by indirection to blame the plan. But the incident showed again that the best of plans must reckon with human impulse and frailty.

The Admiral of the fleet of twenty-three English and five borrowed ships was Sir Edward Howard, second son of Thomas Howard, Earl of Surrey. In the Spanish war the year before, he had redeemed in some respects the degree of English disgrace by his prey upon French vessels. Now his assignment had been to rid the Channel of the French fleet so that the King's army could pass across the Strait of Dover unmolested.

On April 20, 1513, he set sail from Plymouth with plenty of guns and confidence and men, but short of beer and biscuit and patience. He believed he could dispose of the French in swift engagements and return later for supplies if they happened to be needed. "Such a fleet," he wrote to the King, "was never seen in Christendom."[20] It was a sight to put the French to fear, and fifteen of the French vessels fled to port before its majestic approach. "Sir," wrote the Admiral, "we have them at the greatest advantage that man ever had. The first wind that ever cometh they shall have broken heads that all the world shall speak of it."[21] The Admiral in his cheer at the thought of victory again reckoned without the new French strategy.

Pregent de Bidoux, Admiral of the Mediterranean, had been sent to take command of the French defenses of the Channel. "He knew his business. He had laid his hands on 24 huge hulks to launch as fireships upon an English attack. It was clearly Pregent's plan to entice the Admiral into the shallow water of the harbor, where the French galleys could easily overpower any English row-boats which could be sent against them, and at the same time be out of reach of the enemy's ships of line." In the harbor the French galleys were protected by bulwarks on both sides. These bulwarks were planted thick with guns and crossbows that shot square iron bolts known as quarrels. In the face of any attack the "quarrels and gunstones came together as thick as hailstones."[22]

Now Admiral Howard needed nothing so much as victuals. With beer and biscuit aboard his bulky fleet he could have contained the French ships by blockade until the King and his grand army had passed safely across to France. Without victuals to keep his sailors nourished and beer to keep them happy and warlike, a blockade was out of the question. His rashness had led him into a serious predicament, and Howard now decided that he would attempt to deliver himself by still greater rashness. Against the prudent advice of his captains, the Admiral decided to attack the French fleet in four small rowboats. The scheme was to board the main vessel and take possession of it by force of arms. The

Admiral went in person on this foolhardy and tactless tactic. He succeeded in boarding Pregent's ship but, doing battle fiercely to the last in the manner of the best of knights, he was thrust overboard by morris-pikes.

Likewise in this act ended the heroic plan to free the seas of the French before the great invasion. The English fleet, with its leader lost, sailed home in disorder; nothing but exceptionally vile weather on the Channel prevented the French from pursuing. Lord Thomas Howard, first son of the Earl of Surrey, was sent down to take up his brother's office as head of the fleet. He reported that it was "the worst ordered army and furtherest out of rule" that he had ever seen.

It was scarcely a month before the main host of the King's army was scheduled to cross the Channel. What else might be wrong? The preparations were pushed with tense earnestness, all the greater because of the new disaster, and with increasing attention to the problem of co-ordinating the diverse strands that would pull the enterprise together. It would do little good to have provisions and troops if the two could not be assembled; all the salted oxen on earth would avail the King's cause scantily if they were not in the proper place at the proper time. Still the Almoner had not given up.

Meanwhile the defiant death of Sir Edward Howard at Brest proved a boon and a blessing to the King's cause. Careful planners could not have anticipated its sharp effect upon the English mind. Up to now the English had been engaged in packing beef and paying taxes and spinning tents and brewing beer. Preparation had been a commercial enterprise, beneficial to some, annoying to others, but a cold affair at best. The Admiral's death suddenly gave the war meaning, for it was a display of personal courage of the sort Englishmen and Europeans had understood and admired throughout the epic of the past. Working day and night to mold great cannons or to stitch tents was one thing; to hear of a Howard who mounted a French galley from a rowboat, called to his men to follow him, and met death personally and not abstractly in the Spanish sun—this was quite another. War was suddenly no longer a business enterprise but a tournament in which brave men, brave Englishmen, did great deeds of valor.

CHAPTER III

Under the spell cast by the news of Howard's bravery the English nation became at last a cohesive mass, more than a combination of plans and procedures. By the time Henry got ready to cross the Channel the fleet was able to throw a threatening cordon about the whole unprecedented spectacle and carry out the transport besides.

On June 30, 1513, Henry arrived at Calais with the main body of his troops. The vanguard had already crossed under the command of Charles Brandon, now Viscount Lisle, a commoner by birth. His father, plain William Brandon, had been Henry Tudor's standard-bearer at Bosworth and had been killed defending the future King—some said in personal encounter with Richard III. His son Charles was "a bluff Englishman after the King's own heart. He shared, as none else did, in Henry's love of the joust and tourney." In the hierarchy of England's nobility he had been given the title and rights of a viscount, a rank above a baron and below an earl. In manner and heartiness he was dear to the King, standing for the healthy overtness that Henry identified with the Englishman at his best. With the King on the expedition there were said to be "two obstinate men who governed everything." One was Wolsey, unforgettably a commoner, and the other was Brandon, emblem of the new nobility. And in the invasion of France in 1513, designed to display a nation's might, England's nobility, new and old, was on display along with all else that might impress the French.

In intent and purpose the army of the King went to invade; but first and foremost it went to parade. Or so it seemed, for here was a rich and tapestried pageant of the old and new England for all of Europe to see. The Earl of Northumberland carried with him a feather bed and mattress for his pavilion, "with cushions of silk, hangings of worsted, twelve dishes, six saucers, twelve silver spoons, two or three folding stools, a folding table, a close carriage with seven horses, two chariots each with eight horses, four carts each with seven horses, not to speak of a steward, a chamberlain, and a treasurer of the household, a treasurer of wars, two chaplains, a gentleman usher of the chamber, a master of the horse, carvers and cupbearers, a herald and a pursuivant."[1]

Northumberland's accouterment was but a sample of the costly encumbrances which, without regard for military aim, were transported across the Channel. And Northumberland merely brought up the rear. First into Calais came the King's household to the number of three hundred. Next came England's only Duke, the Duke of Buckingham. His banner was followed by Mr. Almoner with two hundred in his train; Ruthal, Bishop of Durham, with one hundred; Fox, Bishop of Winchester, with the same number. "Next came the King and his banner and guard of 600 men, the priests and singers of the chapel to the number of 115, secretaries, clerks, sewers, grooms and pages of the chamber, with Peter Marmelanius, his lutanist," and the most important members of the Council. Henry had 14 fine horses "with housings of the richest cloth of gold and crimson velvet with silver gilt bells of great value."[2] He had brought with him his Master of the Jewel-house; also a "house of timber went about with him in fourteen wagons."[3]

Wolsey not only rode high in the procession; he was also in close attendance upon the King despite his paltry rank. For once the great body of all the King's horses and all the King's men was safely across the Channel and on the hostile soil of France, it was clear that he had left nothing undone. He had managed the beer and the biscuits and the mares and the tents (for all the host was snugly under cover); his genius lay in the fact that he had thought too of the artistic touches and the aesthetic fillips that gave the whole display its proper opulence. He had even chosen "the shade of the colour of the satin for the King's doublet." And three months before the King crossed to Calais, Mr. Almoner had given instructions to Sir Gilbert Talbot, deputy at the port, "to have a tun of a certain wine ready against the King's coming at the house where he is to lodge."[4]

The war must be a clean and courtly affair, carried on with aplomb and under the highest rules of chivalry. To this end Mr. Almoner displayed his greatest refinement in the preparations, for he caused to be printed 1600 copies of *The Statutes of War,* done in a proper manner by the King's printer, Richard Pynson, and at a cost of £16 13s. 4d. In this book was set forth the manly and sportsmanlike code of arms which must not be violated any more than the rules of a tourney. The war would be played by rules, and here was the book with the provisions plain for all to see. "Murmurs or Grudges against the King or the Officers of his Host" are of course strictly forbidden. "Everyone, except he be a Bishop, is to bear a Cross of St. George, 'suffysaunt and large.'" There follow stern injunctions against such acts of unknightly warfare as "sacrilege, robbery, pillage, violence toward the inhabitants of the invaded country, firing of houses . . . all of which offences are punishable with death." There are rules against dicing, card playing, and other games of chance. And finally with a thought to morale and the rivalries of unruly men from all parts of the kingdom, it is stated that "no man is to give reproach to another, because of the country he is of, that is to say, English, Northern, Welsh or Irish."[5]

Considering all the grains of detail Mr. Almoner had winnowed out for the care of the King's men and the comfort of the King's person, small wonder that he enjoyed in the procession at Calais a position far above his rank, or that in the consultations he was, along with Viscount Lisle, hard by the King's side. He stood ready to remedy any error in the line of march, to dispatch messengers who were needed to do the King's immediate bidding, to prompt the actors if they faltered in their appointed parts. He was present to give feet as well as wings to Henry's conception of conquest, to execute faithfully the dreams of a young King.

Henry arrived at Calais about an hour and a half before sunset. According to John Taylor, one of the King's chaplains, who did a chronicle of the whole campaign, Wolsey, as became his station and as a stratagem of his priestly humility, rode in plain cassock—and on a mule, not on a richly caparisoned horse. The cavalcade moved from the quay to the Lantern Gate of the fortress, the gate with a beacon marking the port from the sea. For weeks soldiers in Tudor white and green had been pouring into Calais. Now Henry was here in person to give the inhabitants of the portside city some sense of English might and color. The inhabitants were descendants of the English colonists planted there 160 years before, mostly from County Kent. Their contacts had been only with English merchants and traders, and this was to be their first sight of the stupendous pageant which marked the pomp and circumstance of the homeland.

Henry bore their homage well. He received the plaudits and respectful tokens from maidens and men at the windows of houses that overhung the streets, the greetings of the Merchants of the Staple and the mayor, well appareled, at the Staple Hall. But he moved with the grim intent of a true crusader to the Church of St. Nicholas in St. Nicholas Street, which he entered just as the day was waning. There he made offerings to the church and its clergy and "prayers to God and His Saints—for the safe passage of himself and his armies across the perilous seas, dedicating both to the services of the Almighty and of His Church, in the great enterprise he was entering on in vindication of the rights of the Holy See against the sacrilegious insolence of Louis XII."[6] The King and the priest were at one in pageant and in prayer. Thomas Wolsey had at last become the fleshly shadow of the King.

Henry kept his portly character as an armed apostle bent on the Lord's work in the nondescript engagement which followed. When some German soldiers in his hire burned some churches at Ardres, "the king, mindful of the sacred character of his expedition, had three of them hanged."[7] His exemplary personal conduct—in such matters as practicing archery with his archers and surpassing them all and in refusing one rainy night to undress, insisting instead upon riding about camp encouraging the watch—all was calculated to impress his soldiers and the people of France.

It was a lofty and chaste performance, all told, in which the business of bashing men's heads seemed out of place. There was, of course, a certain amount of fighting, all conducted according to *The Statutes of War,* but not much. In skirmishes around Thérouanne, French chevaliers and English knights challenged each other to single combat, their followers looking on.

War began with this crusade, however, to change subtly in character. The use of great cannon, which would belch and fume at one place and destroy men and property at a distance, was part of this change. Fighting was beginning to be industrialized. It was a convenience to be able to set off a great gun and have the gun do the work of destruction. War was taking on a faintly impersonal character. The obsession with its preparation and financing showed among other things that the design was not so much to conquer the enemy as to intimidate him.

In the case of this war Henry had so advertised his might abroad that he expected France to quail before his coming. He was not disappointed. Weakened by the series of disasters of the year before, France had no heart for the affair and seemed merely to go through the motions of defense. When Henry decamped from Calais on July 21 and arrived before Thérouanne August 1, Louis XII—he who had seemed such a ferocious threat to Christendom a year before—drove out from Paris in a carriage, but he was ill and feeble and lacking in heart and he took no part in the action to defend Thérouanne. In common with almost everyone else, he seemed but a spectator at a war that never quite came off.

Thérouanne fell August 22, the first French city to be captured by English arms since the days of Jeanne d'Arc. And before it fell, the English had accomplished a disastrous rout of French cavalry sent to supply the town. This engagement, in which the French unceremoniously took to their horses' heels, first at a trot and then at a canter and then at a gallop, came in English lore to be known as the Battle of the Spurs. Henry was mounted for this fray, but his staff kept him at a safe distance until the French cavalry had been thoroughly routed. Then "he had the delightful experience of chasing a defeated enemy as long as his horse would go, and of capturing dukes and counts and the Chevalier Bayard himself. He never forgot this exhilarating afternoon—but he had no chance of repeating its joys in all his life."[8]

Protected from actual encounters, Henry had all the glory of war and none of the gore, a circumstance which colored his views of Europe for years to come. He was the man on horseback, the strong deliverer. At Lille he received all the honors of a conquering hero simply by riding through the town, riding "with as much pomp," to quote from Taylor's diary, "as ever he did at Westminster with his crown on." The people, Taylor continues, "crowded out of the town to meet him in such numbers you would have thought that none could have been left behind; girls offered crowns, sceptres, and garlands; outlaws and malefactors with white rods in their hands sought pardon. Between the gate of the town and the palace the way was lined with burning torches, although it was bright day, and there was scarce room for the riders to pass. Tapestries were hung from the houses, and tents erected at frequent intervals, where histories of the Old and New Testament and of the poets were acted."[9]

But if the burly and puffing Henry played only a supernumerary role in the engagement, he managed to be on hand for the official ceremonies of surrender, and he got the credit for the behavior of his troops.

It was plain that the French now had no desire to engage the English troops directly. Henry was full of confidence. And when Thérouanne fell and the walls by his order were destroyed, foreigners began "talking respectfully of the renewal of English might. Ferdinand, who had sent only regretful messages in answer to Henry's appeal for help, now sent a special envoy to draft plans for a grand joint invasion the next year."[10]

The campaign served to show Henry that as a sovereign ruler he rated with the best. And to complete the picture, Emperor Maximilian of the Holy Roman Empire showed up one day in his camp in the guise of a common soldier and volunteered his services and those of his troops —for pay, of course. Taylor described the Emperor as "of middle height, with open and manly countenance and pale complexion. He has a snub nose and a grey beard; is affable, frugal, and an enemy of pomp. His attendants are dressed in black silk or woolen."[11]

It was a touching scene, this homage paid by the Emperor to the King. True, he was Emperor in title only and not quite that, for he had never been crowned, having been refused passage through the territories of Venice when he set out to Rome for his coronation. His empire, which ostensibly embraced the German states under the Hapsburgs, Switzerland, the Netherlands, and Burgundy, was tenuous and scattered, stitched together by marriages, a coat of many colors and endless seams. Known as "the man of few pence," Maximilian never stayed long enough in any one part of his putative dominion to govern, being forever occupied with ambitious intrigues, all designed to bring him ready money. He exported his services. He found it easier to raise money by large-scale chicanery than by attending to the grubby business of taxation. He was full of ideas for reforms, many of them good, but never carried out; the task of actually governing his empire or any part of it seemed to be beneath his dignity.

But still and all he was the Emperor of the Romans, in line of succession with Charlemagne, a genial and likable fellow in all his personal dealings, which were many, and it was no small tribute to the young and virtuous King of England when the great man appeared in his camp and offered to serve as a common soldier. Besides, Maximilian, whatever his cash balance at any one time, was well connected, and one could never tell when one of his relatives might stand a King in good stead. His daughter Margaret was regent of the Netherlands, and she had in her tender care the upbringing of the Emperor's grandson, Charles, who in turn was the son of Joanna, ruler of Castile; and Charles, when he reached beyond the age of puberty and old Ferdinand died, would become King of Castile and Aragon. Joanna was mad, to be sure, having been inconsolable since the death of Maximilian's son and her husband, Philip, who had ruled the Netherlands until his death a few years before. Still she was head of Castile all the same.

To him Europe was more or less a family affair. He was in his vague way a good man to know and to cultivate. And while Henry was in France and the Emperor was in his hire, he visited Margaret to arrange for the marriage of this young and potential Charles to his sister the Princess Mary.

After the fall of Thérouanne, Henry turned next to Tournai, then held by the French, "the wealthiest city," writes Tuke, the clerk of the signet, "in all Flanders, and the most populous of any on this side of Paris . . . The gates were of iron, the towers of stone, and the heavy guns of Lille were requisitioned for the siege."

In the fall of Tournai on September 24, well ahead of schedule, Henry marked up the greatest triumph of his campaign. Tournai was a city of carpetmakers and a place of wealth, with the legend THE UN-SULLIED MAIDEN inscribed over its great gate. And in its fall, too, Master Almoner displayed the crowning genius of his thoroughness. Indeed his preparation proved to be too thorough, as far as practical needs were concerned, but it shone all the more spectacularly in the galaxy of English commercial grandeur because it was not necessary. He had prepared for a long and strenuous siege. Knowing from the days he had visited Maximilian something of the vagaries and unpleasantness of Flanders weather, he was not content to trust the army of the King to canvas. Instead he had ordered the building of an immense number of wooden huts, "of which a great part had chimneys"—huts "sufficient to shelter the whole English army of 40,000 men. They were so numerous and ample that they covered a space around the walls of Tournay as extensive as the area covered by the town itself, which . . . harboured no less than 80,000 inhabitants."[12]

It was a fanciful scheme. The town capitulated quickly; there was hardly time to put up the huts. They were in practical terms a costly military waste. But they left an impression of English skill that was not only immediate but durable. For they were standing long after the English army returned to its native land, and they served as suburban homes for laborers engaged in the industries of the city.

In the fall of Tournai the French campaign ended, and, leaving a garrison of 6000 men to hold the city, the English army slipped safely home before the rigors of winter set in. Everything had gone according to plan, and since the war had been nine-tenths preparedness and one-tenth fighting, it was Thomas Wolsey who got the credit with the King. He had confirmed at every turn his master's faith—a faith all the more remarkable because of his signal failure in the Spanish campaign the year before. Here was a man whose worth to the kingdom must be reckoned in thousands of pounds.

There was a tide running now in the destiny of this Ipswich fellow. For the moment when his powers were fully recognized by the King was also the moment when the fortunes of England in the realm of war and national might and prestige turned triumphantly for the better. Thomas Wolsey and the King and England at one and the same time had arrived at the moment of ascendancy. Their images assumed a strange identity, molded by a oneness of purpose—the assertion of might. England would no longer be the laughingstock of older nations in Europe, or her King regarded as a cherub who might best attend his lute, or his new councilor a paltry and officious priest.

To make matters firmer than the campaign in France had made them, the English, while Henry was jousting in Flanders fields, had gained a decisive victory over the Scots at the battle of Flodden. There was nothing polite or courtly about this affair. It was bloody, attended by frightful slaughter. In the bitter scheme of things it supplemented the pageant in France and the display there of the nation's wares of war, for it demonstrated that in the hard tasks of war the English soldier was not to be counted glibly out as a military man. Upon the carnage wrought at Flodden, no less than on the elaborate and pretentious siege of Tournai, England's new reputation rested. And by one of those odd twists of circumstance that bring greatness by association, Henry and Wolsey found themselves enhanced by Scotland's slithering downfall. Its defeat contributed to the notion of the greatness of England and by indirection to the power of the young King and his ubiquitous aid.

The Scottish invasion of England while Henry was in France vaunting his supremacy and his wardrobe came as no surprise, in spite of the habitual English effort to make every move of the Scots appear to be an act of treachery. Wolsey had been bound to admit to the seventh Henry that in the matter of border raids the English had given the Scots more provocation than the Scots had given the English. At least, the solemn old Henry had set up diplomatic means by which the traditional differences between the two countries could be made into talks, if not altogether amicably settled. He had even given his daughter Margaret as a hostage to the future relations of the two countries. The young King Henry had changed all that, or if he had not changed it he had notably neglected to carry forward his father's efforts. He had studiously ignored a proud land of six hundred thousand people to the north. Bent on the assertion of his own manliness and regality before the audience of the Holy See and the rulers of Europe, he had been at no pains to develop friendship with his estimable brother-in-law, King James IV of Scotland. To Henry, Scotland was not a country but a quarrel. A quarrel he could understand and handle. But a country which was hospitable to foreigners, even partial to influences from abroad, a country having chimneys and windows when these items were by no means common in England, yet a country not given to manufacture and industry—this sort of country, or any country other than the one he inherited, Henry could not understand and did not aim to try. It was easier to fight a problem than solve it.

The Earl of Surrey had been appointed Lord Lieutenant of the North and left behind when the main force of Henry's army crossed to France. Preparations against the Scots had even been calculated in Wolsey's plans for the invasion of France, and if they were less showy they were more practical and thorough; for by September 1, the Earl of Surrey, old Thomas Howard, now in his seventieth year, who had fought with Richard at Bosworth but had been loyal these twenty-eight years to the Tudors, was able to assemble an army of 26,000 men—and within a week after James had delivered his ultimatum to Henry in France. The levies, tough men all from the northern counties, "were given conduct money from their homes and taken into the king's pay as from 1 September."[13] Wolsey had made his plans big enough to include provisioning the army that would be needed to guard the Scottish border. Everything was in readiness for the surprise. Even the royal artillery had been sent north and was at Newcastle ready for use when the troops arrived there.

During the summer of 1513 Catherine the Queen had kept up a lively and resilient correspondence with Mr. Almoner. "She arranged to write once a week and to have every courtier bring back a letter, at least from Wolsey if Henry was too preoccupied with war. She worried about Henry's rashness in battle, and his tendency to get overheated and catch cold . . . She pestered Wolsey about her husband's health and remembered to send fresh supplies of linen for him." Her letters were labored in language but full of solicitude on personal matters and vocative with detail on matters of state, particularly touching the impending Scottish invasion and the last-minute preparations for it.[14]

She had been left as Henry's regent in England, and as such she was responsible officially for the defense of her adopted country. But her devotion was to Henry, and if she wrote confidently of the defense against Scotland and the busyness of the people with it, it was more to set Henry's royal mind at rest than anything else. She was a woman and wife before she was a ruler, and her feminine mind knew that through the King's Almoner and steady companion she could keep in touch on those daily trifles that have such vast significance to a solicitous female. She wrote Wolsey on July 26, 1513, begging him "to take the (pains) with every of my messengers to write to me of the King's health, and (what) he intendeth to do, for when ye be so near our enemies I shall never (rest) till I see often letters from you . . ."[15] Again she writes to Wolsey on August 13: "Ye may think when I put (you to) this labour that I forget the great business that ye have in hand, but if ye (remember) in what case I am that is without any comfort or pleasure unless I hear, ye will not blame me to desire you (though it be a short letter) to let me know from you tidings as often as may be . . ."[16]

Apparently Wolsey performed his task well, for on August 25 she wrote again: "Master Almoner, for the pain ye take remembering to write me so often, I thank you for it with all my heart . . ."[17]

Even her personal letters to Wolsey and Henry offer picturesque information to ease the royal mind about affairs at home. She wrote Wolsey to tell the King that "all his subjects be very glad, I thank God, to be busy with the Scots, for they take it (for a) pastime. My heart is very good to it, and I am horribly busy with making standards, banners, and badges."[18] There is no doubt that the Scottish war was Catherine's war. She was "the soul of the enterprize. She quieted Henry's dangers by occupying herself with warlike occupations."[19] When the Scottish invasion struck, it was Catherine who by virtue of the authority vested in her summoned 40,000 men from the south to meet in London, while Surrey collected his men according to plan in the north.

James crossed the Tweed into England with a large Scottish army, strong in artillery and adequate in provisions. It was said that a token from the French Queen, "who besought James as her true knight to advance three feet into English ground and to strike a blow for her honour," swayed the King at the last moment of indecision. Wise men in his council sought to stay the step, but gallantry prevailed over wisdom. James was not a man to let an impulse pass or to let a lady down. He was not a man, as James Gairdner puts it, "to think lightly of any provocation he received." Well educated, a good Latin scholar, he could not only "talk Gaelic with the Highlanders as well as lowland Scotch, but he (also) had the command of all the leading European languages."[20]

With all his accomplishments of the mind and his amiable temperament in dealing with his people, he was essentially a volatile Scotsman who loved a fight and whose measure of personal bravery was the willingness to die against odds. The main course of his life, however, had been to forge Scotland into some semblance of a nation. He had given his country status, so that it had diplomatic dealings with other nations and a voice that was coming to be respected in the courts of Europe; it sent accredited representatives hither and yon and played at the game of diplomacy as well as at the games of war. More, he had given the Scots some measure of unity, as great a measure as anyone could hope for.

In scope and extent the Scottish move into England had all the aspects of a diversionary move made to divide English energies and take the pressure off France. With all his vast army, James spent the first few precious days of his campaign destroying castles, including one owned by his episcopal highness the Bishop of Durham. But beyond this the King of Scotland did not go; his tactics were the tactics of endless years of border raids, and on or near September 1 he drew up his army in a strong position on a hill facing south at a place ten miles west of Wooler.

The hill was called Flodden Edge. There he awaited developments, the plan apparently being to draw Surrey and his army as far north of London as possible. Whatever his plan or motives, and no one knows, the fact remains that he did not move more than fifteen miles into English territory.

It was far enough to provoke a battle. On September 9 the battle was joined.[21] By nightfall it was mercifully over, and the victor had begun stripping the dead, which numbered 10,000 Scots and by all accounts only 1500 Englishmen. Effective artillery fire from the English had maddened the Scots, so that they forsook their commanding position on Branxton Hill. At first the fury of undisciplined border fighters swept the English before it, but the King's men, holding the center of the line, were also lured down the slope. His men carried spears fifteen feet long and marched in a solid phalanx, so that the effect was like a porcupine. But the spears proved of no use at close quarters, where English broadswords won the day. By an expert maneuver, Howard swept to the rear of the King and his men while they were fighting at close quarters with the English. Attacked on all sides and "forced to fight in a ring," the Scots went down, resisting to the last man. James fell "not a spear's length from Surrey's standard, riddled with arrows and gashed with swords and bills." Godwin tells us that "his necke was opened to the midst with a wide wound, his left hand almost cut off in two places did scarce hang to his arme."[22] With him there died his natural son, "the youth of twenty who had been a pupil of Erasmus, a bishop, two abbots, twelve earls, fourteen lords and representatives of most of the families of consequence in Scotland."[23]

When Henry heard the word from Flodden he shook his head and said with pompous magnanimity that James had paid a higher price for his perfidy "than we would have wished." But another dragon had been slain, even if he had not been there in person to attend the matter. It was his queen, the daughter of Ferdinand, who had accomplished this feat, and she let him know the significance of the victory when she wrote: "But to my thinking, this battle hath been to your grace and all your realm the greatest honour that could be, and more than if ye should win all the crown of France."[24]

It was a tactless thing to tell a husband, much less a King—and one who was still puffing from the pursuit of the fleeing flower of French chivalry, but Henry had a great capacity for enfolding honors, for absorbing credit. It was part of being a King to construe what happened under a reign to be an evidence of God's favor, what with one's fighting solidly on God's side. A woman may have been as regent technically responsible for the victory, but the effect was something that Henry could gather to his growing bosom and meditate on. In a single year Henry had emerged from the chrysalis of obscurity and failure to be feared throughout Christendom. It was this that mattered; all else was detail.

Except the succession, of course. In September of the eventful year 1513 the Venetian ambassador announced the birth of another son. But it was a son Henry never saw. Either it was stillborn or it died immediately after birth. Henry went home from his triumph in France to a Queen who had not borne him an heir.

CHAPTER IV

How rapidly Wolsey rose to acknowledged power after the ponderous invasion of France and the repulse of Scotland may be seen from the fact that three bishoprics were bestowed upon him in a single year. It is said that Erasmus decided to dedicate a book to the ascendant Wolsey, but before the book could be readied for the printer he was forced to change the salutation three times. The priest who had hitherto borne such petty titles as bursar, chaplain, and almoner now went about the business of collecting titles and tokens of esteem like a man starved for recognition.

First, and in direct and open acknowledgment of his administration of the French war, Wolsey was made Bishop of Tournai. Henry had captured the city in a holy war, and he considered it within his royal prerogative to take the bishopric, vacant at the time the city fell, and bestow it as he chose. Then the diocese of Lincoln fell conveniently vacant through the death of its occupant. Wolsey being already dean of the cathedral there, it was within the logic of the text "To him that hath shall be given" that the zealous servant of the King should now be elevated to the bishopric of Lincoln. There followed some spirited correspondence between Wolsey and Sylvester de Giglis, the English agent at Rome, about reducing the fee to be paid the Pope for the rights to the see, but Rome replied that the church at Lincoln was rich and must pay the tax. De Giglis did say, however, that the Pope would forgo the customary annates expected from another honor conferred on Wolsey, the deanery of the Church of St. Stephen, which stood hard by Westminster. There would also be a reduced fee for expediting the bulls to this deanery, due to the insistence of the Pope, though, de Giglis adds, "the officials are angry with him for having brought it down so low."[1]

Within a few months Cardinal Bainbridge died in Rome, his death attended by more than a suspicion of poison, and Thomas Wolsey succeeded him as Archbishop of York.

All of the honors that had befallen Wolsey up to this point had been granted by the authority of the King and sanctioned by the power of the Pope. From the very beginning of his service at the court, but particularly now in this period of the enhancement of his honors, there was duality, a double recognition and a double leverage at every move. Theoretically, bishops were elected by the clergy of their dioceses. In practice bishops were named by the Crown. If a bishopric fell vacant, a writ was immediately issued to vest its temporalities in the Crown; the property connected with it, in a word, became the property of the Crown for the time being. Then a candidate for the bishopric was proposed by the King. If the candidate was acceptable to the Holy See, he was then consecrated and invested in the episcopal see, having first been required to take an oath of allegiance to the Pope and the Holy Catholic Church. This oath of obedience to the Pope contained clauses "not easily reconcilable to the duty of a subject or the rights of secular princes."[2] Hence in this situation the bishop, duly consecrated and invested by the Holy Father, must next apply to the King for the restoration of his temporalities. And before the temporalities of any archbishop or bishop could be restored "he was obliged to disclaim and renounce all clauses in the Pope's bull prejudicial to the rights of the crown or the King's prerogative."[3]

It was a double deal, a system that rested on contradictory oaths solemnly taken and ceremoniously denied. To become a shepherd of the Lord's work in England a man who should have stood as an exemplar of morality and honesty in office was by his very induction disqualified for any but the temporal care of his flock and see. He served two masters and was sworn publicly to do so. This followed hallowed custom, and Wolsey was not one to question procedure or depart from order; his genius lay in the extraordinary energy with which he carried out what was expected, and there is no indication that a ripple of concern over the curious relation between Rome and England ever rolled across his mind at this stage. He had above all else a sense of the immediate; and he had a sense of the Pope. To serve both the King and the Pope became his chief concern—to use both when needed, to play upon the favor of one to gain favors of the other, to identify himself subtly with the interest of both, to choose to see their interests as at all times identical and his own interests as supreme. This policy he continued indefatigably for years until at last his own interests could be served by neither and he was compelled to make a bitter choice between the two oaths he had taken.

From the very moment of his ascendancy, Wolsey began to press for honors beyond those that the King had the power to bestow. Shortly after his consecration as Bishop of Lincoln, he sent Polydore Vergil to Rome. The ostensible purpose of the trip was to let a man who had been resident in England for twelve years "visit his old home and kiss the feet of the new pope."[4] But the real mission was confidential. Wolsey had already set in motion the forces which were designed to make him a cardinal, not unmindful that the word derives from the Latin word meaning *hinge*, on which the door of the Church and other important matters turn. As a cardinal he would be technically a member, if not in residence, of the governing body of the Church, and a visible—nay, conspicuous —representative of the Church in England.

The stratagem suggested by Wolsey called for Vergil to pay his respects to Cardinal Hadrian, a man Wolsey had in 1511 recommended for the papacy at a time when to all appearances Julius II might give up the ghost. Julius had lived two more years, and there had been no occasion to elect a new Pope. But Vergil was to refresh Hadrian's mind of events not long past, and, if Hadrian showed himself disposed to recall gratefully Wolsey's recommendation, then and then only was Vergil to broach the matter of Wolsey's own election to the College of Cardinals.

The flanking attack for the cardinalate went well, for Hadrian broached the matter to Leo X, who thought not ill of it, seeing how by this time the Archbishop of York stood with the King of the English. England was regarded in Rome, in the words of one of the popes, as "our storehouse of delights, a very inexhaustible well; and where much abounds, much can be extorted from many."[5] The question, as Pollard phrases it, was not whether Wolsey was worthy of the cardinal's hat but whether he was worth it. When the time that suited best the circumstances at Rome dictated it, Hadrian was to write to Wolsey and Wolsey was then to secure the royal assent. Meanwhile, not a word was to be said, "and the affair was to be so managed as to appear the spontaneous offer of Leo X, 'as,' remarks Vergil to Wolsey, 'your reverend lordship told me it was to be done.'"[6]

Nor was this sufficient unto the day. An archbishop might be made a cardinal and still he would not enjoy plenary powers befitting the good right arm of the King. There still remained the Archbishop of Canterbury, dry and dull perhaps, but in the residue of his vigor nonetheless Primate of All England. Wolsey foresaw that if his own position were to be safeguarded by the proper bastions of power within and without the realm, he must be made a papal legate in England. Not a nuncio, for such an official had but temporary powers deriving from a special mission; and not simply a legate either, for Warham by virtue of his rank was already legate *natus*. What Wolsey would have to become was legate *a latere*—and for life. This position would make him the Pope's permanent representative in the kingdom of England, invest him with the right to reform the Church, which obviously needed attention in view of the undercurrent of criticism that had been mounting for the past fifty years, and give him the right to make judicial decisions on religious matters without forever referring these matters by laborious correspondence and slow messenger to Rome.

Wolsey had not trusted the request for the legateship to Vergil but had routed it through Sylvester de Giglis. It was better to have two agents than one and to exercise pressure through a squeeze. De Giglis wrote to Wolsey that His Holiness had the matter under favorable advisement and that, with certain conditions accepted by the Archbishop of York, he might be made legate *a latere*—if not for life, at least legate *a latere* for successive periods, the matter to be renewed each few years.

Thus tentatively assured how matters stood at Rome, Wolsey now thought it propitious to send forward the King's letter of request that he be made a cardinal. The letter was drawn on August 12, 1514. It sang in eloquence the worth of Wolsey, adding from the royal hand the remarkable statement that Henry could do nothing of the least importance without Wolsey and referring to him as "our most secret counsellor."[7]

This letter was a secular request made by the secular power. There is no reference in it to the spiritual qualifications of Wolsey for the high office in store. These qualifications are assumed or ignored. The King wants his "counsellor" honored and supported by the Church. And if it was true that the King could do nothing of the least importance without Wolsey, it was doubly true that Wolsey could do nothing without both the King and the Pope. His advancement and maintenance under the system of his time depended upon their joint will and approval. With the power vested in him by them both he could do what he chose.

The Pope in his deliberations delayed a full year, and if there was any doubt in Wolsey's mind as to whether the King or the Pope was the greater in power to grant his wishes, this year, a sobering one, must have resolved the doubt. With all the King's approval, he could not win the hat. But that he won it in the end assured him more profoundly than ever of his ability to manipulate even the greatest person in Christendom. If there was any power stronger than that derived from a Pope, it was the power to influence a Pope and make him do one's bidding. The year of waiting and maneuvering for the hat, whatever else its effect, fixed his mind more than ever on Rome as the primal center of his authority; and certainly his success in wresting the hat from the obstinate Leo left in his thinking the lingering impression that by proper blandishments and stratagems he could do all things through the Holy Father.

Leo's reluctance was partly due to the atmosphere of scandal in which the enemies of Wolsey linked his name with the murder of Cardinal Bainbridge, but it rested on other foundations besides. Grave understanding of Wolsey's aggressiveness and ambition underlay much of the reluctance. "Men say an English cardinal ought not to be created lightly, because the English behave themselves so insolently in their dignity," wrote in his diary de Grassis, papal master of ceremonies at this time, adding, "as was shown in the case of Cardinal Bainbridge, just dead. Moreover, as Wolsey is the intimate friend of the King, he will not be content with the cardinalate alone, but, as is the custom for those barbarians, will wish to have the office of Legate over all England."[8]

Meanwhile, and during the course of his strenuous negotiations for the hat, Wolsey faced exacting problems in England. One was the increasing hostility toward the Church. In handling this problem there is no indication that the Archbishop, busy with the new dignities he enjoyed, was stirred to thought or driven to perception. Wolsey's life was a round of activities that left little time for reflection and deadened him to the vital forces moving in the current of his day. Wolsey thought like a knight in a joust, his mind a lance to use in unseating his opponent or in preventing himself from being unhorsed; and in the sweat and urgency which attended all his designs he never seems to have paused to inquire whether jousts were necessary or wise or an essential part of the divine nature of things. His was not to reason why, to raise abstract questions for which there was no practical answer.

Since history bears small trace of his introspections, it is not possible to tell whether his incessant concern with the practical was invoked consciously or unconsciously to protect him against matters deeply disturbing. Whatever the reason, we do know that the man whose most distinguishing mark was that he came from the common people did upon his accession to power surround himself with all the paraphernalia of success and did sever in his daily manner of living all connections with the commonalty and did cushion himself extravagantly against the abrasive cares that made up the life of the average Englishman. He who was a rebel and in revolt against the nobility took on all the manners of the nobility as if eager to establish his worth beyond dispute by the outward station of his living.

His duties as a man of influence, of course, took an ever larger measure of his time. He began to charge fees for professional services rendered. As early as June 11, 1513, he received a substantial annuity from a Lady Margaret Pole for such counsel as he might give in handling money matters for her ladyship. It was said that more than ever, after the affray in France was over, he encouraged Henry to entertain and pleasure himself with jousts and the hunt and his beloved lute and to leave "old men's work" to his servant's willing hands.

In this business, with its infinite shuffling of papers, Wolsey was diligent beyond compare. George Cavendish, who in later life became his gentleman-usher, tells of one occasion which illustrates his power of pre-occupation and his capacity for sustained application. Cavendish says that the Archbishop rose one morning about four of the clock and sat down to write letters, "commanding one of his chaplains to prepare him to mass, insomuch that his said chaplain stood revested until four of the clock at afternoon; all which season my lord never rose once to——, nor yet to eat any meat, but continually wrote his letters with his own hands, having all that time his nightcap and keverchief on his head. And about the hour of four of the clock, at afternoon, he made an end of writing, commanding one Christopher Gunner, the king's servant, to prepare him without delay to ride empost . . . with his letters, whom he dispatched away or ever he drank."[9]

Here was diligence fit to serve a King. "Writing," admitted Henry, "is to me somewhat tedious and painful." When Wolsey thought it "essential that letters in Henry's hand should be sent to other crowned heads, he composed the letters and sent them to Henry to copy out."[10] He was the one, an enemy admitted, "who knew more and could do more than all the rest of the King's council put together."[11] Leo, who by all tokens had good intelligence at the court of England, said that Wolsey had the King so much under his influence that Henry would sign state papers without knowing their contents.

With manifold duties in high places, a private practice in canon law, and his sees to supervise, the Archbishop was as busy as the forces of evil. Earlier it had been his duty to conduct the preparations of war, not to sit around and think whether the war was justified in the sight of God or ethics. And now when he confronted his first great problem as Arch-bishop, he met it on practical grounds. He had no time and he was in no position to feel the impulses of the people of England or to understand the assertiveness of a mass of laymen in revolt against the clergy; he had time only to hear the clamor and to treat it as a watchman might.

On the early morning of December 4, 1514, the body of a well-to-do merchant-tailor, by name Richard Hunne, was found hanging from a beam in the prison of the Bishop of London, a place known as the Lollards' Tower in St. Paul's. It was announced by Richard FitzJames, Bishop of London, and by his chancellor Dr. Horsey that Hunne had died of his own hand while being detained in the prison to stand trial for heresy.

The announcement of Hunne's suicide met with no favor or credence among the laity, for the deceased was known as a man who held strong views on the privileges and pretensions of the clergy; who had read the New Testament in English and had referred to priests and bishops as Scribes and Pharisees. Stories began rapidly to circulate and to gather flame as they went. It was said that Hunne had refused to give the priest who buried his infant son the child's bearing-sheet as a mortuary. Under the custom of mortuaries the Church claimed the best article belonging to the deceased as a burial fee. Hunne had resisted on the ground that his son, being only a few weeks old, "had no property in the bearing sheet which the parson claimed."[12] It was further rumored where men congregated and reviewed the case, which gained daily in common interest, that the priest had sued Hunne for the fee in a spiritual court and that Hunne had countered with a suit in the Court of the King's Bench, charging that the spiritual court in which the priest's suit had been entered was a foreign tribunal and that those who sat in it were guilty of a breach of praemunire.

The use of the term "praemunire" excited the greatest antagonism among both the laity and the clergy, but more particularly among the latter: loosely it meant treason, but it also meant a peculiar kind of legal treason instituted by the allegiance of the Church in England to the Church at Rome. The term came from the first word of the summons issued to the defendant to answer the charge, a harmless Latin word but colored and poisoned by years of painful use. An act of Parliament had been passed in 1353 called the Statute of Praemunire. It enacted specifically that all who appealed abroad any plea which might properly be tried in the King's courts were in danger of being guilty of offense against the King.

The clergy were sensitive and touchy on any charge that hinted an action of praemunire, and it was said bitterly in London that Hunne had been haled into prison for his audacity and arrogance in charging the spiritual court with foreign origins and thus invoking praemunire; that the Bishop of London and his officials had examined him for heresy and imprisoned him on the basis of preliminary evidence and, once he was jailed, had done him to death.

So the stories ran. And they were given some fuel when a coroner's jury examined the body of Hunne, ruled out the official announcement of death due to suicide, charged Dr. Horsey and two of his servants with murder, and ordered them to stand trial. "The text of the inquest, with subsequent additions, was circulated in pamphlet form, and the air was full of inaccurate and untested surmises."[13]

The jailer, Charles Joseph, had fled the day after the coroner's jury was impaneled. He first had taken sanctuary in Westminster and then had escaped to a secluded village in Essex. This escape made the task before the coroner's jury, "24 right honest men," as Thomas More described them, all the more difficult and heightened the feeling of those who were already convinced that Hunne had been murdered.

The officials of the see of London, seeing how things stood in the matter, now faced the question of whether Richard Hunne should be given Christian burial. To accord him this privilege would be tantamount to admitting that he was not a heretic and that he had been unjustly held for trial. Thus on the Sunday following Hunne's death a fresh list of charges was read out against the deceased, all pointing to heresy. On December 16 the corpse "was solemnly tried in the presence of the mayor and aldermen by an ecclesiastical court, the bishop of London presiding with the assistance of three other bishops."[14] The dead man was "pronounced a heretic, and his body handed over to the secular power to be burned; and burned it was at Smithfield on December 20, to the grief and indignation of the people."[15]

The Church had triumphed again over heresy, but still the coroner's jury patiently continued to sift the evidence. Joseph, the escaped jailer, when finally brought back to London from Essex, sought to establish an alibi for himself, saying that he had spent the night on which the murder was alleged to have been committed in a house of prostitution; and in support of his claim he brought two whores before the coroner's jury, one being the madam of the house. But other witnesses, less disreputable, swore that they had seen him making his way from the Lollards' Tower in the twilight of the December morning when the body was discovered. "He then made a confession in which he accused Dr. Horsey, the bishop's chancellor, and Spalding, the bell-ringer, as his accomplices."[16] The three were ordered by the jury to stand trial for murder at the next assizes or in the King's Bench.

It was at this point that FitzJames turned in desperation to the Archbishop of York who had the ear of the King, and it was the royal ear that FitzJames felt he must have. It would be futile, he said, to expect a London jury to do justice in the case, "so set were they on heretical depravity."[17] His plea and his appeal put the whole question at issue plainly. He was concerned for Horsey alone, who held orders in the Church. It would not do for Horsey to be tried by a secular court and before a jury. Even if he were convicted, he would not be hanged but could claim benefit of clergy and be handed over to Warham of Canterbury for custody. But what FitzJames sought was to avoid the indignity of having his chancellor tried for murder by a lay court. He concluded his plea to Wolsey with the plaintive words, as if Wolsey were Pope: "Help our infirmities, blessed father, and we shall be bound to you forever."[18]

Meanwhile, however, Parliament, which had been summoned before the Hunne episode, met at Westminster, and the ground swell of interest had become so marked that the King made no move to intervene.

Here was a chance to study the forces at work in the whole controversy over clerical immunity, involving as they did a definition of the
rights of the Crown. And it was to this problem that the Parliament inevitably addressed itself—the upper House, with the lords spiritual being slightly in a majority over the lords temporal, seeking to preserve
the rights of the clergy against civil molestation; and the Commons,
made up of knights of the shires, squires, and burgesses, boldly asserting
that these rights must be curtailed. Summonses had been sent to twenty-
one bishops, twenty-seven abbots and the Prior of Coventry. There were
thus forty-nine spiritual lords and forty-two laymen in the upper House,
the laymen comprising three dukes, one marquis, ten earls and twenty-
eight barons.

Agitation for revoking the special privileges accorded the clergy in
criminal cases had long plagued the Church in England, and Wolsey
knew it. The issue had come to be a perennial source of bitterness. It
flared up threateningly now and then, but as an old complaint and a
worn theme for orators of discontent; it was not to be taken too seriously. The problem simply needed to be dealt with administratively. It was
only one of the problems Wolsey faced, including that of gaining the
cardinal's hat and the powers of a papal legate. If he garnered those powers, he would be able to work matters out to the satisfaction of all. It
was important that an institution as powerful and permeating as the
Church, which owned one fifth of all the land in England, should regulate
questions pertaining to its rights and not have these questions the subject of irritating public discussion among civil authorities. The Church
could look after itself. The right of the Church to self-reform was the
heart and kernel of its sacred prerogatives; and the contention that religious practices and decisions should be regulated by laymen acting
through a lawmaking body must be resisted at all costs.

Yet the Parliament meeting in 1512, assembled essentially for the
purpose of granting the new King funds by which he could rush to the
rescue of the fiery Pope Julius from his enemies the French, had passed

a law which denied benefit of clergy "to all those clergy who murdered people in their own homes, in hallowed places or on the king's highway." A clergyman who did murder, being duly convicted in a civil court, could no longer escape the penalty imposed in civil law. He would be sentenced like any other criminal; not merely placed, if he successfully pleaded benefit of clergy, in a bishop's prison from which he might easily escape.[19]

In all cases the civil court had to convict the holy man of murder; what the act of 1512 did was simply to remove the benefits deriving from his sacerdotal character after his conviction. It seemed not unreasonable to Parliament to do this, seeing the daily increase in robberies, murders, and felonies. But although Parliament had passed this legislation, it had seen fit to qualify it. The act was to be in force only until Parliament met again and must be renewed then. Furthermore, it withdrew privileges only from those in lower orders and left all the old benefits in force among clergy who enjoyed the rank of priest, deacon, or subdeacon.

Now so shortly after the death of Richard Hunne, and with a man high in holy orders held for his murder, Parliament met again. Plainly an old controversy would this time take on new force and meaning, and both sides to it were arrayed for battle. The Lords, with a majority of bishops and abbots and priors over the dukes and marquises and barons, fired the opening shot of the battle before Parliament assembled. They did not use one of Henry's Twelve Apostles, nor yet a canon, but they did choose an abbot who could thunder. He was the Abbot of Winchcombe, and he rejoiced in the name of Richard Kidderminster. He was to preach at St. Paul's Cross on the Sunday, February 4, 1515, before Parliament opened and set the tone of the deliberations. Meanwhile Pope Leo X in the previous May had declared that, "according to the law of God as well as the law of man," laymen had no jurisdiction over churchmen. The good Abbot of Winchcombe followed the same high line, but he came down to earth enough to apply it to the troubled situation in England. "He denied the distinction drawn by that act [of 1512] between holy and lesser orders: all orders, he said, were holy orders, and any clerk in any order was immune from punishment by lay tribunals for criminal offenses. His doctrine was that it was for the church and not for parliament or the crown to determine the limits of criminal and coercive jurisdiction."[20]

The Abbot's sermon may have lacked some qualities, but it did not lack clarity. It stated the case for the Church, but it overlooked the deep basis of popular complaint: there were no corresponding privileges accorded laymen. A priest could murder, but a layman could not think for himself. A man in orders might commit crimes of violence against his fellows and not incur the punishment prescribed by the law; but a man outside of orders could not even read what he pleased or think the way he chose without incurring the censure of the Church, and, if this censure was strict enough, without paying for his thoughts with his life.

The question of clerical privilege was indissolubly tied up with the corresponding question of lay privilege. All other matters left aside, the rankling fact remained to give overtones of bitterness to the whole controversy that Richard Hunne, a man in charity with his neighbors and respected as a freeman of the city of London, had been brought to heel for heresy, and, after he had met death while in the custody of the Church, his body had been ceremoniously burned for heresy. And full many other bodies had been burned before they were dead, and full many others might be burned any day.

There had been no need of a warrant to arrest Hunne for heresy. An act of 1401 "had authorised any diocesan synod, which meant the bishop and (or) his officials, to condemn heretics without appeal, and had made it part of the routine duty of sheriffs to carry out the sentence without recourse to chancery or the King's council for any special warrant."[21] Nor was there any clear or statutory definition of heresy. What was heresy rested on local judgment, and the threat of heresy and its penalties was always present to disturb the citizen. It might be used as a pretense to cover the anger of Church officials on some other cause, as so many believed it to be in the case of Hunne; for it was still a bruit far and wide that he had been lodged in the bishop's prison on trumped up charges of heresy merely because he had seen fit to charge the officials of the bishop with acting in behalf of a foreign power.

In the face of the fact that the civil rights of laymen could be invaded at any time by officials of the Church, the claim of the Abbot of Winchcombe that the clergy had privileges which could be invaded at no time had a hollow sound and made music only to the ears of those who had put him up to preach. The course of their action in the convening Parliament was easy to see anyway. On February 10 the Lords considered the statute of 1512 and, by letting it drop after a single reading, made it be known that they would not renew it. Even so the Commons were not daunted. They spiritedly passed a bill to renew the act which the Lords above had dropped.

The two Houses being at loggerheads over the issue of extended clerical privilege, it came about that the scene of the controversy shifted to the presence of the King. For the rights of the Crown as well as the rights of Parliament were at stake. Besides, the idea of a public debate in the royal presence pleased and flattered Henry. He was not averse, as Fisher puts it, to presiding over a tournament of learning. It would be well to have the whole matter, raised by the act of 1512 and given fresh significance by the case of Richard Hunne, aired and propounded by advocates of both sides of the issue. Hence the King acted with favor on a proposal made by Sir Robert Sheffield, who had been Speaker of the Parliament of 1512 in which the act against clerical privilege had passed, and ordered the learned men of the land to appear before him and his councilors in the great hall at the Abbey of the Blackfriars.

Being busy with the King's affairs, Wolsey could not give the full weight of his attention to the controversy set off by the death of Hunne. He was a diplomatist as well as a churchman, and hardly had Parliament assembled than he faced a crisis in the Council that might upset the delicate balance of Europe. Louis XII of France died and was succeeded by his nephew, who took the throne as Francis I. Francis was a youth of twenty-one and of unknown qualities, although it was generally believed that he was reckless and might play havoc.

The death of Louis was a personal blow to Wolsey, for in the months following Henry's invasion of France the Most Christian King had become an ally. And to seal the matter, Mary, the sister of Henry and one of the most beautiful women of her day, had become the wife of Louis and the Queen of France. The match had been a turn of fortune little to be expected, a great diplomatic feat. And if only Louis had died with issue planted and quickening in the body of the Queen, England and France might have been forever joined in blood and even united later in kingship. Instead, the marriage had killed off the doddering Louis, old and worn-out at fifty-three, and now the hopes so patiently fashioned were set at nought.

To compound the complications, Mary, soon after the death of Louis, had married Charles Brandon, who had gone to the French war as Viscount Lisle and had been made Duke of Suffolk by Henry after the war was over. Henry had sent him back to Paris to offer Francis I formal congratulations at the beginning of his reign. While there Suffolk had married Henry's sister, secretly, without the royal consent.

Nor was this neglect of the royal consent the only bad feature of the marriage. It removed from the list of those eligible to form other profitable alliances two persons of immense value. Mary might, as long as she remained single, serve as a queen in the hole to win England some other worthy ally. Charles Brandon, Duke of Suffolk, had been hopefully groomed by Henry for a marriage with Margaret, regent of the Netherlands. There was widespread disgust among wiseacres around the court that so beautiful a princess as Mary "should be wasted on a mere love match when she might have purchased a substantial political alliance; and the council was full of men who clamored for Suffolk's ruin."[22]

The King himself was furious. Charles Brandon, according to Godwin, had been "rather a companion than a servant to the young Prince of whose household he was." He was a commoner made noble by Henry and a close personal friend. There was no assurance that Henry would ever forgive Suffolk's presumption or Mary's offense.

Wolsey placed himself boldly on the side of Suffolk; became his only advocate and friend at court. Here was a chance to pit his mind and might against the arrayed hauteur of the nobility of England. It is not singular that he chose to defend the romantic right of Charles Brandon, Duke of Suffolk, who held the highest rank in the hierarchy of the nobility but was the son of a commoner. For my lord of York, so close to the King that the King had written the Pope that it was impossible to do anything without him, was the son of a commoner, too. And if he won the King's approval of the outrageous marriage, he would give a further intimate and convincing sign of his hold on his master's favor.

Also Wolsey had been closely connected with the arrangements for the marriage of Louis and Mary, and it was natural that she as well as Suffolk would turn to him in their extremity. After the triumphant invasion of France in 1513, Henry had planned with both Ferdinand and Maximilian to invade France again the next year. But both had treacherously and secretly formed an alliance with France. Henry had learned of the deceit, and Catherine, in piety and devotion as well as in fact still the daughter of Ferdinand, had borne some of the brunt of Henry's rage. The King had reproached her with her father's abandoned faith, and some attributed the premature death of Catherine's fourth son to the brutality Henry displayed toward her at this period.

Henry had decided to make a firmer peace with France than the peace made by the sovereigns he had counted on as allies against France. When in January of 1514 Louis's queen died, Henry had proposed that Mary, a gay and graceful girl of seventeen, be pledged to the French King. But it had not been reasonable to base an alliance upon a matter as insubstantial as the life of Louis. "Being of an amorous disposition, which his advanced age had not entirely cooled," says Hume, "he was seduced into such a course of gaiety and pleasure, as proved very unsuitable to his declining state of health."[23] Reports from France told how Louis "loved to observe the good old French custom of dining at 8 of the clock in the morning; and going to bed at 6 in the evening; but now it suited his young Queen that he should dine at noon, and not go to bed till midnight."[24] The physicians had warned that this change in his mode of life would cause his death. Whether because of the change in his way of living or the strenuous effort to repeat his youth, Louis had inconsiderately lived less than three months. And his death had left Mary, the beauty of the house of Tudor, with her rich belongings, stranded in France; and it had left Henry, pride of the house of Tudor, with all his ambitions and schemes, stranded in England.

Wolsey had been the father and confessor of Mary in the affair of the marriage and in the confusing events that followed its dissolution by death. Hardly was the wedding over when Mary found her English servants dismissed. This dismissal she attributed to the Duke of Norfolk, who had been sent along to look after her household. Mary wrote: "Would God my Lord of York had come with me in the room of my Lord of Norfolk; for then I am sure I would have been more at my heart's ease than I am now."[25] It had been made plain also in a letter from Suffolk that Norfolk had dismissed Mary's servants because they were of Wolsey's choosing.

In the bitter aftermath of the marriage, Wolsey had continued to act as Mary's father and confessor. Immediately following the death of Louis, Wolsey had written her stern advice. "And if any motions of marriage or other fortune be made unto you, in no wise give hearing to them," he had said. But the counsel of the prelate could not prevail with an impulsive girl freed by death from a marriage she detested and at the same time romantically inclined to the manly Suffolk. Nothing would deter her—not even a proposal from the new King of France. At first flip and flirtatious, Francis I had suggested that he might free himself from other commitments and marry her. But Mary had merely written to her brother Henry to tell him of "the extreme pain and annoyance I was in by reason of such suit as the French king made unto me not according to mine honour." She feared he would "take courage to renew his suits unto me." And she said to her brother again that, having obeyed him in marrying the old King, "now I trust you will suffer me to marry as me liketh for to do."

She had not waited for an answer. She had gone ahead in the manner of a headstrong woman and married Suffolk. And one of the weighty problems before the Council in the spring of 1515, when Richard Kidderminster was thundering against the plea of laymen that criminous clerks be tried and sentenced in secular courts, was the acceptance or dissolution of the marriage Mary had made.

Wolsey's position as a go-between in a royal family quarrel called for judicious juggling at every turn. He must keep the lines of communication free and open, but there must be no doubt, even when he winked, about the chief object of his loyalty. This was ever the King. In reply to the early letters of entreaty which Mary and Suffolk sent him, he could only counsel patience and report to them how matters stood with the royal will. He wrote to Suffolk to say that the King had called him apart after sittings of the Council and had bade him "use all effort to obtain from Francis Mary's gold plate and jewels; until this was accomplished, Suffolk and the Queen would not obtain license to return." In his letter to Suffolk he continues: "I assure you the hope that the King hath to obtain the said plate and jewels is the thing that most stayeth his grace constantly to assent that ye should marry his sister; the lack whereof, I fear me, might make him cold and remiss and cause some alteration, whereof *all men here,* except his grace and myself, would be right glad."[26]

The negotiations dragged on, and tempers grew warm, and Suffolk bumbled and failed lamentably to get from the French what Henry sought. Meanwhile, no reply or assurance was given by the King of England to the repeated requests of the lovers that their marriage be approved. Suffolk's letters to Wolsey, along with those of Mary, are full of lamentations and bewilderment that the suit of the great matter within their hearts is brushed aside disdainfully by the King. One finds no trace in Henry's acts and no hint in his words to indicate any disposition to believe that the passion of a man and a woman and the desire for marriage should be reckoned with in affairs of state. Thus did bluff King Hal behave in the spring of 1515. Love was one thing and government was another. If there was a conflict between the two, love could wait.

It was up to Wolsey, when he received the intelligence of the secret marriage, to explain as best he could the King's mind to Suffolk. The King, he said, had taken the news "grievously and displeasantly." He is careful to remind Suffolk of his origins and of his dependence on the King for his station, bewailing that "ye hath failed to him which hath brought you up of low degree to be of this great honor." The sign of the importance of this point in the mind of my lord of York may be seen from the fact that the words "low degree" were inserted in the place of "nothing"—the only editing Wolsey did in the letter.[27]

Having wagged his head and clucked his tongue in the first part of the letter, Wolsey gets down to business: if there is anything that will soothe the outraged sentiments of the King, it will be an obligation to assume an annual payment to the royal household. He closes with the warning to Suffolk that "ye put yourself in the greatest danger that ever man was in."

Henry's policy, if it was policy rather than stubborn inaction, seems to have been to keep the couple dangling and enlist their uncertainty for whatever it was worth in the procurement of money and jewels. Mary finally received permission to return home the week after Easter. Even then the way was hard and the reception uncertain. From Calais Mary wrote to Henry. Her letter is preserved in the form it was carefully revised by Wolsey. "I am now comen out of the realm of France," she writes, "and have put myself within your jurisdiction, in this your good town of Calais, where I intend to remain till such time as I shall have answer from you of your good and loving mind herein; which I would not have done but upon the faithful trust I have in your said promise." She then promises to give him "all such plate and gold as I shall have of my said late husband's. Over and besides this I shall, rather than fail, give you as much yearly part of my dower to as great a sum as shall stand with your will and pleasure."[28]

Possibly the letter had some effect. Mary and Suffolk were openly married at the palace at Greenwich in the presence of the King and Queen on May 13, 1515. But Henry took her plate and jewels and obliged her to repay the expenses of her former marriage with Louis in yearly installments of one thousand pounds for twenty-four years, and to give up her dowry, if ever recovered, to the full amount. The terms were firmly made and rigidly enforced.

For Suffolk, it was a triumph discolored by lasting debt. But he still had his neck and his bride, and he could easily have lost them both if it had not been for the good offices of Wolsey, who had managed to circumvent the Council. It was a pretty good indication that in negotiations Wolsey could do anything he chose. Both as a servant and a friend he had been tested and shown his worth.

CHAPTER
V

In the odd ways of history, it was Francis I and not Henry VIII who created the circumstances that made Thomas Wolsey Cardinal.

Neither Henry nor Wolsey properly anticipated the turn events would take in 1515. They knew only that Francis was an untrustworthy ally and that he might cause mischief. He spent much time dawdling in his mother's salon, little time at the council table, and talked volubly about what he would do—so volubly, in fact, that Henry and Wolsey thought he was not likely to do anything. Henry was still redolent with confidence after his own triumphs in France, and he refused steadfastly to believe that Francis would make a move that might incur Tudor displeasure. Even after the Venetian ambassador told Henry that Francis had left Lyons and was on his way to Italy, Henry replied: "The French king will not go into Italy this year. I believe he is afraid of me, and that will prevent him from crossing the Alps."[1]

Nothing, least of all the fear of Henry, prevented Francis from crossing the Alps. Not only were preparations, both diplomatic and military, conducted with such secrecy that the English, under a renewed alliance with France, learned of them always indirectly and always late, but the passage of the Alps itself was carried out with such heroic stealth and fortitude that neither the Italians and their Swiss defenders nor the English could believe it had happened.

Francis started from Lyons for Grenoble in July, 1515. The regular passes in Italy were firmly guarded by the Swiss. The French must employ one of these passes or else plan to abandon their artillery. In this perplexity Francis accepted the counsel of one of his aides and decided that his army and artillery would cross the unguarded and unsuspected Cottian Alps leading to the plains of Saluzzo. It was a masterful suggestion; but there was no road, and the enterprise would be attended by certain losses of men and equipment and by the gravest hazards at all times. Albeit, the French made the passage. They fenced dangerous slopes and dragged their guns with incredible toil to the top of the mountains.

The descent was even worse. As Brewer puts it: "Men in armour fell headlong into the abyss; horses plunged and struggled in vain with their unmanageable burthens, lost their footing, and rolled thundering over the precipice with guns, carriages and drivers. But the French troops, with wonderful spirits and alacrity . . . were not to be baffled. They dropped their artillery by cables from steep to steep; down one range of mountains and up another, until five days had been spent in this perilous enterprise, and they found themselves safe in the plains of Saluzzo."[2] Meanwhile the men-at-arms had followed various passages as best they could, and the Swiss, who had never imagined that such a passage was possible, were caught entirely by surprise and were so dismayed by this display of French bravery and tenacity that, though they fought with their usual vicious skill at the battle of Marignano, the French, with Francis the dawdler performing marvelous feats of individual bravery, won the day.

Europe was topsy-turvy again and the hated French were again in command of Italy. With this situation before him, Leo acted on the request that Wolsey had so long kept before him, a request he had resisted on moral grounds and against royal pressure. Events had come to his aid, but Wolsey left nothing to the course of events. He warned Leo pointedly, saying that he wanted a cardinal's hat mainly "to make the king fast to the pope."[3] Henry, he explained, wanted the hat more for Wolsey than Wolsey wanted it for himself. He warned Leo that if Henry forsook him Leo would "be in greater danger on this day two year than ever was Pope Julius." And as Francis descended into Italy, Wolsey had reminded Leo that he as Archbishop and friend of the King, "no earthly man helping thereto," had prevailed upon Henry to consent to the league with the papacy "on the red hat being sent."[4]

Leo showed signs now that he would yield. Indeed he swung full circle, and word came early in September that he would insist on the promotion of the Archbishop in spite of all the cardinals, hastily summoned from their vacations for a consistory to deal with the threat to Rome. At last, on September 10, "Leo X notified Wolsey that the creation had taken place; and in ten days a royal courier arrived in London with the important document."[5]

There had not been a cardinal resident in the realm of England since the death of Morton fifteen years before. Meanwhile the color of the court had enhanced, and opportunities for display were increased a hundredfold. The splendor of the court and the nobility was to less fortunate mortals one of the entertainments of the time. Government, with all its exactions, was still a pageant, and a fully bedecked cardinal and his train would embellish the pageant and give the people a little more for their tax money in the way of public show.

The arrival of the hat, then, was not to be treated casually. Here was an opportunity for drama, and from the days when he superintended the interment of Archbishop Deane, Wolsey had never missed seeing the force of drama. Well ahead of the invasion of France, he had sent to the Deputy Collector of the port of Calais and had asked him to procure "some French black for his own wearing," that he might be dressed in a garb appropriate to the position of the King's Almoner. Now he sent at once to Rome "for a pattern of the exact texture and shade of red of the cloth worn by the Cardinals in the Eternal City."[6] He was not one to overlook a detail.

There was another reason why the arrival of the hat must be treated with the fullest dignity. The hat formally signified the promotion of this Ipswich fellow in rank above all the nobility of the realm. It was the position and not the man who filled it that carried the honor. Wolsey did not create the system or arrange the order of precedence. He simply benefited by it. He saw that the same man who six years before had been a mere chaplain to the King was now, by virtue of the authoritative position he occupied, only slightly less than King. Society stood on ceremony and by custom was compelled to acknowledge rank. By the good offices of the Church, the lad from Ipswich had bested the whole nobility.

It was something to celebrate. The ceremony of Wolsey's transcendence over the nobility would be turned on the arrival of the Cardinal's hat. He received word that the hat, together with a valuable ring bearing the affection of the reluctant Pope, was on its way in the care of Boniface Collis, secretary to Sylvester de Giglis. But it was the hat that mattered. The hat mattered more than the man who would walk under it. The Cardinal's hat was distinct.[7] Other ecclesiastics wore a hat of the same shape, but the Cardinal's hat was scarlet, and it was distinguished by the series of fringed tassels that adorned it. It was a kind of crown, having inherent and continuing virtue in itself, and it was not without significance that a proper ceremony for its reception would be known as an enthronement.

Apparently the protonotary of the papal court who carried the precious symbol did not fully perceive its worth. He arrived at Dover, according to some reports, carrying the hat under his cloak and made ready to push on to London like an ordinary courier. But Wolsey intercepted his casual passage, "clothed the ruffian in rich array and sent him back to Dover again." When the hat reached the gates of the city, "the mayor and aldermen of London on horseback and the city gilds on foot were turned out to do reverence as it was borne through the city on Thursday 15 November; and there it reposed on the high altar until the following Sunday."[8] A chronicle of the day tells us that tapers were set about it, "so that the greatest duke in the land must curtsie thereto; yea, and to his empty seat, he being away."

On the Sunday morning after the hat had been ensconced on the high altar of Westminster Abbey and treated with proper deference by the world and the Church alike, a procession formed at Wolsey's palace, York Place. Mounted on horseback were knights, barons, bishops, earls, dukes, and archbishops. In due order all proceeded "from his place betwixt eight and nine of the clock to the Abbey; and at the door aforesaid his grace with all the noblemen descended from their horses and went to the high altar; where in the south side was ordained a goodly traverse for My Lord Cardinal. And when his grace was come to it immediately began the mass of the Holy Ghost, sung by the Archbishop of Canterbury."[9]

Two other archbishops from distant sees had been summoned to attend the ceremonies—the Archbishop of Armagh and the Archbishop of Dublin. The high and the mighty were all there, arrayed in the magnificent trappings and habiliments of their stations or offices, all witnesses now to the ceremonious recognition of Wolsey as Cardinal of Rome bearing the title of St. Cecilia Beyond the Tiber. It was an occasion such "as I have not see the like," says Cavendish, "unless it hath bin at the coronation of a mighty prince." The hour of glory had struck in the clashing cymbals of Church and State. London should be astonied and reminded by this display of sanction and power that the Church was here to stay and not to be trifled with through legislative meddling.

Yet there was one somber figure in all the splendor, and he rose now to sound a minor and dissonant, if not actually discordant, note, in the thundering paean of acceptance. And if my lord Cardinal sought to awe London and remind its citizens of the magnificence of the Church, the man who preached the sermon in the Abbey that day reminded the assembled lords spiritual and temporal that there was more to the Church than cardinals and that the Church arrayed in all its glory might to its grief overlook the simple requirements of Christian virtue.

The man who preached was John Colet, Dean of St. Paul's. He was the son of a London merchant, and he had been sent early to Oxford, being there at the time Wolsey was completing his own work. He had left Oxford, probably in 1494, for several years of travel in Europe. In Italy he had spent some time in the study of the Scriptures, always with a view to an analysis of their meaning and of ways by which that meaning could be made plain to plain men as well as to the learned. He had been in Italy during the pontificate of Alexander VI, when dissoluteness and scandal blackened the system of the papacy and showed that the man mattered as much as the office. He had returned to England sobered in outlook and with a strong ethical message. He had gone straight to Oxford and there delivered a course of lectures on St. Paul's Epistles. Later he had been advanced through the favor of the seventh Henry to be Dean of St. Paul's.

There the common people heard him gladly. "Instead of assuming the purple garments which were customary, he still wore his plain black robe . . . For years he abstained from suppers, and there were no nightly revels in his house. His table was neatly spread but neither costly nor excessive . . . Somehow or other he contrived so to exert his influence as to send his guests away better than they came."[10]

This is the man who, high in the ranks of the Church and exemplary in habits and conduct, stood forth before my lord Cardinal to preach the Gospel. He chose as his theme the doctrine of Christian humility, and in expounding this doctrine he chose to stress the spiritual side of the cardinalate. He acknowledged the honor that had come to Wolsey, but he went on to say—directly to my lord Cardinal: "Remember that our Savior in his own person said to his disciples that he came not to be ministered unto but to minister; and he had said also that he that is greatest among you shall be your servant. And whosoever shall exalt himself shall be abased; and he that humble himself shall be exalted." The exhortation rolled forth across the heads of the nobility and clergy in sonorous and cadent Latin: *Et qui se exaltat humiliabitur, et qui se humiliat exaltabitur*. Then as if the Scripture were not enough, Colet closed with these words: "My Lord Cardinal, be glad, and enforce yourself always to do and execute righteousness to rich and poor, and mercy with truth."[11]

It was straight talk, simply made, carrying the authority of a good life. In pointed terms it suggested to the Cardinal that there was more to his jurisdiction than the administration of the temporal affairs of the Church; and to those present it served notice that, whatever the just criticism of the Church for excessive privileges, there were still among the clergy men of moral fiber and stern will who dared assert on the enthronement of a cardinal the revolutionary precepts of the Carpenter of Galilee.

It was noted that as William Warham, Archbishop of Canterbury and still Primate of All England, passed down the nave of Westminster Abbey after the ceremonies were over, no cross of gold to herald his rank was borne before him. What went on inside Wolsey during Colet's sermon he never made a matter of record. But as he passed down the nave, two great crosses of gold were borne before him by comely priests, one cross signifying that he was Archbishop and the other that he was now Cardinal. These crosses would precede him hereafter wherever he went. None was ever borne again before Warham in the presence of Wolsey.

Wolsey's hour had come. Crowned with the red hat, he was the leading Church dignitary of the kingdom, and even though the Pope had not seen fit to make him legate *a latere*, he had by his rank lordship over the nobility. After the ceremony he was conducted back to York Place by eighteen temporal lords. And the procession of state was led by the Dukes of Norfolk and Suffolk. Not bad for the son of an innkeeper of Ipswich.

It had been a part of the cunning of Wolsey's program for the arrival of the hat that the event would distract public attention from the debate over the rights of the clergy which still raged, indeed with greater vehemence than ever, in the fall of 1515. A massive display of the Church's power manifest in England and now vested in the person of a common son of the kingdom might also be hoped to overawe the aroused laity. The hat arrived and the enthronement took place just as Parliament convened from an adjourned session in the spring and just as Convocation, the term given to a separate meeting of the ruling body of the clergy, assembled also. The question before both bodies—the question on everyone's mind—was that raised by Richard Hunne's death: the rights of secular courts to have jurisdiction over men in orders.

It was a question too deep and vital to be shunted, and, from the standpoint of public interest, the vast ado over the hat and the enthronement proved actually to be only a sideshow to the main events. The Commons met and promptly passed again the bill limiting the benefits extended to criminous clerks, but the Lords cavalierly took no action on it. The Commons presented another and more pointed bill making it a matter of record that "clergymen declined to bury their parishioners unless they were rewarded by the most precious jewel, suit of clothes, or other possession of the deceased person; and it prayed that every incumbent should be compelled to bury the dead or administer the sacrament to the sick upon penalty of £40."[12] Again there was no action in the Lords. Nor was there any when the Commons impatiently passed the benefit of clergy bill a second time and sent it to the upper House.

The Houses were obviously deadlocked over the issue. Frequent adjournments were necessary among the Lords in order that the bishops and abbots might attend sessions of their own order separately in Convocation. Moreover, the scene of action had now been transferred significantly to the presence of the King again. The matter was to be laid before the throne again as it had been in the spring. But this time the issues would be more sharply drawn, and the meetings before the King would be more than splendid tournaments of learning. The young Henry, greatly instructed by the debates and sensitive as Tudors always were to the currents of popular feeling, showed that he was beginning to know his own mind and see his own future.

In the spring the Abbot of Winchcombe had appeared before Henry at Blackfriars to state the case for the clergy. The interests of the State had been represented by Dr. Henry Standish, warden of the Grayfriars in London. He was a favorite preacher at the court of Henry, and in these circumstances and with the King's protection he felt free to speak his mind and to offer the case against a strict and unreasoning interpretation of the Church's position. The Abbot of Winchcombe urged the sanctity of a papal decree which forbade calling criminous clerks before a secular tribunal, but Standish pointed out that the decree had never been accepted in England.

The joust between Standish and the Abbot had been so unequal that some of the members of the Commons had sought to have the Abbot offer a public recantation for his sermon. At this point, however, Parliament had been adjourned until the fall. During the interim Dr. Standish had continued to advance his views in a series of public lectures, all of them distasteful to the lords spiritual and all inclined to give aid and encouragement to the members of the Commons who sought to bring clerks within the jurisdiction of the regular courts. Thus when Convocation met again at the time of the arrival of the hat, the lords spiritual haled Standish before them and began meticulously to inquire into his views. What he had said in the presence of Henry was protected, but what he had said publicly might be made the basis of procedure against him. He had said in effect that "a papal decree could not stand against the continuous usage of a country."

Serious and searching questions were propounded to Standish at the convocational inquiry. Can a secular court convent clergy before it? Are minor orders holy or not? Can a temporal ruler restrain a bishop? These were questions which, if answered to the displeasure of the lords spiritual, might lead Standish into something resembling the fate of Hunne. But he answered them in favor of the State by refusing to plead his answers at all and by appealing to the King for protection. By this very act and by the acceptance of responsibility by the King under his coronation oath, the direction of events could be clearly seen. For Henry now summoned Standish to Blackfriars again "to plead before his majesty in the presence of the judges, the king's counsel, the temporal and spiritual lords, and some members of the lower house."[13]

Here again Dr. Standish acquitted himself to the full satisfaction of those who agreed with him anyway. His answers to the charges brought against him in Convocation exalted the rights of the Crown and Parliament. So enthusiastic were the judges present that they eventually declared the clergy present at the Convocation which had cited Standish before them to be guilty of praemunire. It was an opinion expressed to the King and not a judgment rendered by the benches in session, but it served notice of the temper of the temporal authorities, this charge that the Convocation had acted under the influence if not the bidding of a foreign power.

It was a strange and unscheduled reversal of events. The clergy had placed Standish before their tribunal in Convocation to answer for his views. He had refused to state his views for their inspection but had in turn appealed to the King who called Convocation to stand before him. And, supported by the strong arm of his judiciary, the King had heard the Standish case in its fullness, and the judiciary had subsequently declared the clergy guilty of what was tantamount to treason. The declaration had a chastening effect on the actions of the lords spiritual if it did not change their views. They had better seek an audience with the King.

Flanked by the lords temporal and led by my lord Cardinal, the lords spiritual appeared in the presence of the King at Baynard's Castle. There was a sprinkling of commoners there, too. Here was the first official appearance of my lord Cardinal after his elevation. And his first official act as Cardinal was to kneel before Henry in the presence of the assembly and offer the explanations and apologies of the clergy. In his dual role as friend and adviser of the King and as representative of Rome by virtue of the cardinalate, he could do the job as no one else could. He explained humbly that the clergy had not intended to do anything which might reflect on the prerogatives of the Crown. Far from it. At the same time he declared that the conventing of "clerks before temporal judges seemed to all the clergy contrary to the laws of God and to the liberties of the church, which they were bound by their oaths to maintain."[14] Then my lord Cardinal followed this repetition of the stated beliefs of the lords spiritual with the astonishing suggestion that Henry—to avoid the censures of the Church—let the whole question be referred to the Pope and his counsel in Rome.

Henry shook his royal head. "It seems to us," he said in reply, "that Dr. Standish and others of his spiritual counsel have answered you on all points." There was an outcry from Fox and Warham, but Henry closed the proceedings with prophetic vigor and firmness. "Kings of England have never had any superior but God alone. By the Providence of God, we are King of England . . . and I would have you take notice that we are resolved to maintain the rights of our crown and temporal jurisdiction in as ample a manner as any of our progenitors."[15]

Clearly Dr. Standish would not have his case remitted to the dubious mercies of Convocation. And the decision on matters of clerical and temporal authority would not be referred to Rome. Kings of England had no superior but God alone.

My lord Cardinal made a poor spokesman for the clergy that dreary November day in the drafty reaches of Baynard's Castle. He stated the clerical case clearly and well, beating a kind of refrain to what had been said before. To no avail. Henry addressed him like a child: "It seems to us that Dr. Standish and his spiritual advisers have answered you . . ."

With all his red robes and gold crosses and tasseled hat, he had failed, for he spoke as a Roman and not as a subject of the King. He encountered that duality which was to prove his doom. His position as Cardinal exalted him above the nobility, but when he displayed himself as a churchman he ran head-on into Henry's imperious will. Whether his plea that the question before the nation be referred to Rome came from his own initiative, or whether he was prompted by Convocation to advance it, we do not know. In either case, the plea was incredibly misguided and tactless, and it fell upon ears that were already listening to the sounds of the future.

The humiliation of the Cardinal, a commoner beneath his vestments, had in it many lessons. The role Wolsey played best was not the role of a debater. There is no record that he accomplished anything by means of public speech. He bore the talent but not the will of an orator. His voice had the ring of authority, and his sentences had the rhythmic breathing of eloquence; there was in his style a melody that comes from the love of words as music. But in pleading publicly he was out of character. The matter before the kingdom was too important now to be left to a forum. It would be well to deal privately with the King in this matter—to dispense with forensics.

Although my lord Cardinal failed in his address to the King at Baynard's Castle, he persuaded the King soon after the meeting to dissolve Parliament. The session came to an end on December 22, in time for the holidays, and with no action taken on the bill for limiting benefit of clergy. The act of 1512 was not renewed. Both Houses had been in session six weeks and had accomplished little. The chief item they were called to consider had been referred to the King. If the court was to be the scene of action and the King the source of authority, why keep Parliament around? If the Church was not to guide England's legislative program, why should the Commons? Let Henry, now so assertive of his rights, take control; let the government be centered firmly in him. And let Wolsey be his aide.

Three days after the dissolution of Parliament, William Warham, who as Archbishop of Canterbury held the Great Seal of England by long tradition, surrendered this emblem of authority to the King, who conveyed it at once to Wolsey. Warham had advocated the frequent meeting of Parliament. The change meant, among other things, that from now on the King would reign. And on Christmas Eve, 1515, Thomas Cardinal Wolsey became his prime minister, succeeding Warham as Lord Chancellor of England.

CHAPTER VI

There was something meet and fitting about Thomas Wolsey of Ipswich seated on a sack stuffed with wool. The woolsack was the throne, so to say, of the Lord Chancellor of England, and now the Chancellor was the son of a man of sheep in a land of sheep which owed its wealth and daily living to sheep, with sheep outnumbering humans three to one. Dealing in cloth occupied men's thoughts daily. Many figures of speech came directly from it. One spun a yarn, carried a thread of discourse, unraveled a mystery. A thing was fine-drawn or homespun. Unmarried women were spinsters. The government concerned itself gravely with every detail of the trade in cloth; the import of foreign-made hats and caps was forbidden; the prices of articles produced at home were fixed; the export of more expensive kinds of cloth was not to be allowed unless the cloth was fully finished.[1]

The woolsack was a healthy and solid reminder of an ancient fact. It survived ceremonially out of a time when woolsacks had been occupied in Parliament by high dignitaries of the Crown. Now the highest councilor of the Crown still occupied it. With all his glory, and though a Cardinal, the Chancellor of the realm accepted as his symbol a sack stuffed with wool and covered with rich and appropriately red cloth. It gave him, this emblematic sack, some kinship with the common people and some basis for concern with their daily problems. The connection might be tenuous, as it is in any ritual, but it was there just the same. The King existed above and beyond the commonalty; the Lord Chancellor was of it: an audience for the complaints and aspirations and pleas of the lowborn and the bedraggled. The Chancellor stood between the throne and the people, and the woolsack signified that he was of the people.

Wolsey took his woolsack seriously. It is true that he had little or nothing to do with the actual symbol of his office, for the woolsack was the seat of the Chancellor in Parliament, not outside of it, and Parliament sat but once during the fourteen years he occupied the office. But if Parliament was not to meet for its endless snarling and backbiting, there must still be hearings for grievances, and there must be some machinery by which the law could be put into force.

The Parliament of 1515 had passed an act to restrain the rise in the cost of labor. The first draft of this act was in the handwriting of Wolsey. Humbler artisans and traders were beginning to demand some voice in the organization of trade and in the conditions under which they worked.

This situation was highly irregular and would of course, if not restrained, lead to riot and civil commotion. In London there were strikes among the shearmen, the saddlers, the shoemakers, and the tailors. There was implicit in all this unrest the threat of government by mobs.

Persons of low degree might by severity of punishment be kept in their places; but there was to be noted also a restlessness and eagerness for betterment to be found among the slightly more privileged classes. These classes showed a tendency to dress and eat beyond their appointed station. The whole question of dress needed to be reviewed; and the Parliament of 1515 passed an Act of Apparel, fathered and furthered by Wolsey, which restricted the burgesses to their appropriate homespun and defined in more precise terms than did the earlier laws what men of the several classes would be permitted to wear.

The Act of Apparel went further. It set up regulations in another area where the tendencies of persons of low order to ape their betters had begun to show themselves—the area of food. Those who stood in the ranks of gentlemen were permitted to have three dishes at a meal; lords of Parliament, Lord Mayors, and Knights of the Garter could have six. In the proclamation issued by my lord Cardinal to make this law known, it was pointed out that, since a cardinal ranked above the nobility and even above princes of the realm, he himself would be entitled to nine dishes; and it was further made a matter of record in the same proclamation that the number of dishes allowed would be "determined by the rank of the most distinguished guest."[2]

It was plain from this Act and from the proclamation accompanying it, that Wolsey as Lord Chancellor intended to inspect and oversee every detail of the common life of the people of England. Regulation had become an established Tudor principle; it was a part of the heritage of the seventh Henry, who had set the land in order after chaos, that government in its essence meant making people behave according to the wisdom of those charged with the responsibility of governance. The English were quarrelsome and unruly, wild and restless, addicted to factions and fighting, assertive and independent. They needed a strong ruler, who would hold them firmly in check and exact obedience. Their society was based fully upon the principle of rank and authority by rank. The King stood above all ranks—that much Henry VII had made painfully clear. And as he had brought law and order to the profit of one and all, so his successor must continue that government by law and edict lest the land fall again into weakness and decay. And the King being busy with many matters and with the ceremonies of the throne, it would devolve of necessity upon his chief aide to see that orders from the throne for the good of all be severely enforced.

The office provided my lord Cardinal with all the appurtenances of authority. Theoretically he had scant connection with the law courts, save that he was entitled to name the justices of the peace in the shires and could in this wise keep a finger on their conduct. But the personality of Thomas Wolsey overflowed any polite bounds of tradition. The King must be made the center and focus of the whole life of the people, and the royal prerogative must be exalted above royal factions, "and even above the law, if necessary."

There was, of course, an elaborate web of courts spread across the kingdom. These courts were under the sitting of men of rank, as a rule, for it was part of the English tradition that the privileged and the titled should condescend to administer justice. For example, it was provided that there should be a court held in every market. It was composed of merchants, but it was deemed best that it be presided over by the mayor. This was the Court of Piepowder or *Piepoudre*—"dusty feet"—so called because "the chapmen or merchants came straight in without ceremony to have their differences adjusted on the day on which they happened, and to have offenders punished without delay."[3] Any notice of a fair always carried with it the announcement of a Piepowder Court, with the assurance of swift adjudication.

It was a court of dusty feet, with its rough-and-ready decisions of equity arrived at promptly and without haggling over the technicalities of the law, that Thomas Wolsey of Ipswich now instituted on a large and lordly scale. The place of its sitting was the Star Chamber in the palace at Westminster, where a court had commenced to sit in the early and turbulent days of the seventh Henry, designed to bring recalcitrant lords to heel and obedience. It kept its purpose and tradition; all Wolsey did was to extend the purpose and amplify its jurisdiction in line with his high intent of disciplining the people.

The Star Chamber had long been a place where the King's Council sat in judgment. It withdrew there to resolve itself into a judicial body. But its meeting had been only occasional before the time of the seventh Henry. Parliament "authorized the king to establish a court of judges chosen from the Privy Council to relieve the Council of its judicial duties. The particular function of these judges was to seek out offenders among the barons, to summon those to trial and to punish those whom they found guilty . . . The activities of the new tribunal were gradually extended. In 1495 it was given jurisdiction over 'heinous riots', perjury, and appeals in criminal cases. Still later such unrelated subjects as usury, enclosures, and quarrels between merchants trading beyond the sea came within its competence."[4]

Over this Court of the Star Chamber Wolsey, by virtue of his office as Chancellor, now came to preside; and it was this court which, by virtue of his personal capacity and his great disposition for official meddling, he converted into an instrument that brought him in touch with every quarter of life of England. He stretched out his judicial hand and drew into his venue every conceivable kind of dispute, settling it without the embarrassment of recourse to the awkward procedures of law. In the awkward procedures of law my lord Cardinal had never had a whit of training, neither in canon nor civil law. His training had been in the sturdy principles of philosophy, and to these, as he pontifically sat, he had recourse. His court was a court of equity and a court of conscience, and his dual role as the King's chief minister and as a high official of the Church vested his decisions with no small measure of sanctity among his countrymen, accustomed as they were to bow before princes and to accept the edicts of those who stood above them. In effect, the court over which Wolsey presided was the court in which the King was judge, and if the King cavalierly delegated his authority and prerogative to the richly robed Cardinal, it did not lessen the honor of appearing before a tribunal in which the sovereign with his inherited wisdom was the supreme symbol of justice among his subjects.

Precedent aplenty could be found in the attic of the past for the use Wolsey made of the Star Chamber as a court of conscience. In his own thinking he drew a sharp line between law and conscience, a line so sharp that the two would appear to be antithetical. He had no odd moments during his frantic administration to formulate his principles, but he acted them out every day, and after his fall he wrote his sentiments to Mr. Justice Shelley. In giving advice to one of the King's advisers, he says: "... for when ye tell him this is the law, it were well done ye should tell him also that although *this* be the law, yet *this* is conscience; for law without conscience is not meet to be given to a king by his counsel to be ministered by him nor by respect to conscience before the rigour of the law ... The king ought for his royal dignity and prerogative to mitigate the rigour of the law, where conscience hath the more force; and therefore in his princely place he has constituted a chancellor to order for him the same ..."[5]

With such a philosophy and with abounding confidence in his own conscience, Wolsey provided a court that was welcome to the hearts of the people. Actions were prompt, delays at first rare. Counsel fees were moderate and, in the case of the poor, dispensed with entirely. A poor man who because of his poverty found it difficult to engage in litigation could come before the Star Chamber at will. Here was a court open to one and all, superior in rank and dignity to all the old-fashioned and creaky courts of common law. And it was a court where, as Pollard puts

it, justice "was rarely denied merely because it might happen to be illegal."

In no other phase of Wolsey's life does one find such a daily, sustained, unrelenting interest as he showed in sitting as a judge of other
people's problems. He taught that decision should at all times be vested
in a person and not in a procedure or a rule of conduct. His court, and
those that broke off from it with delegated authority when the docket
grew too heavy even for Wolsey to handle, established plainly in men's
minds that conscience was king, that supreme authority lay within a
man, or at least within a man of rank.

In this respect the Chancellor never forsook the woolsack. With all
his pomp and glory and his insatiable appetite for position and the emblems of authority, he remained seated on his origin: a local wiseacre
with a talkative mind, full of opinions of right and wrong, sharing them
fully with his fellows in a moment of respite while waiting for the pack
train to come.

It was an odd twist in the character of a Cardinal. Wolsey had risen
above princes in a society where princes ruled by right of inheritance.
Yet somehow he could not rise above his station; there was too much an-
cestry in him. He would remain until the day of his fall from the King's
grace, until the day of his reversion to nothingness when he would walk
about in empty robes, a bright and meddlesome mind ceaselessly at work
where people congregated to air their grievances; a man who knew it all
and could solve any problem other than his own; a bumpkin with a vo-
cabulary and a fluency far beyond his station, always seated on a sack
stuffed with wool and able to prate the solution to any difficulty, however
complex, or offer the government free advice on any policy, however
great the crisis.

Whatever Wolsey did, he could not do simply. He was incapable
of simplicity or directness. If he remained inwardly a peasant, the fact
was disguised better from himself than from any of his associates. He

overlaid his personality with vestments, with layers of assurance, and he could never get enough to be sure that his nakedness was covered or that the body of the man would not be detected by others or by himself. The elaborate manners of the day aided and abetted him in this and sanctioned his behavior as well. He could not perform a commonplace act such as going from one place to another; if he went anywhere his going became a procession; he was flanked and escorted by priests bearing maces and poleaxes and the ubiquitous hat.

Thus, however much he might descend into the market place to hear men's disputes from all over the King's realm, he made his attendance upon the Court of the Star Chamber an act of regal condescension. Wolsey was usually ready to set forth from his house about eight in the morning. Cavendish, his gentleman-usher, describes Wolsey's procedure of getting to the scene of equity, taking pains to tell us first how my lord Cardinal was attired:

"His upper garment was of either fine scarlet, or taffety, but most commonly of fine crimson satin engrained; his pillion of fine scarlet, with a neck set in the inner side with black velvet, and a tippet of sables about his neck; holding in his hand an orange whereof the meat or substance within was taken out, and filled up again with part of a sponge, wherein was vinegar and other confections against the pestilent airs; the which he most commonly held to his nose when he came among any press, or else that he was pestered with any suitors."

Thus fortified against the smells of the common people, my lord of York, late of Ipswich, moved forward to his chamber of presence. "And before him was borne first the broad seal of England, and his Cardinal's hat by a lord or some gentleman of worship, right solemnly. And as soon as he was entered into his chamber of presence, where there was daily attending upon him, as well noble men of this realm, and other worthy gentlemen, as gentlemen of his own family, his two great crosses were there attending to be borne before him; then cried the gentlemen ushers, going before him bare-headed, and said, 'On before my lordes and masters, on before, and make way for my lord cardinal.' "

In this lofty manner did my lord Cardinal fare forth from his dwelling to hear disputes and dispense justice and equity in behalf of the common man. He rode, as became the Christian humility which Dean Colet had urged upon him at the time of his enthronement, a mule, a lowly commoner among beasts of burden and one with long and honored traditions of simplicity. Yet the mule which bore the Cardinal's festooned carcass was disguised out of all recognition in crimson velvet, and, lest there be some discomfort to the posterior of the Cardinal, the saddle was of like material. The stirrups for my lord Cardinal's feet were of gold, no less.

"Then marched he forward," Cavendish reports proudly, "with a train of noble men and gentlemen, having each his footmen, fewer in number about him, bearing each of them a gilt poleaxe in his hands; and thus passed he forth until he came to Westminster Hall door. And there he alighted, and went after this manner up into the chancery." Usually he would stay a while "at the bar, made for him, beneath the chancery, on the right hand, and there commune sometimes with the judges, and sometimes with other persons; and that done, he would repair into the chancery, sitting there until eleven of the clock, hearing suits and determining of other matters." [6]

This stately procession to the Court of the Star Chamber was Wolsey's routine every Monday, Tuesday, Thursday, and Saturday.[7] The court itself was as public as his going to it. It met in the outer Star Chamber as distinct from the inner chamber where the King's Council sat to discuss matters of policy. Any who wished could come in off the street and watch the great Cardinal perform his acrobatic feats of judgment and throw his conscience around. In the early days of his administration, Henry himself occasionally attended. Wolsey was always sure of an audience. Indeed the attendance at the Court of the Star Chamber was so great that the King complained at times of the scanty attendance at his own regal court. It was quite a show, and Wolsey was so much the center of it that the people gained the impression that the Cardinal himself had created this majestic court. He had a talent for doing a thing as if it had never been done before, even though the practice was hoary with custom and precedent.

That Wolsey's efforts in the Star Chamber met with popular favor and filled a current need is the common testimony of his day. Giustiniani, the Venetian ambassador who was no admirer of Wolsey in the area of diplomacy, spoke eloquently of his role as a judge, reporting that he had the "reputation of being extremely just; he favors the people exceedingly, especially the poor, hearing their wants and seeking to dispatch them instantly."[8] He also noted the Lord Chancellor's policy of making lawyers plead gratis for all paupers. Edward Fox, Bishop of Hereford, said that he had never known so painstaking a judge, adding that he was "always on the side of the poor man when opposed by the rich or unscrupulous." And when he decided against the claims of a poor man, he gave assistance to the poor man in money or employment. Sir Thomas More declared that no Chancellor of England ever acted with greater impartiality, deeper penetration of judgment, or a more enlarged knowledge of law or equity.[9]

Dealing as he did with all manner of problems and quarrels, Wolsey naturally made enemies. Sir Robert Sheffield, who had been Speaker of the Commons in the Parliament of 1512, was sent to the Tower "on a charge of having said that, if the temporal lords had only been of one mind in the last parliament, they might have made Wolsey's body as red as his cardinal's hat." And rumors were spread among vulgar folk that Wolsey "had threatened to burn all common beggars in a barn, that Henry had refused without Warham's consent, and that Warham would consent only if Wolsey were put in the barn and burned as well."[10]

Wolsey's ignorance of the law made him in popular fancy a superior judge, enabling him to arrive at common notions of justice without circumlocution, by rule of thumb and rule of tongue. He had a natural penetration which enabled him to discern false from true evidence and to select the most practical mode of judging a case. Wolsey made his own opinion the law and enforced it by the King's writ. And it was not only in thus setting up his conscience as the arbiter of moral action, but also in arrogating to his court all manner of disputes, that he revealed the temper and bent of his mind and the nature of his procedure. His court had validity for the simple reason that the common law was in decay; yet there is no indication whatever that he sought to reform common law courts. His method was rather to show that he personally, sitting in London, could handle cases better than all the legal population of the realm.

The nature of his court, being as it was a part of the King's household, freed it from the common afflictions of perjury and bribery. Local trials throughout the country often ended in travesty because judges and juries were corrupt and could be bribed or bullied by the more powerful party to a suit. Trial by jury was often "a contest in perjury, which itself was hardly an offense at common law."[11] Bribery occupied a public part in community life. "The whole complicated system of local administration had long been kept in working order by a generous system of bribes—bribes given largely and openly, registered in the public accounts and granted indifferently to any official, great or small, who might be induced by a timely gift to 'show his friendship' . . . At the appearance of the King's harbinger the first thought was to collect a sum which might induce their formidable guest to limit the number of troops billeted on the town, or even to march them away altogether. Counted among the usual incidents of government, and reckoned in the ordinary expenditure of the municipality, the payment of such bribes was to all concerned merely the customary mode of defraying some of the expenses of administration."[12]

With bribery an official practice sanctioned by long tradition, court procedure might be made a farce if the two litigants were of unequal station and one could outbid the other for the favor of the court. Added to bribery and perjury was the delay encountered in the common law courts, making litigation hopeless among men of few farthings, who needed its benefits most. Changes which had been irresistibly in process since the end of serfdom some two hundred years before had brought into prominence and into the courts a whole new range of crimes and mischiefs that were not even contemplated in the common law. For the law of the land was the law of land lords; it was not common at all. An accused person was tried by "a jury of his peers." The presumptions and procedures of the law were ill suited to adjudicating the claims of those in the lower orders of society, especially if these claims were urged against the upper classes for which the law was originally intended. It was the right of serfs and villeins to appeal above manorial courts directly to the King that had begun to change the law. The serfs, in a word, had begun to achieve legal status in manorial courts of equity presided over by men of common sense, not in courts of common law.

Wolsey took this fact and this tradition of manorial justice and with his usual vigor extended it to a series of courts around the King, all under the close supervision of himself. What he did was to assist and amplify a trend, not to start one. The plain man could not get what he called justice in his dealings with the high and the mighty as long as he sought it in a series of common-law courts designed for the nobles and the gentry. He could and did get it in the Star Chamber, in the King's court of equity. Wolsey's sense of history was sufficient to see the role he might play in speeding up "the halting process by which the law for the gentry slowly broadened down into the law for all."[13]

Common plea might be moved from the common bench into the Star Chamber "on the ground that the plaintiff was too poor or weak and the defendant was too rich or strong for justice to be had at the common law." The Duke of Suffolk even appealed to Wolsey on behalf of a servant on the ground that the poor man "is not able to sue against Lord Dacre or abide the long process of the law."[14]

Once haled before Wolsey in the Star Chamber, a lord or gentleman found himself on the defensive, and Wolsey showed delight in finding some fault with his case. As a noble ex officio he acted against the nobles by birth and weighted what he called justice heavily on the side of the poor. He went further and began actually to make effective the laws which had been set upon the statute books sternly in the reign of the seventh Henry and then in many cases blithely ignored. The plowing under of special privileges among those who exalted themselves above the King was the central means by which the Tudors sought to cultivate a new land for England.

In a like manner Wolsey dealt with survival of livery and maintenance, those twin practices that had cohabited to make the Wars of the Roses possible. Even in the middle classes the number of idle servants impressed foreign visitors unfavorably. "Owing their existence to the ostentation of their masters, they aped the vices and extravagances of those above them, gambling, swearing and living riotously. Even in their dress, they aimed at show rather than use, wearing long coats that were nothing but a nuisance when they had to ride and doublets with such pleatings and puffings of sleeves that if they had to defend their masters or themselves they must throw off their garments before they could draw a bow."[15]

Men of distinction were judged by the number of servants they kept. And as long as great households were required by the King and custom to be attended by hangers-on who served mainly as emblems of rank, it was but a step to the employment of the coterie of servants for private wars or for the intimidation of lesser men. This was the threat of livery and maintenance. The Duke of Buckingham was one of those who maintained a lavish establishment. In November of 1520, Buckingham instructed his agent to tell the Cardinal that it would be necessary to take three or four hundred armed men with him on a trip to Wales.[16]

To humble such men and exalt the King became one of the Chancellor's games. The last Parliament of Henry VII had complained that little was being done by way of punishment for giving liveries and keeping great bands of retainers. Wolsey of Ipswich would set that matter right. Here in the Court of the Star Chamber he had both the law and conscience at his disposal. Edward Hall, one of the chroniclers of the times, writes: "He punished also lords, knights and men of all sorts for riots, bearing and maintenance in their countries, that the poor men lived quietly."[17] None could escape the wrath of the man of the red hat as it was expressed in behalf of both the King and the common man, directed as it was toward the maintenance of peace in the realm and the maintenance of the King's supremacy over all his nobles. This was the only kind of maintenance that Wolsey would allow. In 1516 when he began his vigorous execution of the law, the Earl of Northumberland was examined before the King in the Star Chamber and sent to the prison known as the Fleet. The Marquis of Dorset, the Earl of Surrey, son and heir of the Duke of Norfolk, hero of Flodden, together with many others of rank, were called before the Star Chamber for keeping retainers.

Wolsey reveled in the role of one who to poverty born had wealth as his habit. That he overplayed his part, as if to ridicule his rivals, there is abundant evidence. During the fourteen lavish years he served the King as aide and Chancellor, he did not unbend in public or take off his mask of arrogance or show a trace of modesty in the presence of any but the King. He was without the confidence that makes condescension possible. He was unwilling to release his hold for one moment upon the amulet of office and the properties of his role. He had both the imagination and the histrionic bent to outdo the nobles at their own game of ostentation and needless pageantry. Yet he lacked the security of self that would enable him for a season to relax his insistence that he was as good as any man save the King and the Pope. He had the pride of a man who is afraid other men will forget his worth.

Giustiniani, the talkative Venetian ambassador long resident in London, sized up Wolsey's determination to be recognized at every turn and in every deal and remarked: "Were it a question of neglecting His Majesty or His Right Reverend Lordship, the least injurious course would be to pass over the former." Even Fox, who had discovered Wolsey's shining talent and done much to deliver it to the throne, once said of a matter: "We shall have to deal with the Cardinal, who is not Cardinal, but King; and no one in the realm dares attempt aught in opposition to his interests."[18]

The painful consciousness of station and position allied to grandeur never deserted my lord Cardinal. During the visit of the Emperor of the Holy Roman Empire to England in 1520, "Wolsey alone sat down to dinner with the royal party, while peers like the Dukes of Suffolk and Buckingham performed menial duties for the Cardinal, as well as for Emperor, King and Queen."[19] When he performed Mass at a great meeting of the Kings of England and France at a place that came to be known as the Field of Cloth of Gold, "bishops invested him with his robes and put sandals on his feet, and 'some of the chief noblemen in England' brought him water to wash his hands." A year later, at his meeting with the Emperor at Bruges, "he treated the Emperor as an equal. He did not dismount from his mule but merely doffed his cap, and embraced as a brother the temporal head of Christendom."[20]

Wolsey set a new mode for elaborateness of dress among the clergy, arraying himself in dainty silken garments and requiring that bishops and lesser clergy in attendance upon him do likewise if they were to enjoy the richness of his favor. The appropriateness of the attire required of his minions or the implications of that attire in a time of the increasing unpopularity of the clergy did not seem for one moment to trouble his conscious mind. He was the great imitator, a conformist who excelled, who broke the mold only to make it larger and fill it richer again. No one would say that he did not behave and dress as well as the best.

CHAPTER VII The hostility toward the nobility which the Cardinal showed at every twist of the screw of his power was far from abstract: it was also personal, directed openly against the most powerful. And the resentment he aroused among the nobles in turn showed itself not merely in gossip but in insult. Those who looked upon him as a wanton upstart, a Wat Tyler in silks and velvets, did not quibble to say so. In particular, the loftiest lord of the land looked with icy scorn upon this worm the King had made his Chancellor. The Duke of Buckingham, Edward Stafford, could afford to show his spleen even to the King's favorite councilor. Ensconced as Lord High Constable of England, he boasted royal blood among his forebears, being descended through his father from Thomas Woodstock, sixth son of Edward III. A man of prudent wealth, lending employment to a wide host of retainers, he appeared to be hedged with security. His father had rebelled against Richard III and had lost his head for his pains. The young son Edward, now the haughty duke, had merely had his own head shaved by his protectors and had been spirited from place to place in disguise and in the hands of a kindly farm woman until distracted Richard lost interest in the chase.

When Henry Tudor came to the throne as Henry VII, Edward Stafford was restored to the dukedom and ranked high in the esteem of the King. The young Duke had been brought up "almost as a member of the royal family." He became a companion of the young Henry, and he was in the procession which had set out to meet Catherine of Aragon when she came to wed Arthur. At that time he had been the only duke in the realm. He was a smooth and captivating courtier—"handsome, charming, extravagant, a little rattle-brained, a little stupid, with an exalted idea of the privileges and security of his position, but a great gentleman, none the less."[1] And later, when Henry and Catherine were married, he was close to them as a friend. Particularly did Catherine cherish him, for he had been one who had sent her fruit and venison in the days of her adversity after Arthur's death.

Being born to the purple, Edward Stafford, third Duke of Buckingham, showed by many acts that he could not tolerate with equanimity
the person of Thomas Wolsey of Ipswich, merely elevated to the red.
Wolsey stood in his arrogance as a threat to the whole social structure
with which Buckingham was unconsciously familiar and in which he was
comfortably fixed. It was a world that, with all its turmoil, had stood
obediently still for the nobles during the past hundreds of years. It had
its postulates and standards and shibboleths. One of these was that a
man was born to what he was destined to become; he had no control over
it, any more than he had over his birth. There were certain things a nobleman did; and there were certain things a plain man did not do. Into this
fixed preserve now came the Cardinal, a man who, stripped of his vestments and the position to which these entitled him, was a plain Ipswich
fellow, whose father was a butcher and grazier and innkeeper and whose
grandfather, if the truth were known, was probably a serf.

Collision was inevitable. The Duke took no pains to conceal his disdain, and there began a rivalry in snobbery. In due course the two descended to childish rebuffs which, had they taken place among school-
boys, would have been punished by Latin verses or the cane. Chroniclers
report that on one occasion the Duke of Buckingham was holding a
ewer of water for the King to wash his hands in. The story goes that into
this basin Wolsey had the effrontery to dip his hands after the King had
finished. The Duke, outraged at the presumption, "shed the water in his
shoos."[2] Wolsey, in turn outraged, said in a burst of eloquence to the
Duke that he would "sit upon his skirts." The next day Buckingham
came to court without the skirts of his doublet, thinking thus to put a
jest upon the Cardinal. When the King asked him why he appeared at
court in a short coat without skirts, he replied that he was resolved to
disappoint the malice of Wolsey.

Thus continued the prattle and peevish scuffling between England's
haughtiest nobleman and proudest churchman. It is likely that the stories of the "fumes and displeasures" between the Duke and the Cardinal

were exaggerated in retrospect, seeing what happened later and how people often reach back and put a bold interpretation on incidents that had not even been noted in the first place. But whether this antagonism had any relation to the event, nonetheless it came to pass that reports of rash and treasonable utterances by the Duke reached the sensitive ears of Henry, son of another Henry whose main concern had been the security of the throne. These reports now in the light of history appear signs of indiscretion rather than treason, but the King displayed toward them a close and attentive interest and, after examining those who bore the reports, gave grave credence to what he had heard. It was the King and not the Cardinal who closeted himself with the bearers of the news, and it was the King who sent letters to the Duke at his pleasant estate in the west of England, summoning him to come instantly to London.

The Duke's diary shows that he had no suspicion of the royal displeasure as he started toward London. He had for the past few months been puttering in his garden, and otherwise engaged in wholly domestic matters. He kept a faithful and careful account as he moved toward London of his expenditures along the way. It was like any other journey until he approached Windsor. Then he began to note that armed men were watching his movements. "They seemed to hover in the distance: at every winding of the road, as if to cut off all hope of escape, real or imaginary, they drew more closely upon him."[3] Still the Duke did not suspect, but toward Windsor some twenty miles from London, some of the men he had seen even went so far as to take up lodgings in the same hostelries as the Duke. This seemed an impertinence to the lofty nobleman and aroused his anger. The morning after he arrived at Windsor, as he was sitting down to breakfast, he noted a royal messenger loitering about and demanded what he did there. "The messenger replied that his office lay there, by the King's commandment." Then for the first time the Duke discovered that he was a prisoner. "The news fell on him with the abruptness of the headsman's axe. He turned ashy pale, the untasted morsel dropped from his lips, death was before him, escape was impossible."[4]

The indictment the Duke faced was based on the testimony of discontented servants. One, Robert Gilbert, "deposed that he had heard the duke say that my lord cardinal was an idolater, 'taking counsel of the spirit how he might continue to have the king's favor,' and that he had ministered to the king's vices . . . The duke had complained in Gilbert's hearing that he had done as good service as any man and was not rewarded, and that the king gave offices and fees to boys rather than to noblemen . . ."[5]

On May 13, 1521, Buckingham was brought into Westminster Hall to be tried. The Duke of Norfolk was the chief judge. As Buckingham was led into the Hall the axe of the Tower was carried before him. The indictment was read, and he vehemently pronounced it untrue and forged to bring him to death. He was allowed no counsel save his own eloquence, which weighed little against the testimony of the witnesses. Their depositions over, "the duke was allowed to retire to a house called Paradise, to consider his defense."[6] Later he was brought back to the bar, and the Duke of Norfolk, as chief judge, pronounced the sentence of death for treason: "To be drawn upon a hurdle to the place of execution, there to be hanged, cut down alive, your members to be cut off and cast into the fire, your bowels burnt before your eyes, your head smitten off, your body to be quartered and divided at the King's will, and God have mercy on your soul." Norfolk had demurred at reaching the verdict, and now his voice broke down and he wept as he pronounced the sentence upon an intimate friend and one of the great noblemen of his day.

When Norfolk had finished, Buckingham spoke: "My Lord of Norfolk, you have said unto me as a traitor, but I was never none; but my lords I nothing laigne for that you have done to me; the eternal God forgive you my death as I do; I shall never sue the king for life; however, he is a gracious prince, and more grace may come from him than I desire. I desire you, my lords, and all my fellows, to pray for me."[7] After he had spoken thus to his peers and judges, the axe of the Tower was turned significantly toward him to show the edge of death, and he was conducted from the Hall. As he passed through the city, there were great lamentations among the people that he should die, and in a comely manner the Duke with dignity asked that the common people pray for him. This made a great impression and added to the wonder of the populace that so upright a man should be sent to his death by his peers.

It was said that if he would but seek the royal mercy he might escape death, but Buckingham refused to pray to any but God and not to the King for mercy. He expressed no regret save for the manner in which he was to die, this being so far beneath the dignity of a duke that he marveled at it, and before his death, four days after his condemnation, the King relented and graciously consented that the Duke not have his bowels burnt before his eyes but that he be merely decapitated. So he was, on May 17, 1521, to the astonishment and sympathy of the people far and wide.

Catherine had entreated the King to spare the Duke, her oldest and closest friend in England. But Henry was in no mood to listen. The words laid to Buckingham that rankled him were that God would not suffer his issue to prosper. For now there appeared to be many signs that this was so. Not less than five children borne him by Catherine had died. Only one, a puny child born in 1516, five years before Buckingham was disposed of, now lived. And she was a girl, a girl named Mary, after Catherine's affection for the King's sister, the Queen Dowager of France. A girl. Henry of the House of Tudor and the hope of England—all that stood between stability and the chaos of a repetition of the Wars of the Roses —had no son. It would not do for any whisper in behalf of a rival to find its way to the ears of the people. Now was the time to assert, with all the eloquence of a swinging axe, that this Henry would brook no pretender.

The part that my lord Cardinal played in the proceedings against

Buckingham was far from conspicuous. It was certain that he did not intercede with the King, for it was the King's interest that was at stake and in the cultivation of this interest Wolsey always showed himself blameless and sedulous. But the lesson of the sequence of events was plain for all to read. Buckingham had been an enemy of the Cardinal, had resented him, had spoken against him, had taunted and insulted him. This same Duke was now dead, and though he had been Lord High Constable of England, he was dead all the same, his goods attainted, and the very office which he had held abolished as a token of the obliteration of his line and memory.

So fully and anxiously had the Cardinal allied himself with the King and so subtly were the two identified that an attack upon one was now an attack upon the other. Or so it did appear: barbs thrust at Wolsey would seem to be arrows intended for His Majesty. It was a warning to the nobles. Not merely in functions had he, my lord of York, taken on the position of King and left the King free for pleasures. More insidiously, he had made the King's interests identical with his own, so that when one was offended, the interests of the other might be offended too.

It was said that the Cardinal had bewitched his royal master, that he exercised over Henry some power of necromancy and held devilish fellowship with the spirits to maintain it. That he had some strange hold over the King to be explained only in terms of his communication with evil spirits was a view that persisted long and found wide currency. As late as 1532 there is record that the supposition so ran. In that year a dabbler in the black art said that Sir William Neville had asked him if it were not possible "to have a ring made that should bring a man favour with his Prince; seeing my lord Cardinal had such a ring, that whatsoever he asked of the King's Grace, that he had." In another and earlier case a man sought to summon up a spirit, but the spirit refused to speak because "he was bound unto my lord Cardinal."[8]

There had been nothing like it seen in all the realm, this man who ruled the ruler and seemed to make him do his bidding. Earlier kings had had great advisers and men who at the council table or by whispers in the King's closet had doubtless swayed them, but in the case of Wolsey and Henry it appeared that the two were but parts of the same person.

The explanation need not have been sought in the world of spirits. There were evident grounds for the King's confidence—and many of them must have been plain to rational observers. Thomas Wolsey had no thought as minister but to serve his King, to fashion the realm to the King's liking, to make the King supreme, to keep the nobles in an enclosure where they could not dispute his prestige or threaten his succession with their quarrels. That was all. There was no mystery about it, for Wolsey's purpose ran like a thread as conspicuous as his Cardinal's robes through all he said and did. His decisions in the Court of the Star Chamber, subtly and elaborately reasoned and supported by learned garrulity, weighted justice on the side of the Crown and against the ever-present threat of the ascendancy of great families and aggregates of wealth.

In matters of policy Wolsey sought to determine but one point: what was the royal will? If this could be found, and finding it was not difficult, then the policy of the Lord Chancellor was fixed. By habit under the seventh Henry and by appointment under the eighth Henry, the man who had received part of his training as chaplain to the Archbishop of Canterbury plied a course that aimed to show that the King of England could run his country like a monarch and not merely be suffered by the nobles to reign. Wolsey was born to make a king see what he was fit for and capable of.

Nothing could distract Wolsey from the labors that must attend the onerous execution of the King's business—not even the mysterious return of the dread disease known as the sweating sickness two years after he became Lord Chancellor. This dire epidemic had fallen upon the people first in the autumn of 1485, soon after the battle of Bosworth. Nor was its return a coincidence. It had come into the country with Henry

Tudor and his French mercenaries. Known among the French as the Picardy Sweat, it had long persisted on the Continent in mild and somnolent forms; but once loose in England, where there was no immunity to it, it had taken on a violent and virulent character. In its first visitation just before the coronation of Henry VII it had lasted only a month, but in that time it had boiled the blood of those afflicted and made the blood run cold among those who saw its effects. The sweating sickness fell upon victims with the suddenness of a beast of prey. One chronicler, Forrestier, a doctor of medicine and a native of Normandy who tarried for a while in London, said that many died while walking in the streets, without being confessed. Dr. Gaius, a physician of the day who recorded the devastation of the disease, wrote of the victims: "As it found them, so it took them; some in sleep, some in wake, some in mirth, some in care, some fasting and some full, some busy and some idle; and in one house, sometime three, sometime five; sometime all; of the which if the half in every town escaped, it was thought a great favor."[9]

So shattering were effects of the sweat that accounts of it doubtless took on some of the panic of the disease itself. It is hard to believe with Gaius that it "immediately killed some in opening their windows." But the exaggeration with which the disease is reported tells more than accurate statistics. There was a sly malevolence about the way in which it pointed the finger of God at the realm of the Henrys, for "it followed Englishmen as the shadow does the body" into other countries. In Calais and Antwerp "it generally singled out English residents and visitors, whilst the native population were unaffected."[10] It raged throughout the greater part of England, yet it stopped short of the Scottish border and it did not spread to Ireland. And to cap the mystery, it seemed always to pick out persons who were in the prime of health, and, unlike the bubonic plague, it attacked the favored classes and the well-to-do rather than the impoverished.

The masquerade of the evil was all the more complete because there were no carbuncles to mark the disease, no purple spots to taint the body. As Bacon puts it: "Only a malign vapor flew to the heart and seized the vital spirits; which stirred nature to strive to send it forth in an extreme sweat . . ."[11] The course of it lasted from a few hours to twenty-four. "The attack began acutely, with high fever, palpitation, rapid pulse, difficult breathing, and a sudden, copious general sweating; nausea was common, vomiting rare. In nearly all cases there was delirium followed by an uncontrollable desire for sleep. Gaius says the poison 'moves the mind with madness and oppresses it with heavy sleep.' "[12]

After the first visitation in 1485 the sweating sickness disappeared from England almost as rapidly as it had descended. Then it returned stealthily in 1506 after an absence of twenty-one years—an absence as inexplicable as its return. Again it made its grim appearance in April of 1516, more of a feint this time than an attack, when it appeared that it might pass over without its full choking effect. What violence it showed subsided with the approach of winter, this tendency to retreat from winter being one of the few reliable traits of behavior it showed. But that winter was severe. The weather itself seemed to bear malice to man. A drouth bleached the country, beginning in September and continuing through a winter of shattering cold. On January 12, 1517, a freeze came upon London so severe that the Thames was thick with ice; men and horses could cross it. Then as the spring of 1517 came to bring some hope back to life and the earth seemed habitable again, the sweat returned, this time with silent and creeping fury. "Houses and villages were deserted. Where the sickness once appeared, precaution was unavailing; and flight afforded the only chance of security." Nor could plans of flight always be carried out. Ammonius, the Latin secretary to the King, was dining one day with an acquaintance. "They had arranged to meet the next day and ride to Merton to escape the infection. The next morning, before his friend had time to get out of bed and dress himself, a messenger arrived to announce the death of Ammonius. He was carried off in eight hours."[13]

London as a city suffered the suspense born of horror. This time the sweat continued off and on through the spring and summer and into November. During the winter, when the drouth was broken at last, it abated, as its custom was, hiding from cold; but early in 1518 it resumed like a ghost men thought had been laid, and its apparition stalked the roads, and its vapors seeped through the walls of houses. "Not only business but amusements ceased in a great measure; crowds and places of public resort were carefully avoided; the noblemen broke up their establishments and every one in dread of the infection hastened, as best he could, to isolate himself from his neighbours . . . No lord, except during his necessary attendance at court, was suffered to keep servant or staff in his chamber . . . Fairs were put down; and at Oxford, so long as the court resided at Abingdon, orders were given by Sir Thomas More in the King's name that the inhabitants of infected houses should keep in, hang out wisps of straw, and carry white rods in the same way that the king had ordered the Londoners."[14]

In the midst of the consternation the King moved from place to place, alarmed at every rumor and report of a disease that did not deign to spare the elite. Who knew that it might spare a King? And to the King's concern was added that of Catherine, who was not only solicitous of the health of her young husband but now had the worry of the Princess Mary, a child of two and a half and the only issue of the royal pair. Yet even movement and dodging and hiding did not suffice, for the disease, as if to tease, invaded the transient palaces established by the King. The pages that slept in the very bedchamber of the King died of this insidious plague. Henry further stripped his establishment, ridding himself of all his servants save three trusted gentlemen.

With the King in flight and the court stripped of suitors and attendants, the government might well have been at a standstill save for one man, and that was my Lord Chancellor, the one official who remained steadfastly at his task during all the depredations of the disease. The King's business could not wait, and the duties he had taken unto himself could not be stayed or suspended or neglected. The Court of the Star Chamber could not meet, for presses of men were forbidden lest the contagion spread. But day after day Wolsey wielded the Great Seal of England, now like a club, now like a wand, and carried forward the business of the kingdom, administering personally the details of government. It was as though he had made the occasion of the disease but another occasion of his unflagging loyalty and devotion to the King.

For this he was abundantly rewarded in the esteem of his royal master, for Henry during this period of madness, which threatened the succession as no war had, put himself on the record of history. He said that "he was no less contented with the Cardinal's contentation than though he had been his own father." Here was a tribute from a young king to his middle-aged minister that might in future centuries explain more than could be guessed at that time of the unshakable hold that the Lord Chancellor had upon Henry. In 1517 Henry was twenty-six, and Wolsey was forty-six. A difference in age might make less difference later—and none at all when the King felt the full sinews of his power. Now it did. With steady application the older man stuck to business in the presence of danger and left the younger one free to move as he might in the fond hope that he could flee the affliction of the sweat.

To the lords Henry said "that there was no man living who pondered more the surety of his person and the common wealth of his realm." And as if this did not serve sufficient notice upon the lords to show the Cardinal what full confidence the King reposed in him, Henry addressed to Wolsey the following letter in his own hand:

"Mine own good Cardinal, I recommend me unto you with all my heart, and thank you for the great pain and labour that you do daily take in my business and matters, desiring you that when you have well established them to take some pastime and comfort, to the intent you may the longer endure to serve us; for always pain can not be endured. Surely you have so substancially ordered our matters, both on this side the sea and beyond, that in mine oppinion little or no thing can be added . . ."

He continues in this vein, touches with approval on certain specific items of business, and adds: "The Queen my wife hath desired me to make most hearty recommendations to you, as to him that she loveth very well, and both she and I would feign know when you will repair to us."[15]

The King knew well the value of his Chancellor, and he might well have been concerned for his health. With all his fidelity and bravado, Wolsey did not escape the sweat. The first severe attack came in June of 1517, and it was so harsh that his life was despaired of—to the undisguised delight of those who had been "compelled to pay their just debts to the Crown and submit to the impartial administration of the laws." In July of the same year he suffered from quinsy, and in August he had the sweating sickness again. This time many of his household died. Giustiniani reports that the affliction told heavily upon his appearance.

After the second attack the Cardinal felt that it would be necessary to find some surcease for a season, and he proposed a pilgrimage to Walsingham, hoping at the shrine of Our Lady for some aid of the spirit that might forfend other attacks. But even here he stuck to business, and in the course of his journey he went on to Norwich, "and settled a dispute between the citizens and the monks over a piece of ground in that city." The next year he suffered again from the sweat. Meanwhile the royal solicitude continued, not only in prose but in paste, for Henry was a great amateur medicine man and full of royal home remedies. One of these, designed for the sweating sickness, was called *Monus Christi,* made in part of coral and a half pound of some unidentified preventive, probably flour. But neither the sweat nor the King's remedies could kill the Cardinal.

All the while, Henry and his court and Queen and the Princess Mary moved restlessly about. Wolsey, when he was well enough to attend to business, and often when he was not, gave a certain stability and order to government, but not enough. London suffered when the court was not there, and its lawless elements and its discontented apprentices stirred with mischief as the court moved from Richmond to Reading, from Reading to Abingdon, to Woodstock, or Wallingford or Farnham.

Discontent in London had a focal point—one for which the King himself was held responsible—and it was natural that trouble would occur while he was away. For it was whispered, and later openly said, that Henry had been of aid to foreigners. In 1516 a statement had been posted on the door of St. Paul's "reflecting on the King and his council." It insinuated that strangers obtained money from the King "and bought wools to the undoing of Englishmen." The King had made foreign loans in order that merchants might do business in England, and his whole policy, like that of his father, had been to encourage foreign trade. He had lent money to Florentine merchants in particular. These and other foreign merchants in turn used the money lent by the King to buy goods and wools in England, often competing sharply with their better bargaining power against Englishmen.

The whigmaleeries and involvements of foreign trade were no less a mystery to the overworked apprentices and workers of London than they would be to future generations, and the gossip of the King's doings caused grumbling and growling. What Londoners saw in the atmosphere of gossip was a band of overprivileged and often oversexed foreigners who infested the city, had no fellowship with the citizens, and took every advantage of their position.

Even under pleasant and moderate circumstances the English did not like aliens. Froissart had written a hundred years earlier that the English felt that foreigners "were neither on a level with them nor worthy of their society." A visiting Italian, who in this period accompanied the Italian ambassador on his rounds, said: "They have an antipathy to foreigners and imagine that they never come into their island but to make themselves masters of it, and to usurp their goods."[16] The matter was complicated further by the fact that English kings tended to favor aliens, either for the encouragement of trade or alliances or through a broadened sense of the world by means of international marriages.

Not so the ordinary English of the streets. The Italian observer wrote: "The English are great lovers of themselves and of everything belonging to them; they think that there are no other men than themselves, and no other world but England, and whenever they see a handsome foreigner they say that 'he looks like an Englishman,' and that 'it is a great pity that he should not be an Englishman'; and when they partake of any delicacy with a foreigner they ask him whether such a thing is made in his country."[17]

All of these natural antipathies toward foreigners were now brought to a focus like the sun's rays caught in a magnifying glass. The sweat had demoralized the watch commonly kept over the city. Business was depressed, English artificers being out of work while foreigners continued to flaunt their wares and parade their privileges. Even when the sweat subsided, its return was always a threat, and the King had withdrawn his court and suspended most of the activities connected with it. Trouble crouched ready to spring.

In the Easter season of 1517 a preacher was found and briefed who would stand before the people, the sweat having abated for the moment, and plead the plight of the artificers. He would report that even in that very season of Lent there had been seen no less than six hundred strangers shooting at the popinjay with crossbows and enjoying other hilarities and pastimes of a frivolous nature while honest Londoners suffered from the invasion of competition. Perhaps through a sermon reciting the enormities of the time the mayor and aldermen might be aroused "to take part with the commonalty against the strangers."

The sermon had its calculated effect—not on the mayor and aldermen but on the populace, who were urged by the preacher to defend their country against hordes of aliens as birds might defend their nests. May

Day was at hand, and a rumor spread that on that day the Londoners would rise up and slay all who were aliens. The court had withdrawn to Richmond, but Wolsey took every precaution. He called the mayor and the corporation together. "We are informed," he said to them, "that your young and riotous people will rise up and distress the strangers. Hear ye of no such thing!" The mayor assured my lord Cardinal that all would be well. But to make doubly sure, the Cardinal called upon the old Duke of Norfolk and his son the Earl of Surrey. They brought thirteen hundred men "in harness into the city . . . 'Then proclamations were made that no women should come together to babble and talk and all men should keep their wives in their houses. All the streets that were notable stood full of harnessed men, which spake many opprobrious words to the citizens, which grieved them sore.'"

The precautions merely tightened the tensions. In one ward an alderman found a crowd of apprentices watching two playing at bucklers. He ordered them to disperse and they refused. He then made the tactical blunder of taking one of the apprentices by the arm. This was the incident upon which the event had been waiting. "Instantly the cry of *Clubs! Prentices!* was raised; and in a moment the streets were thronged with a motley crowd of watermen, serving-men, and apprentices, swaying hither and thither, bent on mischief . . ." The plan of attack, ill-organized but definite, followed the sermon and the threat. On the night of April 30, the rioters sacked the houses of the Flemish and French artificers. Then they swept on to the Italian quarter, but there the foreigners had fortified themselves with arms and artillery, and, facing real opposition, the apprentices withdrew and moved on to indiscriminate attacks upon stray foreigners less well defended.

The situation was now out of hand, being much greater in its dimensions than the mayor and aldermen had supposed it would be, and these officials were themselves overpowered and compelled to open the jails and release the prisoners. Now the Cardinal's second line of defense went into action, and Norfolk and his son seized the offending preacher, twelve of the ringleaders of the riot, and some seventy other persons that could be handily taken. The Earl of Surrey laid rough hands on all offenders, and he and his retainers showed in word and gesture their contempt for these lowborn rebels. Some were ordered hanged, drawn, and quartered, but the severity of the punishment had not the desired effect or the one which the upholders of law and order had anticipated. Not merely the apprentices but also the entire city of London was aroused.

Public sentiment was such that the whole matter was taken and laid before the King at Greenwich, where a body of aldermen attended him, they being arrayed in black, to ask his mercy on the offenders. He declined their petition and referred them to his Chancellor, "without whose counsel he would do nothing," as Stow, one of the chroniclers, observed.

Eleven days of suspense followed, and then, in spite of the momentary threat of the return of the sweat, there was staged in London a scene which beggars both description and understanding. The denouement would suggest that either Henry or Wolsey or both had resolved to use the occasion to show the power of the Cardinal. At any rate, the King, attended by the lords spiritual and temporal and by the Council, came to London and with great ceremony took up his position on a lofty dais in Westminster Hall to hear the matter reviewed. Not only were the lords and the chief citizens there. The King had also at hand three Queens—Catherine his own; Mary the Dowager Queen of France, now Duchess of Suffolk; and his rampant sister Margaret, Queen of Scotland. "The king commanded that all the prisoners be brought forth. Then came the poor younglings and the old false knaves, bound in ropes, all along one after another, in their shirts, and every one with a halter about his neck, to the number of 400 men and eleven women." It was noted that good Queen Catherine, "with her hair loosened in the traditional gesture of a suppliant, knelt before the King for the lives of the young men whose riot had spilled the blood of her Spanish countrymen." The other two Queens, long on their knees before the King, begged pardon for the rioters. Henry showed no signs of relenting.

Then the Cardinal besought His Majesty to grant them amnesty. Henry still refused, and the Cardinal turned to the wretches and announced the King's decision. Thereupon there arose great lamentations from the ranks of the prisoners, and those who scarce three weeks before had gone hither and yon about the city on errands of mischief, and fiercely and bravely, now fell upon their quaking knees and cried "Mercy! Mercy!" This appeared to be, as if by pre-arranged and carefully staged clemency, the signal for the Cardinal to fall in turn upon his knees and to entreat the King's compassion. The mercy was slow in coming, but it came at last and brought such gladness and rejoicing to those who were about to die that, as one witness put it, "it was a fine sight to see each man take the halter from his neck, and fling it in the air; and how they jumped for joy, making such signs of rejoicing as become people who had escaped from extreme peril."[18]

Even so, the Cardinal did not let the prisoners go without a stern and stately schoolmaster lecture on the importance of good conduct, enjoining them in his best manner to be obedient subjects, "and not to oppose the will of their Prince, who had resolved that all strangers should be well treated in his dominions."

It was well that the King and the Cardinal had made a stentorian uproar showing at once displeasure toward the culprits and a measured leniency to restore peace. For the whole occurrence dismayed the hearts of Londoners. The foreigners had gained the better part of the bargain, being in the last analysis championed by both the King and his favorite. Matters were not improved in the public mind, either, by the sight of festering parts of mutilated bodies around the city after the first vindictive executions. An eyewitness reports: "At the city gates one sees nothing but gibbets and the quarters of these wretches, so that it is horrible to pass near them." And there was talk where men gathered, talk that did not reach the ears of the King or the Cardinal but did reach the ears of history, talk against the way Surrey and his men had behaved toward the citizens of London.

Five months later the rebellion swelled again. This time the aldermen and the mayor were alert and it was quickly stayed, this rising against the aliens, with three of the ringleaders brought to heel. Outwardly the King and the nobility had triumphed over the citizen. But occurrences of this sort are not to be measured or reckoned in immediate effects. The resentment which had shown itself in the Richard Hunne case, a resentment against special privileges accorded representatives of a foreign power, now showed itself again. England did not propose to be tied up by cords of Church or finance to a foreign world across the waters. She was by God independent, sufficient unto herself, and she would be free of foreign entanglements. England was for Englishmen. The portmen of Ipswich, as shown by their annals, were no less resolute than the citizens of London. The time had come when England would be free. Those who could read the meaningful, angry glances and hear and interpret properly the murmurs in the streets and alehouses could see this as plainly as if they had been handwriting on the wall.

CHAPTER

VIII

As for my lord Cardinal, he was too busy to see or read anything but documents thrust under his nose in the urgent business of running the kingdom for Henry. Busyness was his answer to every problem created by an old world shedding its skin. The kingdom would get justice, and men rising in the world would enjoy the blessings of their improvement and adjust themselves to the new order if he personally attended to these matters. He appeared to have, over and beyond his childlike devotion to Henry, a pathological sense of personal responsibility and a belief as strong as forged iron that he could discharge that responsibility by doing the job of ten ministers rolled into one.

Which he was. If a job was important, he was the man to do it. He set about to change England from a kingdom ruled by lords and whims into an orderly state. In this respect he extended and intensified the work which Henry VII had commenced. But he gave it a sense of detail and permanence. The very fact that he was a minister and not a king indicated that change had come about. For a king, with his might and tyranny, to order this or that was one thing; for Wolsey under the King's approval to set up accounts, investigate prices, supervise the coinage, look to export licenses, regulate wages and prices, monitor the diet and dress of the people, devise graduated taxes—this was quite another. The lines of a state which would have continuity were beginning to form.

In his zest for regulation of his contemporaries my lord of York committed many excesses. But he did establish and demonstrate a principle: the conduct of large masses of people within a country could no longer be left to local custom and practice but must be determined by central authority. Whatever his intentions, Wolsey's administration as Lord Chancellor suggested, if it did not fully demonstrate, that a people can be managed by their government.

To the end that affairs might be comely and fitting within his country, he spared no detail, even in dealing with the King's own household. Things must be done in decency and in order. He was meticulous in handling accounts, and he convinced Henry that the King himself ought for his own good to keep a record of where the royal money went. As a result, Henry's Privy Purse Expenses carry a record of his gambling losses and of the lavish gifts he made, including a black satin nightgown given to a favorite.[1] The King should be no less accountable in his handling of public funds. He was no longer above observation by virtue of his position.

Records were essential to supervision, and the extension of supervision was at all times Wolsey's aim. The treasury of the King's household was known as the chamber, and to this treasury funds for the King's use were withdrawn from the national exchequer. In 1515 payments made by the chamber amounted to £74,006. In 1518 and 1519 they had dropped to £50,000 a year. There were still leaks, and Wolsey complained of "the way the king's money goes out in every corner." Many items to ministers ordered by the King merely carried the explanation, "the king's business." In 1522 Wolsey proposed an extensive reform of the whole system of handling the accounts of the chamber and a systematic audit of the chamber accounts every quarter. One set of books was to be submitted to the King, while the other was to be kept in the chamber for reference and for auditing—to be available for inspection at all times. Wolsey's idea, says Richardson, "was to introduce the same regularity in chamber audit as in other departments of finance."[2]

Nothing around the court seems to have escaped Wolsey's eye. In 1526, "for the better avoiding of corruption and all uncleanness out of the King's house, which doth engender danger of infection, and is very noisome and displeasant unto all the noblemen and all the others repairing unto the same," it was ordained that "the three master cooks of the kitchen shall have every one of them by way of reward yearly twenty marks, to the intent that they shall provide and sufficiently furnish the said kitchens of such scullions as shall not go naked or in garments of such vileness as they now do, and have been accustomed to do, nor lie in the nights or days in the kitchens or ground by the fireside; but that they may be found with honest and whole coarse garments, without such uncleanness as may be the annoyance of those by whom they shall pass."[3]

All who were entrusted with the receipt of revenue were brought under strict audit. In this reform Wolsey gave offense to many, and it might be said that those he did not outrage in his decisions as a judge he humiliated in his demands as the King's minister of finance. One who felt the lash of these demands was the Duke of Suffolk, he whom Wolsey had befriended and defended when he married without permission the King's sister while she was Dowager Queen of France and yet on French soil. Suffolk owed the King heavily—and not merely in the continued payment of the moneys Henry had demanded of him upon his return with Mary to England; he also held certain public funds. These he could not pay, and he had to retire from court and lead a frugal existence until he could accumulate enough to cover his debt. By way of thanks Suffolk became a lasting enemy of the Cardinal. But nothing concerned Wolsey in the flush of his administrative efficiency but the orderly conduct of the King's affairs. The kingdom alone mattered. Let incidents fall where they might; his purpose was to bind the nation to its King with hoops of regulation.

These hoops were not in themselves sufficient. But they were the means by which the government began to pull the discordant elements of the kingdom together. Wolsey's steady and relentless insistence upon regulation and responsibility, while it was often misguided, established gradually the consciousness of nationhood. That consciousness was still dim when he came to power. Men were primarily loyal to their class or their locality, not to their country. Their loyalty lay naturally to what was close at hand. It was not that they were disloyal to the King either as a person or as a symbol of the larger weal; there was simply nothing in the range of their experience to encompass the land of England as a whole, save at times of crisis. A king in silken robes in far-off London who was still a laughing matter among the men of the border; the intense local loyalty which in the days of Wolsey's childhood could regard his father as an "alien" because he came from a village ten miles away —these attitudes showed what men felt and how limited was their sight. The State was an abstraction just beginning to emerge in men's minds, and it certainly had not yet the power to evoke strong emotion. To the King some feasible loyalty had in theory already been shown, so that the enlargement of the concept of the King was the easy and natural way of developing the lines of what was to become the State.

The State was still a person, and how much of current thought was draped around the State as a person may be seen from the publication of Niccolò Machiavelli's political cookbook, *The Prince*. This book was finished in 1513, and there is no evidence that Wolsey ever read it—or any analytical book, for that matter. He was first and last and day and night an administrator. But there is much in *The Prince* that adumbrated the work of Wolsey as Lord Chancellor of England. The book and the Cardinal were both part of the same drive to make a great body of people behave according to the will of those who were set to preside over them. Men were virtuous or lacked virtue as they contributed to the power of their Prince, emblem of government. Men were therefore viewed as political beings rather than as human creatures with inherent rights. Equity and justice must prevail because these contributed to the wealth of the whole land. What Machiavelli wrote, Wolsey practiced. The aim and design of the ne'er-do-well of Florence and the pride of Ipswich were akin: to show how a whole country might be given cohesion and solidarity through an allegiance that transcended local obligations.

Wolsey the pragmatist, the man of deeds, was in a position to act out his ideas. His work lay in straight line with, and in continuity with, the startling attempts toward centralized government undertaken by Henry Tudor right after the battle of Bosworth. *Thomas Wolsey was in a sense the real Henry VIII, and the man who swaggers through history under that title was in effect Henry IX,* a king whose performance was made possible by the work of Wolsey, just as Wolsey's work had been prepared for and outlined by the seventh Henry. A valid judgment of Wolsey, or even a partial understanding of him, can be reached only through a due regard for the sequence of events and pageant of persons in his own day. In methods and intentions he stood in direct succession to Henry Tudor. Wolsey was the man who put the principles of control formulated and announced by Henry Tudor into telling effect, and a good deal of the support and confidence shown in him by the eighth Henry was due to the fact that Wolsey as Lord Chancellor carried forward ably and vigorously the work of the eighth Henry's father. By all the tokens of coronation and ceremony, the young Henry came to the throne on the death of his father. But in Thomas Wolsey, a man in the full vigor of maturity and twenty years older than Henry, the father-king lived on in the royal household until Henry, ever watchful and ever learning, saw that he could succeed the Cardinal-father.

Henry began his reign with an assembly of advisers called a Council, but it had no special form, and when Wolsey became Lord Chancellor it had no form at all. Affairs were delegated to an executive committee consisting of the Chancellor, of course, the Treasurer, and the Lord Privy Seal. The Treasurer was the Duke of Norfolk, who was content to look to the mending of his family fortunes and interfered very little with the business of the kingdom. The Lord Privy Seal was Ruthal, whose character was attested by his contemporaries in the statement that he sang treble to Wolsey's bass. Not until 1526, when it began to be clear that the days of the Cardinal might be numbered and the King might at last come of age, was a true Council formed. In that year Henry chose twenty councilors to attend his royal person. Of these, ten were to "give continual attendance in the causes of his said council, unto what place so ever his highness shall resort."[4] But even then the Council existed chiefly in proclamation form, its very existence still tenuous, and Wolsey managed to stave off the formation of a real Council for another few years. He was all the King needed.

Turn any corner in the maze of administration and there you would find the busy body of the Cardinal. All ministers incarnate, Wolsey subdivided himself for special tasks requiring special skills. His labors included even the admiralty. There he regulated the wages of seamen and investigated those paid to servitors on the King's ships. In 1526 a warrant was issued to Wolsey (and doubtless by Wolsey) authorizing him to supervise coinage. He was given full powers, and he acted on the advice not of members of the Council but of a committee of goldsmiths. The aim was to reduce the value of English money to the standard of foreign coins, since it was said that, "owing to the enhancement of value abroad, money was carried out of this realm by secret means."

Once he had his commission, he was not able to stop at ordering a new standard of twenty-two carats fine gold alloyed with two carats sterling silver (known as Crown gold). Rather he went on to imprint his Cardinal's hat under the King's arms on the coin known as a groat. This act gave great offense to those who were his enemies anyway, the groat being regarded as the King's special coin. He had transcended fitness, and while some signs of his arrogance might be considered transient, in this case he had stamped his excess permanently in metal. An archbishop's prerogative would allow his emblem to appear on a half-groat; but Wolsey had to do something better than custom allowed, and again and insidiously he now ranked himself co-equal with the King.

And why not? No problem, however complex, caused him more than executive hesitation. Before he had received the King's warrant and permission to reform the coinage, he had sent commissioners to the Low Countries "to require that all monies valued too highly should be reduced to a real rate."[5] He was not versed in economic theory any more than he was trained in law, either common or canon; but as he did not balk at sitting as the chief judge of the realm, so he did not think it unfitting that he should unravel the skein of trade.

Yet as his problems multiplied and their complexity increased and the interests of the kingdom grew more intersticed and gnarled, even Wolsey had to admit that he could not do it all. He would undertake any task unabashed, but he was compelled gradually to delegate parts of its performance and content himself with the role of supervisor. And while it was true that he started much that he did not finish—much that was not finished for generations—still he did have the initiative to pose a question and get it on the conscience of the kingdom. He made the people aware of difficulties he did not meet or solve. The very delegations and commissions which were named to carry out his purpose began to form the shoots of a government that was to grow and spread like ivy.

Jealous and disdainful though he was of any mind but his own if it threatened to be the equal of his own, he issued commissions right and left as his tasks increased. Some of these were to deal for him with passing matters; some with issues that affected the whole of the society of the day. And every time a commission was issued and a body of men went to work, it meant that through the tyrant's interest further interest was being stirred and men were gradually being trained in the practice of government. A commission of inquiry meant that at least a small body of men heard and entertained complaints and that those they touched by the inquiry began to have some idea on a scale larger than local that government was responsible for man's good.

Consider the attack my lord Cardinal made upon the growing practice of enclosing large bodies of arable land within hedges for purposes of sheep farming. This attack ran its course from sturdy initiative to ultimate failure. The situation could not be met by decree, and the King's wish was as a whim before the forces making for enclosure. Yet the vigor with which Wolsey faced the threat and the interest he stirred up over it asserted beyond doubt the fact that the central government in London would not look with equanimity upon the aggrandizement of lords and wealthy landowners. In his attempt to handle the practice he made a magnificent gesture toward government.

The hedging of land for pasture carried with it insults and grievances that touched every part of the population. Even London was outraged by the enclosure of land north of the city. In 1514 hedges and ditches had been erected where men were used to walking and hunting. The practice reached a point, says Grafton, where "neither the younge men of the city might shoot, nor the ancient persons might walk for their pleasure in the fields."⁶ With urban indignation that open spaces nearby had not been left intact, Londoners murmured and prepared. One Sunday a mass of people assembled in the city, and a turner attired in a fool's coat ran among them crying, "Shovels and spades!" It was the signal for the attack on the offending hedges. People from the city swept beyond the walls, armed with implements to fill ditches and cut hedges. When the people returned to the city at night, they had left the fields open.

Elsewhere the rebellion was not as forthright. Among those dispossessed and thrown on the roads to become drifters and beggars, grievances festered. And the sad effects were plain on every hand. "Where forty men had their livings, now one man and his shepherd hath all."[7] So the lament ran. There was something merciless and unrelenting about the encroachments of the sheepmen. A picture of the process which had been insidiously at work for almost a hundred years is given by Barnard: "The arable land of England was mostly 'open field,' a mass of strips, scattered among various holders, each strip separated off by nothing but a balk of unploughed ground."[8]

Agitation had reached formidable heights when Parliament met in 1489 and two acts were passed with the hope and design that the enclosure of land would come to an end. The acts proved to be hardly more than expressions of social piety. Enforcement grew lax at best, largely because the men who were to carry out the orders of the authorities, when authorities existed, were themselves involved in the malevolence of enclosures. Thus the movement toward the hedging of more and more tillable land crept on and on. The sheepmen were like a band of grazing sheep, moving restlessly forward, ever moving.

When Henry VIII reached the throne, the threat had again thrown the country into turmoil. Great were the grievances laid before the King. Henry had issued in 1514 a proclamation against the "engrossers" of farms, "forbidding them to hold more farms than one and ordering that all the houses of husbandry decayed since his father's reign should be once more 'put to tillage' . . ."[9]

Enclosing went on as before. Henry might be King and a King might be worth fighting for or fighting over. But he had not the will to prevent the spread of sheep when the prices paid for the fleece they bore were good and men could fashion cloth and draw good wages from the business of harvesting it. Wool was everywhere, and most of all it was in men's minds and pockets.

Since the King's will did not suffice, Parliament was invoked in the cause. The Parliament of 1515 was persuaded to pass an act "directing the restoration to tillage of land enclosed since 1485."[10] But it neglected to authorize any means of carrying out the law. The letter of the law became a dead letter almost before it was scrawled on the statute books. The agents who under normal procedure would put it into effect were the justices of the peace, and these were often engaged in the rich profits of enclosing remnants of land. Also the law was so constructed that in many particulars it invited evasion. For example, it was enacted that no man could own more than two thousand sheep, but each member of a family, and even servants, might in theory and did in fact own that number of sheep. The destruction of farm buildings was forbidden; but the statute might be satisfied if a man kept a single room for the shepherd or the milkmaid. "A solitary furrow driven across newly laid pasture satisfied the law that it should be restored to tillage."[11] And if these tactics failed to comply with the requirements in the light of the justice who administered the law, exemptions might be purchased or breaches might be satisfied by light fines.

It was in this disheveled state of affairs that my lord Cardinal decided to intervene. He made a national campaign to defend the farmer, to hold the line against the invasion of great landlords and barons upon the small holdings of men who tilled the soil. What he did amounted to an attack by the national government upon a grievous social problem that could not be attacked piecemeal. The act of 1515 had been left to local administration. Wolsey stepped in now to make the matter a concern of the King. And the method by which he proposed to enforce the laws was characteristically vigorous, and it followed the pattern of his procedures in the Court of the Star Chamber: he would invoke and use the authority of the King instead of the authority of local justices of the peace.

The first step was to appoint on May 28, 1517, a commission of inquiry into all enclosures of land made since 1485. The commission was armed with more than rhetoric. It was directed to bring those who offended before the King and his Council in theory and before my lord Cardinal in fact. The Council was to have coercive power to enforce the decisions of the commission. This was a move strongly resented by those who troubled their minds over the delicacies of law and justice. But it was in this case effective, for the national government stepped in where the local government had failed or had proved itself too flexible. The next year Wolsey issued a decree ordering the destruction of all enclosures that had been made contrary to statutes. The Crown instituted proceedings against even great offenders, including some of Wolsey's friends, among them Bishop Fox, who had so lavishly commended him as a fair-haired boy to Henry VII.

In this and all other questions that had to do with a sense of wholeness in the kingdom Wolsey used authority to the discomfort of friend or foe. Spare the rod and spoil the nation.

CHAPTER
IX

One whose soul was less feverish and tumultuous than Wolsey's might have been content to reign over the realm in the name of the King. But there was another kingdom in England: the kingdom of the Church, a transcendent realm with borders beyond England's shores, a superstructure of conscience to which kings and emperors made obeisance.

Of this vast state of the mind, this vision of spirit made flesh and mortal, Thomas Wolsey showed at all times and in all respects a guiding awareness. From the moment he stepped across the threshold from obscurity into power, the Church engaged his faculties and his concern. Not only did it serve as a vehicle of his progress; it proved also the magnet that drew into some focus and order the wild diversity of his thoughts and policies. Wolsey resided in Rome, although he never so much as visited the Eternal City. In the Church was some *mystique* which could never be fully comprehended and must never be ignored. The Church was shadow and substance combined; it gave architecture to a dream.

Consequently, Wolsey could not be satisfied merely with secular assignments. Once he became Lord Chancellor he set about restlessly to become also head of the Church in England, to gather unto himself the weapons of power in religion. And once he had made himself the chief churchman of England, superior in station to the Archbishop of Canterbury, he sought the papacy itself. In the midst of all his manipulations and circumlocutions one can get an occasional glimpse of an inward conscience. In all his petitions for power his avowed aim—however poorly carried out—was to reform the Church in the presence of its enemies. For such a task he firmly needed full papal authority, and it was for such a task that he sought the steady increase of his powers. As Archbishop of York, Wolsey was Primate of England. But as Archbishop of Canterbury, Warham was Primate of *All* England.

There was a mountain of difference in that one word. It is true that, as Cardinal, Wolsey trailed additional clouds of glory. The office of cardinal, however, gave him dignity rather than power. It signified hardly more than an umbilical connection with Rome. Considering the distance from Rome and his busy inability to take any part in the deliberations of the Roman consistory, Wolsey was not a functioning Cardinal. He was Cardinal in name only, enjoying a deferential form of address made compulsory by tradition. Being Cardinal did not add one ounce of strength to his episcopal muscles. He was not, for all his flowing robes and sacred hat and costly ring and poetic title of St. Cecilia Beyond the Tiber, head of the Church in England.

Indeed the Archbishop of York was a country cousin within the Church. He had under his surveillance and jurisdiction only three dioceses which seemed remote from London, and the seat of the see was detached and far from London too. Various invidious details conspired to point up the difference between Canterbury and York and to keep the Archbishop of York in his place. Among these was the location of the residences of the two. The Archbishop of Canterbury resided at Lambeth Palace, hard by Westminster and the court and the King. He was near a teeming mass of perhaps five thousand people clustered around the court and the noble Abbey of the Benedictines at Westminster, a busy and thronging place. But York Palace, where the Archbishop of York officially resided when he came to London, was far down the river at Battersea. Such details were clear and significant to those who knew the hierarchy of the Church, and my lord Cardinal knew the facts perhaps better than anyone.

It was essential to my lord of York's avowed purpose of energetically reforming the Church that he made himself loftier in station than the Archbishop of Canterbury. With this aim in view he did two things. First, he built a better house in a more desirable location. He abandoned the decrepit and distant York Palace in Battersea and, with all his architectural talents, commenced a handsomely appointed abode near the King's palace at Westminster. The new house was not only more convenient; it was closer to the court than Lambeth Palace, and it was on the right side of the river. It was a palace fit for a king, but Wolsey modestly called it York Place in honor of his see and in the spirit of the kind of humility that made a Cardinal ride a mule. He had the right in building it to impress craftsmen, and in July of 1515 he spent as a matter of record fourpence "for ale given to the plumbers and others."[1] The house, when it was finished, contained vast libraries and picture galleries; its walls were hung with cloth of gold, and the tables were covered with "velvets, satins, damasks of various hues."[2]

Then, having assured himself that in the appointments of his living he would not, though only York, be outdone by Canterbury, he directed his efforts toward persuading the Pope to making him legate *a latere*. Only with the powers of a full legate would Wolsey have the right to accomplish the reformation of the English Church. And this reformation must be accomplished. The bitter and disquieting experience of the Richard Hunne case had sounded a new and ominous note in criticism: the Church might become subject to reform by outside forces, by government, by worldly legislators. The matter on which the Church stood most firm was the right to regulate its own affairs. Yet the state of the Church was such that it would invite increasing outside meddling and lay interference. Reform was in the air and in the minds of men. Strategically, the Church must order its house and its affairs in such a way that it would forfend parliamentary action.

Ample precedent existed to show that churchmen could offer sharp and improving criticism of the Church. Innocent VIII in 1489 had sent a bull to Cardinal Morton, then Archbishop of Canterbury, directing him "to admonish all abbots and priors in his province to reform themselves and those under them, with the threat of excommunication should they refuse to obey."[3] The Pope had heard that monks in some of the monasteries were leading dissolute and lascivious lives. Morton had charged the Abbot of the Abbey of St. Albans with having "laid aside the pleasant yoke of contemplation and all regular observances, alms, and other offices of piety." He accused the Abbot of having appointed as prioress of a neighboring and dependent nunnery "a woman who had already married, and who lived in adultery with the monks . . ." The brethren of the Abbey, Morton further charged, "live with harlots and mistresses publicly and continuously within the precincts of the monastery."[4] Conditions revealed at the priory of Norwich about this time were hardly better. These censures and disclosures had been pronounced by the Primate of All England a quarter of a century before Wolsey sought legatine powers to put the Church in order.

Morton had been as unsparing of the priests as of the monks. He had seen fit to forbid their having swords or daggers, or gold purses or other ornaments of gold, or wearing their hair in such a way as to conceal their tonsure. And above and beyond these strictures on what might have been considered details in which latitude could be allowed, he had remarked upon and reprobated the practice of clergymen failing to live in the benefices they held.

Here Morton had touched a nerve that was still exposed. Throughout the realm parish churches might be served by ignorant stipendiaries who mumbled Masses at stated intervals, little understanding the Latin they used and having no close or real interest in the people who came to the services. The parson who held the benefice, meanwhile, appropriated most of the income from the parish while he lolled in a university or traveled around Italy.

This situation, besides giving rise to an irresponsible body of clergy without stated functions or local roots, lent resonance to the voices of still other critics within the Church. These were the friars, who moved from village to village, preaching and bearing tidings of the outside world to persons who often never left the place where they had been born. Unlike the monks, who stayed customarily within their stately buildings and devoted themselves to piety, the friars identified religious zeal with evangelism. "In theory," Trevelyan says, "the friars . . . lived by begging alms, had no property of their own and preached the doctrine of evangelical poverty so dear to St. Francis. In practise they had now amassed wealth and treasure which they stored in their magnificent convents."[5] But their theory gave them latitude of utterance, and they were among those who protested the sloth of the clergy and the monks.

Notwithstanding the bulls of popes and the monitory letters of prelates, the Church had not substantially changed. While Wolsey had his agents busy in Rome seeking added powers for him, the Bishop of Ely visited a monastery in his diocese and found such disorder that he declared continuance of the monastery "would have been impossible but for his visitation." At Norwich Priory matters seemed worse. "Suspicious women were about, and there was dancing in the great hall by night. Sheep fed within the cloister, the brethren were neglected, there was no schoolmaster, and the number of monks had fallen short by ten."[6]

Apart from confidence born of conceit, my lord of York had small reason to suppose that he could succeed where other agents of the Pope had failed. His ambition was projected far beyond the practical, even beyond the bound of the possible. For all his eloquence, Wolsey often seemed to think in acts rather than words. He left no recorded plan of precisely how he hoped to go about the total job of reform; one step at a time was enough. It looked as if he had staked out a task of such dimensions that failure would be inevitable and yet magnificent in its very scope. He may have unconsciously courted failure, not the failure of inaction but of effort on a scale so extensive that men must admire his audacity in trying at all.

He faced a formidable array of obstructionists. The monastic establishments, for example, had numbers, wealth, and power. There were over seven hundred of them in England, and their wealth in terms of land showed that they had many ties and means of resistance in all parts of the kingdom. In Gloucestershire alone there were ninety monasteries, and they held an average of sixty-five thousand acres of land apiece. One had to reckon also with politics and the power of the abbots, for twenty-seven of the heads of great religious houses had seats as lords spiritual in Parliament. "The bishops could not control the monks, whose vows bound them to allegiance to their superiors, generally foreigners. They were directly connected with the Papacy, and the monastic orders came to be spoken of as the Pope's standing army . . ."[7]

The head of a monastery, usually an abbot but in some cases a prior, "was not only absolute ruler within his own domain, but also a person of great social weight outside it. He often had a house apart from the monks and a large staff of servants of his own."[8] In a day when dignity was advertised if not created by a conspicuous withdrawal from the common herd, the abbots set a haughty standard that left no doubt of their power. When the Abbot of St. Albans dined, it was in lordly state. "His table was raised fifteen steps above the rest of the hall, and in serving him the monks performed a hymn at every fifth step. He sat alone in the middle of his table, and when he received any guests of a very high rank they were only admitted to sit at the ends." How seriously would a prince of the Church with such a demeanor and notion of his own importance take the admonitions of a mere Archbishop of York, though he be a Cardinal?

While His Holiness delayed granting Wolsey the legateship, events kept their trend toward convulsive action. The ghost of Richard Hunne had not been laid; it still stalked in the recesses of controversy. The questions it posed had not been resolved but merely silenced for the moment, to be taken up again like an old quarrel. The threat which a man in Wolsey's position could easily detect was that criticism, now an antiphony in the Church and in the Commons, might unite in a deafening chorus of protest.

Reform had become a bone of contention beyond the Church, and it might at any moment become the chief business of those whose business it was not. Rebellion against ecclesiastical authority had slumbered through more than a hundred years of English life. Once before, the hostility had showed itself in Parliament, and only the timely and furious intervention of the King—in this case Richard II, called back from the bogs of Ireland by the alarmed bishops—had prevented the undermining by Parliament of the whole structure of the Church.

That earlier tempest of 1395 had been brewed by the Lollards, a name of derision bestowed upon the followers of John Wycliffe, denoting them as mutterers. Wycliffe himself was no mutterer. He was a man of strong views and trenchant utterance, and he advocated, among other preposterous reforms, the distribution of Church property among poor laymen. His disciples went about the country as Poor Priests, strenuously preaching his views of disendowment. Being of good demeanor and not ranting against lay property, the Lollards made friends among the gentry. In due course they had friends at court, and some of the members of the King's Council were loyal Lollards. It was these well-placed Lollards who sought in 1395 to lay the views of their co-religionists before Parliament.

At the time, King Richard was off on a long and bootless effort to tame the savage Irish with English swords. In his absence the Lollards of the Council wrote out in detail their beliefs, including an attack on "the riches and secular employments of the clergy." Their beliefs, eloquently stated, were not only presented to Parliament but, for good measure, nailed to the door of St. Paul's where the ordinary citizens of London might see and read.[9]

When Richard heard these tidings, he returned to London in haste, "vowing to hang all Lollards." Because of the prompt action of the King, the attempt to give heretical views respectability in Parliament had failed. And the repression was effective. Yet the memory of the views and of the day they had at court lingered on.

English memory lent urgency, then, to the petitions Wolsey presented to the Pope for the authority to institute reform. Both experience and perception showed that resentment might at any time break out like a fire in some unexpected quarter. It might be set off by a trifle, as news of occurrences in Germany at this time plainly told. There Martin Luther, a young friar attached to the monastery of the Augustinian Hermits at Wittenberg, had chosen to protest the sale of indulgences. Men of scratchy conscience had long objected to indulgences sold like wool in the marts of trade, but the practice of raising funds for an estimable cause by the sale of pardons did not stand at the top of abuses for which the Church had been criticized. And the commotion caused by the friar's protest seemed out of all proportion to the seriousness of the abuse criticized. For this reason the news from Germany was all the more instructive and merited observation and study. If an obscure and callow friar, with no status save that bestowed by his own eloquence, could write ninety-five defiant reasons for condemning a practice sanctioned by His Holiness, almost any insubordination might win popular support. Particularly was this so if the reasons were accepted with muttered approval by the laity. It was as if the sound and fury had come back as an echo from events in England. In the whole affair were many elements spotted throughout English history.

The abuses which pinched the conscience of Luther were present in all countries where the Church held sway, and they were abundantly present in England. Occasionally a civic use was made of indulgences, by means of which Church authorities would remit penalties in exchange for work done to improve the community. In one case an archbishop granted a hundred days' pardon to all those "who contributed to the repair and to the building of new bridges at Oxnede."[10] Registers "abound with the details of indulgences granted for the repair or upkeep of bridges and bridge chapels." In many other cases, however, the sale of indulgences was put to less worthy use. An indulgence might reduce the severity of a punishment, and in some cases the punishments were "of long duration; fasting and mortification had to be carried on for months and years." Thus a sinner might for a consideration "exchange a year of penance against three hundred lashes, reciting a psalm at each hundred. Tables of such exchanges were drawn up by competent prelates."[11] Into this complex system pardoners stepped with offers of indulgences which might commute the punishment of the Church authorities when the Pardoner arrived "with his wallet 'bretful of pardons come from Rome all hot.'"[12] Exchanging penance for a money fee blunted the lingering moral perceptions of sinners. Chaucer told of the Summoner, sent to summon delinquents to Church courts, who would, according to Abram, "overlook an offense for a year for a quart of wine, and would warn 'a good felawe' not to fear the Archdeacon's curse, for he would be punished only in his purse."[13]

Ideas from the Continent were beginning to permeate England, and there was an audience not only for the fulminations of Luther but for other much less respectable outcries against the Church. There came to be circulated in England about this time a gross satire on the monks under the title of *Epistolae obscurorum virorum*. Its reception could not be accounted for by its worth or style, and the satisfaction which its vulgarity afforded the intellectuals who devoured it showed how sentiment drifted. "It is read everywhere," wrote Thomas More to Erasmus.[14]

Even if hostility toward the Church did not assume the proportions of a national revolt, it was still there to be reckoned with and guarded against as a threat of local violence. Thirty years before Wolsey set out on his tenuous program of reform, the clergy in Convocation had addressed to the throne a petition "complaining that churchmen were cruelly, grievously, and daily troubled, vexed, indicted and arrested; drawn out of church, and without due reverence, even from the altar, by malicious and evil-disposed persons, notwithstanding all the censures, anathematizations and curses, yearly promulgated and fulmined by the holy father the pope, and in all the churches of England; so that they could not be resident on their benefices, to execute duly and devoutly their office . . ."[15]

Gairdner points out the contempt which lay law officials had for the sanctuaries. Arrests were sometimes made by bailiffs in church, "leading to unseemly profanation of the House of God, and scuffles interrupted the parson even while he was saying mass."[16] The Pope cried out against these sacrileges, but the clergy were continually "drawn before secular judges and punished without ecclesiastical authority."

For three years Pope Leo resisted and evaded the importunities of Wolsey for the legateship. Nor is there any indication that he would ever have granted this barbarian Cardinal his request if events had not conveniently arranged themselves so that Wolsey was able to extort the appointment.

It chanced that in the same year that Martin Luther posted his Theses, Leo wrote to Warham as the Primate of All England to say that he planned shortly to send into the realm a legate of the Holy See for the purpose of raising funds to carry on an expedition against the Turks, who were moving closer and closer to the heart of Europe. It would be the purpose of this legate to aid in promoting a five-year truce among the princes of Europe, so that full Christian energy might be expended on the repulse. The letter went unanswered for months, being as studiously and conspicuously neglected as had been Wolsey's efforts to obtain the legateship. In Rome this neglect of the Pope's letter, especially seeing that the letter pertained to so important a matter as the union of Christendom and the protection of the civilized world against the inroads of Muslim hordes, occasioned great annoyance and astonishment. The English agent in Rome reported to England that the Pope "asked him ten times a day" when he might expect a reply.[17]

At last, although he had received no reply, the Pope announced that he was sending on his stated mission Cardinal Lorenzo Campeggio. This Cardinal had served the Holy Father well in other capacities, and he had been created Cardinal the year before. Campeggio set out for England, toward which place he came by slow stages, and finally reached Calais, where he sought admission into Henry's kingdom.

The admission was not granted, but at this time Wolsey, after consulting with his King, sent to Leo the reply so impatiently awaited. It was not the reply Leo expected to a routine request for assistance in the most noble of all causes. It stated imperiously that it was not customary in England "to admit any foreign cardinal to exercise legatine powers in the country." Still, the King was willing to release Campeggio from his detention at Calais and admit him on his mission provided the Cardinal of York be associated with him in the legatine commission and have equal legatine faculties. The dispatch concluded with the astonishing condition that if the Pope did not grant this concession "the King will in no wise allow Campeggio to enter England."[18]

The Pope had no choice but to bow to English stubbornness. It was in this wise, and with the known contrivance of the King, that Wolsey gained the legateship. Campeggio got the royal assent to cross to England. Once admitted, however, he was shown high deference, it being necessary for Wolsey to demonstrate the honors due a legate *a latere.* Hall in his *Chronicle* relates that Wolsey went to great lengths to help equip Campeggio with the splendor becoming his rank and mission. He says that the night before Campeggio entered London Wolsey sent him twelve mules bearing empty coffers trapped with scarlet; "and thus the cavalcade, with eight others belonging to the Legate, passed through the streets as if they had carried so much treasure." In Cheapside, however, "one of the mules turned restive, and upset the chests, out of which tumbled old hose, broken shoes, bread, meat, and eggs, with 'much vile baggage' at which the boys exclaimed, 'See, my lord Legate's treasure!'" Brewer considers the story more malicious than probable; but in any event Wolsey saw to it that Campeggio was lavishly treated and scrupulously honored on his way from Dover to London, that he was accompanied by a cavalcade of five hundred horse and received and dined along the way by the nobility of Church and State.[19]

Having established the importance of Campeggio as a legate, Wolsey next subordinated him and put himself forward in all their dealings, insisting that only his own cross should be borne before them. At their public reception Campeggio was given a seat raised three steps above the floor; but the seat on which my lord of York placed his own ample legatine frame was double that height.

With the legatine commission granted, Wolsey used Campeggio's presence in England to reinforce his demands on the Pope for powers of reform. He sought and secured a bull that empowered both of them to conduct visitations of the monasteries. But Campeggio had no stomach for a longer stay in England, and in March 1519 Wolsey asked that he alone be allowed to conduct the visitations, seeing that Campeggio would return to Rome. He asked at the same time for increased powers, "that I may be able to accomplish some good in the Lord's vineyard and be profitable to all christendom."[20] The powers to reform the monasteries after Campeggio left were granted by the Pope in due course. And at once Wolsey began beseeching the Pope to grant the legateship for life.

What Wolsey sought had at last come to pass, and the result left him with untrammeled power. "In the hand of one man," as Gasquet puts it, "were grasped the two swords of Church and State. One mind directed the policy of secular and ecclesiastical administration in England. Had that man been a saint, the danger of such a combination would have been considerable, but when he was a worldly and ambitious man like Wolsey, it was fatal."[21]

The legateship was granted on May 17, 1518. With all his impatience for it and his vast plans for its use and the continued urgency of reform, almost a year elapsed before the overworked Wolsey took steps toward turning a vague scheme of reform into action. And then his first move was hardly more than an unctuous exhortation of the sort that had been issued so many times and so vainly in the past, calling upon the men of the Church to lead a more pious life. Loftily ignoring the fact that his own personal life was far from exemplary, that he was an overlord and not a practicing priest in daily touch with religious needs, the legate issued statements that had the sound and sentiments of papal bulls. He urged the good to be better still, and he called severely upon the lax to mend their erring ways, talking to them like a schoolmaster full of inexhaustible impatience.

The move was without the advantages of tact, and, seeing that the independence of the bishops and abbots had the sanction of the Holy See, it was not calculated to endear the Cardinal to those he sought to reform. Later he summoned representatives of all the religious orders before him and, "after expressing his goodwill towards them, spoke very

plainly of their defects, and of the desire he had to see them live according to their rules . . ."[22] The Cardinal further stressed his intention of
attending to the business of reform personally.

At the time, he was busily engaged in the machinations of high
diplomacy whereby he and not the Pope would be responsible for the
union of the princes of Christendom. Likewise he was sitting in judgment
and exercising his capacious conscience on the problems of the realm
brought before his court; and he was dealing through a royal commission
with such vast and complicated problems as enclosure, trying to hold
back the stupendous changes that were going on in agriculture and in the
tenure of land. Each of these activities was worth the total effort of a
well-organized ministry, but Wolsey had to cover them all. And now he
proposed to add to his labors a further task that might well absorb the
energies of a generation of geniuses; and he assured the world that he
would attend to the matter himself.

By the very nature of time and movement, his attempt to reform
the Church with the part-time use of his left hand was doomed to futility. It would be marked at best by fits and starts. His schedule was
such that the only visit he made during the year he secured the bull em-
powering him to reform the monasteries took him to Westminster Abbey,
hardly a stone's throw from the busy scenes of the court and his residence
at York Place. The Cardinal Legate treated the monks "with considerable rigour," for which there appeared to be no occasion. The monks
of the Abbey enjoyed good repute; no question had been raised to suggest that they had violated religious proprieties. The Abbey's wealth
might mark it for envy, for its holdings stretched out on all sides to
embrace such areas as came to be known as Hyde Park, Pimlico, and
Covent Garden. But nothing save covetousness could raise whispers
against Westminster. Mainly the Legate's visit to the Abbey at Westminster was a household affair, a show of paternal authority over the
Abbot and the monks.

Next he turned to the Order of St. Augustine; this and the Order of St. Benedict made up the great religious bodies of England. My lord Cardinal chose for his opening fanfare a bull issued by Benedict XII in 1334. In this he but called the attention of the Augustinians to previous admonitions, already accepted as worthy and accepted now as worthy of reiteration. At the same time he added some regulations of his own, the same to be kept in force from the moment they were pronounced, on March 19, 1519, until the Feast of the Holy Trinity two years later.

The didactic detail to be found in the regulations Wolsey visited upon this great order reveals him as a preoccupied lecturer. He instructs them that the Office is to be said neither too quickly nor too slowly. He goes so far as to say that all of the monks are to be present at the services, especially Matins and Mass. And then, as if there were nothing else of more importance on the disturbed earth, my lord Cardinal and Legate proceeds to tell the monks of the Order of St. Augustine how to sing.[23]

Wolsey was a reformer by memorandum, setting forth stately thoughts to the clergy as he set forth devious and complicated directions to his agents in the courts of Europe and at the court of the Holy See. As Archbishop of York he issued resounding *statuta* for his province. In reckoning with the province he needed no legatine authority. In fact, he needed only an audience. Most of his injunctions and benedictions are drawn from the enactments (a term often used to suggest that the mere pronouncement of a Church official constituted a law) of his predecessors. His contribution was simply to draw up and edit these earlier pronouncements and issue them again as if to inaugurate a more vigorous policy. And in many cases he added the vigor of his own phrasing and a freshness of terms which would catch the eye even in a document of religious instruction. Four times every priest with the care of souls was to explain, "in the vulgar tongue and without any subtlety or fantastic turning about of words," the fourteen Articles of faith, the Ten Commandments, the two evangelical precepts of charity, the seven works of mercy, the seven deadly sins, the seven opposing virtues, and the seven sacraments of grace.[24]

Enough high-sounding words, properly arranged for effect, were apparently supposed to jolt the whole Church into a newness of life. In the governing of his own province Wolsey ordered that all clerics must remain in their parishes unless they had papal dispensation or their bishop's permission to absent themselves—a measure that sounded good and struck the keynote of reform; but Wolsey himself knew that permission from the bishop could easily be arranged, and when he issued this edict he had not visited any of the livings which he himself held. The clergy of his province were forbidden to attend unlawful spectacles, "especially duels, tournaments and sports in which blood might be shed."[25] They were also urged to be different in dress and deportment from the laity to call the world's attention to the distinctiveness of the religious life. Yet he himself at the time paraded around London in competitive pomp and appeared to seek by his every act to show that the clergy could not only dress as well as the lords temporal but vastly better. Later the Cardinal ordered all bishops to be in attendance upon their cathedrals at the time of ordinations, yet in his own province of York the ordinations were held by his auxiliary bishop.

In all he said Wolsey seemed to regard himself as the appointed leader of reform; in all he did he appeared to look upon himself as an eloquent exception. He lived in his mind, and the fruits of his mind were schemes so vast that their mere entertainment gave him satisfaction and a feeling of accomplishment. He enjoyed his power and capacity more than his deeds, and in his dreams for the renovation of the whole Church in England he viewed the world from the icy heights of innocence. There was about him and those few who championed his efforts a touching naïveté, as well as a lordly disdain for practical difficulties and complexities.

The obstacles which confronted Wolsey when he turned from words to official action were thick and frustrating. The legatine powers he sought did not come all at once but by degrees, and only through his continued importunities in Rome. Before they were granted to the full, those who opposed "the great tyrant," as Warham's secretary called Wolsey, had prevailed upon the Archbishop of Canterbury to anticipate the Cardinal and make motions of reform ahead of him. Accordingly an official of the province of Canterbury prepared to conduct a visitation of the cathedral monastery in the diocese of Worcester. The visitation was refused admittance. The monks were excommunicated for their refusal, but they maintained that the power of visitation now rested with the Legate.

Incidents of this unhappy sort did little to prepare the way for Wolsey to carry out his commendable and highly commended designs. They represented the jurisdictional disputes which the Archbishop of York, a distinctly ecclesiastical underling,though vested now by the Holy Father with legatine strength, would encounter at all times. When he discovered that Warham had summoned his suffragans to hold a council at Lambeth for "the reformation of enormities," his remonstrance was prompt. If there was anything more important than the reformation of the Church, it was that this reformation should be conducted by the Pope's commissioned representative. To Warham, Wolsey wrote in dignified astonishment "that you should enterprise the said reformation to the express derogation of the said dignity of the See Apostolic and otherwise than the law will suffer you without mine advice, consent, and knowledge . . ." At this stage of his legateship, still amiable in his strength, and confident that there were larger rights yet to be bestowed by the Pope, Wolsey suggested to Warham that the two prelates meet and discuss the whole matter. He selected Richmond as a proper place for the meeting and added with a touch of politeness the hope that this "shall not be much incommodious" to Warham.

Then by way of official reply to the Archbishop of Canterbury and the mischief the provincial Convocation on reform might create, Wolsey summoned a legatine synod to meet at Westminster. The first session had to be postponed because of an outbreak of the sweating sickness, an affliction which upon its return always drove men to cover, whether kings or prelates. The synod finally assembled when the sweat had passed again, but its accomplishments are not a matter of record. The chances are that it was an exploratory meeting designed merely to make out problems, and that the problems which appeared were so many and fierce that they sobered the Cardinal in the matter of general reform through synods, convocations, or any other kind of clerical assembly. He did not understand or trust deliberative bodies, whether they were composed of those who wore the cloth or those who came together as squires and burgesses in the Commons. His idea of a legatine council henceforth was to assemble a few chosen bishops at his residence and deal with them as subalterns.

Four years after the first futile synod on reform met under Wolsey's jurisdiction, the King issued a writ to Warham to summon the bishops and clergy of his province to meet at St. Paul's in London, or wherever the Archbishop might deem it convenient to meet. The call was issued. At the same time a writ was issued to Wolsey to summon his clergy from his own province. But before the two writs were fairly cold, Wolsey moved to show that any assembly held would have to be under his auspices. As Hall puts it: "In this season the Cardinal by his power legatine dissolved the convocation at St. Paul's, called by the Archbishop of Canterbury, and called him and all the clergy to his convocation in Westminster, which was never seen before in England."[26] The Abbey of Westminster, where Wolsey ordered the assembly to meet, was exempt from the jurisdiction of the Archbishop of Canterbury.

After all the arrangements and counter-arrangements, nothing came of the Convocation that contributed to the reform of the Church. It marked the end of Wolsey's half-hearted efforts to institute reform by consent and reduced the government of the Church to what Pollard calls a legatine autocracy. The various divisions of government within the

Church had the right to meet and enact through councils, but it was more of a right than a practice, and, as Sir Thomas More pointed out later, the weakness of the deliberative bodies within the Church had laid the way for their abandonment in the matter of reform. More deplores the fact that there had not been assemblies of the clergy in every province throughout all Christendom. Had this been so, he observes, "much more good might have grown thereof than the long disuse can suffer us now to perceive." He continues: "But of all my days, as far as I have heard, nor (I suppose) a good part of my father's neither, they came never together in convocation but at the request of the king, and at such their assemblies, concerning spiritual things, have very little done. Wherefore that they have been in that necessary part of their duty negligent . . ."[27]

CHAPTER X

In 1524 Wolsey got the legateship for life. There was no remaining excuse now why he should not accomplish the high ends he had announced, save that he was already weary of the task and he had encountered enough difficulties to vex a saint. He had not touched the problem of priests in minor orders who did the clerical work of the kingdom—priests in name only whose privileges were deeply resented by the laity. He had done nought but preach to the general body of the active clergy, all of them under the jealous jurisdiction of their bishops. He had fitfully exhorted some of the monks. It took something more than authority to reform a body as amorphous as the Church.

When next he turned his attention to the friars, they met his advances with a stony eye; for all the good the Legate accomplished among them he might as well have remained only an archbishop. The friars were simply unavailable for reform; they wanted no legatine nose poked into their affairs. To begin with, they were vastly more than English: they were organized on a scale as big as the civilized world. Touched off by the Crusades, each order organized as "an ecclesiastical army with its general residing at Rome and with a cardinal designated there to give special protection to its interests."[1] The Dominicans (Black Friars) had been founded by the Spanish Dominic and had come to England in 1221. The Franciscans (Gray Friars) had come to England in 1224. Both these huge orders were well established, immured in English society, yet active in the whole life of the country and given to valorous independence of action. There were other orders of friars, less powerful but no less assertive.

No wonder Rome advised Wolsey to deal lightly with the body of friars. Before he could announce his intention to visit the Franciscans, representatives of that order had appealed to Rome in an attempt to prevent the visit. When the Observant Friars suspected that Wolsey would visit and reform them, they sent scurrying messengers to their cardinal-protector in Rome and asked him to lay their case at the feet of the Pope. As Hall put it in his *Chronicle,* the Cardinal "would have visited the Friars Observatines, but they in nowise would therein condescend." The appeal to the Pope was not without effect. His Holiness wrote Wolsey, calling attention to the good name the order enjoyed throughout the world and urging the Legate to "make use of gentleness and tact rather than severity in admonishing them."[2] The cardinal-protector also wrote the Legate, asking him to give up the visitation altogether. Both requests were polite and routine, but to reinforce a feeling the Pope could hardly express in an official communication His Holiness sent word the following month through one of Wolsey's agents in Rome that the Legate should "for God's sake use mercy with those Friars," seeing that "they be as desperate beasts, past shame, that can lose nothing by clamor."[3]

Another reason could be advanced for letting the friars go their unreformed way. They were popular with the rank and file, subject to criticism more by the bishops and the priests than by the laity. They identified the service of God with the service of man. Their convents were in or near the larger towns, signifying their mission to the masses, but they had a system of itineracy which sent friars two by two into villages and country districts and to the houses of the gentry and farmers. They heard confessions, and "there were many who chose to confess their misdoings to a comparative stranger, who did not live among them, rather than to their parish priests."

Mainly, however, they were preachers. They preached in churchyards and market places, wherever men and women would gather to listen. Their emphasis on preaching affected their architecture. Their churches had auditoriums where large congregations could hear sermons rather than witness liturgical processions. Their services were designed "to attract the sluggish and popularize religion." They encouraged and produced miracle plays to drive home religious lessons, and their preaching was calculated to influence men's daily lives. "The sermons were practical and moral rather than dogmatic, interspersed with anecdotes, often of a sensational type, and illustrations drawn from daily life . . . To go and hear a friar preach was one of the recognized forms of entertainment in the merry England of the Middle Ages."[4]

The favor enjoyed by the friars was not shared by the monks and nuns, and the houses of these great stationary orders continued to receive Wolsey's legatine attention. If the monastic establishments with their conspicuous display of wealth could be remodeled, the change might enhance in no small measure public good will toward the Church. The priests and bishops would rejoice to see the monks brought to heel. And the laity would nod with satisfaction too, for the monasteries were great landlords, and many of their dealings with people outside the walls were on the basis of business.

A new spirit of commerce in the towns made these institutions seem out of date, an obstruction to progress. They were "rentiers living on their revenues."[5] They stood to gain by keeping things fastened in place as they were. The problem that a reformer faced was not the morals but the immovability of the monasteries. Little concrete evidence came to light to show that the monasteries were dens of vice. Those rare cases in which charges were made were laid before the authorities of the Church by the members of some Church visiting body. This was true before Wolsey's day and in the visitations which he made or authorized. The reform of the monasteries could not be accomplished by an unsparing use of the rod on individual monks and nuns or by instructing them in a redoubled use of prayer and fasting or by a warning against such frivolous practices as the prick-song, which was fancy in its rhythms. Reform involved vastly more than private morals. The Legate was dealing with great corporations of power and wealth "faltering to decay, such as society has to reform out of existence from time to time."[6]

In times past, the monasteries had contributed to the vigor of the common life of the kingdom and had given stability when it was sorely needed. They had been pioneers. They had brought waste lands under cultivation and had set an example to the lay landowners by the use of enterprising methods in agriculture and horticulture, in the growth of food and the development of plants and trees. Cutts points out that they led the way in using streams for waterpower and for irrigation and sanitation. They developed the practice of bringing pure water long distances in conduits. And in all their practices they had worked pleasantly and well with the people who farmed or used their land. Not a few of the tenants of the monastic houses, "seated generation after generation" on their manors, grew into mighty and noble families.

Indeed it was the success of the monastic houses that engendered failure, as is the way with institutions. Their hospitality came to be accepted and then abused. The closeness of Church and State led to royal presumption upon their good offices. In the reign of Edward II the Queen left her pack of hounds at Canterbury for two full years. An Italian visitor writing in the days of the Legate observed that monasteries were obliged to defray the expenses of one, two, or three gentlemen, "and as many horses with their keep, at the pleasure of His Majesty. Because, whenever the King wishes to bestow an easy life upon one of his servants, he makes one of these monasteries pay his expenses."[7]

Abuse was not confined to royalty by any means. To those who visited the great monasteries hospitality was usually extended for two days, but many guests stayed longer. And it was one of the minor problems of administration that outside laymen looked upon the houses of the religious as hostels for their convenience. Often they paid for their keep, and the temptation to turn the houses into something other than places for meditation was great. Abram says that at one nunnery both men and women were received as paying guests, a practice that led to public criticism and, to put it mildly, a diversion of original purpose.

Plenty of provision also was made for the accommodation of wayfarers. Hospitality was regarded as a duty imposed by tradition as well as religious devotion, though it was of course exercised more freely by some houses than others; chiefly, according to Bernard, by the great Benedictine monasteries and some houses of Augustinian canons. At St. Albans's arrangements were made for the stabling of three hundred horses. Abingdon had "a special endowment to meet the cost of new shoes for the guests' horses." The hosteler of one monastery was reminded that "by showing cheerful hospitality to guests the reputation of the monastery is increased, friendships are multiplied, animosities are blunted, God is honored, charity is increased, and a plenteous reward in heaven is promised."

To these ends detailed duties were laid down for the hosteler, and the tastes and peculiarities of wealthy travelers were kept scrupulously in mind. The hosteler was ordered at the Augustinian monastery of Barnwell, near Cambridge, to see that guests had clean towels, "cups without flaws, spoons of silver, mattresses, blankets and sheets not merely clean but untorn, proper pillows; quilts to cover the beds of full length and width and pleasing to the eyes of those who enter the room." The guest house was to be kept clean of spider webs and supplied with "fire that does not smoke; writing materials; clean salt in saltcellars that have been well scrubbed."[8]

Less lavish attention was bestowed upon the comforts of the poor wayfarers who came to the monastery gate, but not less consideration of their needs. "The abbot of St. Albans's entertained every traveler that came to his gate for three days; at the priory of St. Thomas of Canterbury there was a hall 150 feet long and 40 broad, appropriated to the accommodation of poor pilgrims."[9] Monasteries in areas likely to be less traveled usually entertained the poor in the almonry near the gatehouse. Here charity as well as accommodation was dispensed. Often the volume of charity was not great in terms of money. Records indicate that one Benedictine monastery, having in it a community of twenty-two monks, gave only five shillings and eightpence in a year to the poor. The cash outlay was similarly slim in other monasteries, as at Abingdon Abbey. Yet the kindness bestowed probably went far beyond what shows in the cash disbursements. For example, when new clothes and shoes were given out "at regular times in the monastery, the old ones were handed to the Almoner for the poor. All that was left from meals in the refectory and guest-house was reserved for the Almoner."[10]

Those fortunate few who received bounty from the monasteries had some sense of the lingering kindness that came from the principles of their original foundations. But many others came to covet the privileges which the inmates enjoyed. For the comforts the monks bestowed upon visitors they likewise bestowed upon themselves. They lived well when many did not. They had, in the midst of their devotions and meditations and the exactions which their many administrative duties imposed, gradually abandoned manual labor and now maintained numerous servants to carry on the daily grind of their complicated establishments. At St. Peter's in Gloucester during these days there were thirty monks and eighty-six servants.

To those on the outside, the monastic life looked to be only one of comfort and of increasing uselessness in a world that was changing with

the passage of each day. The monks "did too little and got too much."
A writer of the day speaks of a body of "abbey lubbers, which are apt
to do nothing only eat and drink." The Lord Mayor of London used
as his reason for asking royal permission to have three hospitals put
under his care the claim that the hospitals had been founded "for the
aid of poor and impotent people, not to maintain canons, priests and
monks to live in pleasure."[11]

By all accounts the flesh was weaker among the nuns than it was
among the monks. Many of the nuns had been deposited in the houses
by their families as good and fortunate riddance, and few of those who
took the veil in this period seem to have been led or called by an intense religious experience. Most of the occupants of the one hundred
and eleven nunneries in England during Wolsey's time were females un-
wanted at home, women who had not been married off. As Trevelyan
points out: "It was rarely possible to become a nun without a dowry.
In this way English nunneries were recruited and in part financed."

In general, the nunneries suffered the same faults as the monasteries. They had slipped gradually over to the side of the world. They were
bogged down in comforts and had lost their alertness to moral distinctions. The cost of fur trimmings on the mantles of nuns came to be matters of competitive interest and a sign of status. Meetings of some of
the chapters became, according to Gasquet, ecclesiastical pageants, occasions for the display of religious vestments in the latest style and in
high degrees of sumptuousness. It is reported that "for more than six
weary centuries the bishops waged a holy war against fashion in the
cloister and in vain."[12]

What could Wolsey do as he faced the reform of the monasteries?
The noticeable need, the one to which the Legate could address himself
without undue perception of the deeper defects, was a tightened discipline that might call the orders back to their original intent. This course
required that he should gird his own magnificent robes about him and
lecture monks on the dangers of comfort. But he did not stick to do it.

He addressed himself first to the startled monks of the Order of St. Benedict at Westminster Abbey, then to the Order of St. Augustine, with minute instructions on the betterment of their devotions. Next he returned to the Order of St. Benedict in a general chapter. Wolsey approached the Benedictines as he approached all other bodies and problems: with a flourish of authority and with written prescriptions for their ills. He merely told them what to do, what would be required of them by him.

The statutes laid down by Wolsey were accepted, but the monks took pains to point out that many were too severe. Their protest against the moral exactions and monastic severity imposed by the Legate told him what he as a practical man should have known already, namely, that the fierce monastic code adopted and practiced by such bodies as the Carthusians could not be applied to the Benedictines. Severity of this sort would lead to a depopulation of the monasteries; they were, whatever else, great institutions, and they needed numbers to maintain their standards as institutions. The monks besought the Legate to consider well this fact and the circumstances of the day, concluding: "For in these stormy times (as the world now decays towards its end) those who desire a life of austerity and regular observance are few, and indeed most rare."[13]

Having exercised his pen and his eloquence upon the monks with no evident sign that they would mend their ways at his bidding, Wolsey found a solution more in character with his understanding of the whole problem. Empowered by papal bulls for the express purpose, he began to suppress and dissolve the smaller houses, to dismember the Orders by cutting off their extremities, devoting the proceeds of his legatine transactions to the business of founding a college at Oxford University and a preparatory school for this college in his native Ipswich. All told, he and his agents visited and appropriated twenty-two monasteries and three nunneries. These houses which had their property diverted to other ends were all houses in which there were fewer than twelve surviving inmates. They were suffering conspicuously from what afflicted the whole monastic body: a paralysis of function.

Precedent existed for the move Wolsey made. The good Henry VI had dissolved ailing houses to set up King's College at Cambridge and Eton near Windsor. Henry VII had seen fit to replace monasteries with hospitals in London. And Bishop Alcock of Ely had founded Jesus College at Cambridge to replace the nunnery of St. Radegund.

There had been precedent for the acts of dissolution but none whatever for the scale on which the Legate now operated or the ferocious determination with which he went about the undertaking. It was a commentary that revealed much of his mind. Faced with a religious problem, he chose a businesslike solution. He evaded the problem by flying off into an abstraction. Hope lay in one word: education.

There was also the comforting assurance that the lofty end of founding colleges for the improvement of the clergy and the raising of the general level of the common life justified the means and the methods by which Wolsey and his agents acted. They met in many cases with sharp rebukes from the people of the communities where they suppressed monasteries. At Tunbridge in the province of Canterbury the inhabitants appealed to Archbishop Warham that he might cause the Legate to desist from the proposed dissolution of a small monastery of Austin Friars. Warham was asked by the Legate to go to the town and inform the people that it would be better to have "forty children of that country educated and after sent to Oxford" than to have six or seven canons living among them.[14] Warham's mission was in vain, and after discussing the matter five or six days the citizens again met with the Archbishop and let him know that they were of the same mind as before. Warham wrote to Wolsey to say that the murmurs were "very difficult to suppress."

In some places the resistance went beyond words. Wolsey commissioned the Bishop of Chichester to look into Beigham Abbey in Essex and report on certain scandals there. But the Abbey, according to Hall, was "very commodious to the country," and when the Legate started proceedings to dissolve the house the neighbors assembled in a "riotous company, disguised and unknown, with painted faces." They "turned out the agents engaged in the suppression and reinstated the canons. Before separating they begged the religious, if they were again molested, to ring their bell, and they pledged themselves to come in force to their assistance."[15]

Hall paints a stormy picture of the way in which Wolsey as Legate acted toward the monasteries. As he tells it, the Cardinal "suddenly entered by his commissioners into the said houses, and put out the religious and took all their goods, moveables, and scarcely gave to the poor wretches anything except it were to the heads of the house."[16] Whether this statement is overdrawn or not, it is well attested that the two agents he chose for the bulk of the work acted with lack of grace in their dealings and were not averse, if the testimony of their own letters is to be trusted, to the taking of bribes and considerations for exempting houses which had been marked for their master.

These agents were John Allen and Thomas Cromwell. Fiddes portrays Allen as a man who, "accompanied with a great train, and riding in a kind of perpetual progress from one religious house to another, is said to have drawn very large sums for his master's service from them."[17] Brewer reports that "loud outcries reached the king's ears of the exactions and peculations of Wolsey's officers, in which the name of Cromwell was most frequently repeated."[18] More than once the King is said to have had to express his great displeasure at the conduct of the man.

Yet the Legate seemed deaf to all but his purpose. He had no ear for complaint or protest or for the resonant whispers raised against his agents. He was a man possessed of possessions, dealing with matters that he could understand, sure of his aim, and used to outcries stirred by his actions. Other views might differ, but the Legate had come to terms with the problem of reform. Both his sense of property values and the towering dream he had built of his colleges and must now reinforce with stone made him unmindful of the claws of criticism.

In this manner preoccupied, he neglected not only criticism but also all other aspects of Church reform. Education would be the answer. Beyond his stately plans for his colleges he showed no will or talent for the simpler reforms which might have extended the Church further into the good graces of the people—such as might well have come about, for example, by the use of English instead of Latin in its services.

And he turned his eyes also from the thorny problem which had been raised by the death of Richard Hunne. He took no pains to abate the hostility of the laity to religious bodies. He seems to have seen no connection between the laxity of the ecclesiastics and the system of benefit of clergy whereby "the bishops were able to demand from the civil authorities clerics who had been imprisoned by the king's justices for any crime."[19] Punishments by death and mutilation could not be inflicted by ecclesiastical courts. However bad the crime of the cleric, his punishment at the hands of his bishop would be light. Yet these same courts were able to arrogate to themselves cases in which laymen were involved, and if the crimes committed merited death by the laws of the Church the lay offenders were handed over to the secular arm of the government for burning or dismemberment.

What precise powers my lord Cardinal had as Legate, as distinct from those he claimed and flaunted, is a matter still lost in the mists of history. Still, he had plenty to deal with heresy. It is odd that, having gathered unto himself the powers of both Church and State, he did not grapple with the conflict between the courts Christian and the courts of the common law, except that he seemed always to see the world through stained glass. He was a Cardinal of Rome first and last, with all that the cardinalate implied; England was only a province of something larger and beyond, and to that larger thing men gave the name of Rome.

When Wolsey acted, then, it was in the manner in which he thought Rome might act. As Legate he paid no more attention to the betterment

of the courts Christian than he did as Lord Chancellor to the reform of
the courts of the common law. His answer in dealing with both courts
was the same: he ignored existing courts, with all their ancient dignities
and prerogatives, and created a system of his own. As Lord Chancellor
he sat like Solomon on the bench of equity and, without any noticeable
knowledge of his limitations, decided out of hand and with a godly nod
every contention that his fellows brought or fetched before him. As Legate he created legatine courts that superseded in authority the other
courts of the Church, and he had brought before these courts, which is
to say before himself, whatever matter might trouble the heart or the
conscience or whatever trifle—yea, even the fall of the sparrow—that
might need the Lord's attention.

For a well-groomed tyrant he showed astonishing streaks of leniency, especially when his legatine courts dealt with heresy. During the
dozen years when he controlled the religious jurisdiction of the kingdom,
not one heretic was consigned to the flames. This is a fact all the more
remarkable when one considers that his methods in every department
of his activity were haughty and harsh and that he could, with public
sanction and in the best tradition, have burned as many English heretics
as he pleased. He did not change the courts or the practice which made
this punishment possible; before the rise of his own power heretics had
been condemned by the ecclesiastical courts and burned by the State;
and after his fall the practice was punctually renewed and continued.
The whole system of courts and procedures which made the burning of
heretics customary the Legate blithely ignored.

Being apparently ignorant of the intensity of conviction that makes
men concern themselves with heresy, the Cardinal caused to be dismissed or let off with light ecclesiastical punishment those who were
dragged before his legatine courts for this offense. He seemed confused
rather than concerned. Toward the end of his days of power members
of the college he had founded at Oxford were accused. One of them, a
man named Taverner, the organist of the church there, was arrested.

He was brought before Wolsey and charged with having hidden heretical books "under the boards in his school." It was a serious charge, all the more so because books were involved. But, as Godwin concludes the incident, "the Cardinal for his music excused him, saying, that he was but a Musician and so he escaped."

The power Wolsey exercised in his effort to reform the Church had Rome as its source. Here lay, in the long run, Wolsey's greatest disservice. He made Rome more and more distasteful to the English clergy as well as to a laity restive for freedom and feeling in its bones the stirring of nationhood. By bringing Rome to London and by making the power of Rome, once comfortably distant and ineffective by inconvenience, ubiquitous in the realm of the King, he held back the cause of reform until it could be achieved only by parliamentary action and royal violence.

Wolsey was, as Pollard phrases it, more papal than the Pope. And the plaintive and futile ambition he nurtured and pursued to become Pope was only a logical extension of his papal addiction and his subservient attitude toward reform by authority, showing both his faith in the power of the Pope and the power of himself and his boundless confidence in what might be achieved if the two could be conjoined.

He made two full-throated efforts to gain the papacy, each of which failed lamentably. The first was upon the death of Leo X, which occurred December 2, 1521. Thirty-nine cardinals assembled with due ceremony in the solemn conclave to select his successor. No communication was allowed between the penned cardinals and the outside world. Their food was passed through the walls "at a round turning wheel made in the wall." After a few days their dishes were "restricted to one kind of meat, with the prospect of further diminution if they failed to agree within a reasonable time." On the sixth day the food was diminished, though one sickly cardinal had been carried out almost dead from the conclave.

Meanwhile the Roman populace milled around the closely guarded quarters of the cardinals' convention or hung on tenterhooks for such news as might escape. Public interest in learning the name of the new pope was not altogether prompted by piety. It was a quaint custom that the cardinal chosen should have his house ransacked and pillaged before he could return to it, "an offense tolerated and overlooked in the general joy and license of the election."[20] Speculations had been rife long before the conclave commenced, and one of the men considered likely to succeed was Cardinal Farnese, a Roman, and one of the wealthiest and most influential of the cardinals. There were clamorous maneuverings in his behalf, and at one moment it appeared that he had triumphed, for a cardinal supporter cried out, *"Papam habemus!"* Those who opposed his election called for a test of the acclamation, and when a scrutiny was taken it was found that he had failed. But news of the first cry had crept through the guardians of secrecy surrounding the conclave. It was a sign for an attack on the house of Cardinal Farnese, which was duly plundered before the correct news could be spread abroad.

Fourteen disorderly days passed before the deadlock ended. When it had become likely that none of the sturdy contenders would draw enough votes in any scrutiny, a distant pedant, scarcely known and hence highly respected, was put forth. In the last scrutiny the choice fell on this man, Cardinal Tortosa, a Fleming, formerly the tutor of Emperor Charles V. No one in Christendom could have cared less for the papacy than the man who took the title of Adrian VI. He did not refuse it, but he accepted it with reluctance and announced that when he came to Rome he would rid the papal court of corruption.

In the bitter contest which thrust the tiara on the learned and unwilling head of Adrian VI, the Cardinal of York got only seven votes in one scrutiny. So ordinary accounts report the matter. He had been told by his agent in Rome that he had received votes in three scrutinies and that at one time the count had reached as high as nineteen votes. In any case and by either report he had not been elected any more than Cardinal Farnese.

Fortunately for Wolsey's aspirations, the pathetic tenure of Adrian

VI lasted only eighteen months before death released the new pontiff and Rome from their joint miseries and earned him the epitaph: "Here lies Adrian VI, whose greatest misfortune was that he became Pope." He was elected in January of 1522 and did not reach the Holy City until August. Meanwhile the hangers-on had cleared out, among them four thousand papal officials and servants. "The Florentine traders who had swarmed into the city at Leo's accession packed and vanished. Commercial life languished, rents fell, banks closed. The artists migrated."

Adrian's arrival did nothing to allay the worst expectations of Rome. He proposed to abandon the great papal quarters in the Vatican and rent a small house. When he was finally persuaded to move into the Pope's palace, "he took up his quarters in a remote wing . . . His predecessor had kept a hundred grooms; he reduced them to four . . . He lived, not merely in retirement, but in hiding, inaccessible and almost undiscoverable among his books." It was the beginning of a strange interlude in the history of the papacy. "All Rome is horrified," wrote the Venetian ambassador, "at what the Pope has accomplished in one short week."[21]

His death brought not only relief to the Roman populace but also determination that another non-Italian must not ascend the chair of St. Peter. The inhabitants had foreseen clearly the mistake, and after the election of Adrian they had greeted the cardinals as they were leaving their unhappy conclave with "screams, whistling, and shouts of derision." So great had been the disappointment of the populace in the election of an outlander, a barbarian from beyond the mountains, that the lives of the offending cardinals had been in danger.

Plainly the cardinals of Rome would not at this stage accept another barbarian. Wolsey's hope, however, was such that it could not be deterred by precedent or by the ugly facts of the past. England had not had a Pope in Rome since the days of Nicholas Breakspear, who had ruled as Adrian IV in 1154. He had been English by birth, but he had spent only his boyhood in his native country, and his election had taken place before national rivalries had entered into the papal elections. Nor had this earlier Adrian's rule in Rome been much happier than the Adrian's just dead.

Steadfastly ignoring all these difficulties, Wolsey resolved to try again and began to lay his plans with his usual devious elaborateness. He was at The More, one of his great houses, when word of Adrian's death came. He wrote at once to the King, who was then at Woodstock, to announce the news and to say that, while he would rather continue in the King's service "than to be ten popes" and that he felt "unmeet and unable to so high and great a dignity," nevertheless he supposed that the King persisted in the same mind and intent as he had shown before. He notified the King that, on the basis of this assumption, he would draw up papers to be sent to his agent in Rome as before and that he would have these papers in the King's hands by the next post. In the same letter he points out that of course the King's interests will well be served if he goes to Rome.

My lord Cardinal and Legate followed through the next day, relieving the King of any onerous chore in connection with the representations to Rome. He had drawn up for him a letter to the Emperor. As he puts it, it was "a familiar letter in the King's name to the Emperor." The letter is already phrased to suit the purpose, but Wolsey expressed the hope that "it may please your Highness to take the pain for to write it with your own hand, putting thereunto your secret sign and mark . . ."

The letter from the King and in the King's own hand was designed to remind the Emperor of an earlier promise he had made to the King and the Cardinal that he would promote Wolsey's candidacy with all the imperial influence at Rome. Long after the election was over, the Emperor replied with apologies and excuses but in a tone most cordial and with every assurance that he had complied, saying "that you may be aware with what zeal and diligence we have taken up this affair in favor of the said lord Legate, we send you copies of our letters in his behalf, directed to the Duke of Sessa, our ambassador at Rome, written before the receipt of yours, as well as others afterwards sent to the Sacred College."[22]

It developed later that the Emperor had in fact written the letter to Sessa in Wolsey's behalf but that he had also taken the precaution of ordering the courier who took the dispatch to be detained, so that he reached Rome long after the election was over.

Meanwhile the Sacred College met and made its choice. The bitterness of feeling among the cardinals was as great as it had been in the previous election, when the Spanish ambassador had written to his master: "There cannot be so much hatred and so many devils in hell as among the cardinals."[23] A rumor spread that arms had actually been hidden in the conclave. A search was made, then the doors were walled up and the windows locked. For eight days there was no result and no prospect of a decision, though all indications pointed to the choice of Giulio de' Medici. Although a bastard, his name carried the weight of a great house. And he was an Italian. Then on the ninth day three French cardinals turned up, much to the consternation of the Romans. They presented themselves at the doors of the conclave in short coats, which, as Clerk writes to Wolsey, were considered very dissolute; and they came also in boots and spurs. One French cardinal wore a hat with feathers. The French were admitted amid laughter for their attire, and the conclave, after this high diversion and interruption, settled back into quarrelsome tedium that promised never to end.

Wolsey's agents waited anxiously and hopefully that the deadlock within might thrust their candidate into the papacy. It was not until the fiftieth day that the choice that had been anticipated all along was made. The Sacred College had chosen Giulio de' Medici who was to take the papal chair under the name of Clement VII. And in all the scrutinies that had taken place during those interminable fifty days my lord Cardinal and Legate had not received a single vote.

It would have seemed to be enough to crush ambition. But Wolsey kept his ignored hopes alive, always ready to thrust them forward and test them again by means of the apparatus of bribery and intrigue which he kept ready. Wolsey's obsessive effort to attain the papacy, an effort that never reckoned with the certainty of defeat or blushed after failure, went beyond the mere desire for high office. It revealed the defiant insecurity of his nature and his need as an Ipswich yokel to be constantly reassured and propped. He sought always the extension of personal authority, and he rested his claims on the good he could do the kingdom and the Church and by inference the human race if he were but vouchsafed the power.

It can be judged how he regarded himself when one notes the playacting he did whenever he received a fresh legatine commission from the Pope. He would absent himself from court, and then, having passed around the stage and changed his costume, so to say, he would reappear and be received in state as though he were really an ambassador fresh from Rome.[24] By such posturing of his soul he lived, wrapping his nakedness in rich symbols, masquerading among the lords towering above the clergy. If he could not be Pope at Rome he would be Pope at home.

CHAPTER
XI

There was a corner in the capacious mind of Thomas Wolsey which was occupied by intellectual concerns. In this corner he acted not as Lord Chancellor or Cardinal or Legate but as one possessed of ideas, as a man named Wolsey and not as His Eminence. His lively and perceptive approach to the processes of education will bear the most critical examination. There were sober moments, hard come by, when he seemed to escape his showy public character and address himself to the inner spirit of his fellows and to consider well the means by which curiosity could be touched off and the pursuit of wisdom commenced. In these moments he was generations ahead of the prevailing views of his day and so far removed from the turgid presumptions of his official personality that something or someone hitherto unrecognized might be speaking through him. It is not without significance that the only book he wrote was an instructive essay on education. In this field his mind was often clean, unhampered by conceits, direct in its effort, free of irritations of insecurity that kept him driving and grasping for power.

Wolsey had even in his early days at the court a name to be noted in the field of education, and the deference shown him did not come wholly from his alma mater. In 1514, while he was yet only Bishop of Lincoln and not yet Archbishop of York, though a rising young man and obviously of great organizing talent, Cambridge University asked him to become its chancellor. Wolsey declined. The excuse he made to the delegation that brought him the invitation was "the multiplicity of public affairs wherewith he was taken up." He does say, however, that he is sensible of the honor conferred and that he will make it "his endeavor to show his gratitude by doing the University in general, and the several members of it, the best services in his power."[1]

That he was not without some use to Cambridge may be seen by the fact that that university later notified him by letter that because of the many favors he had conferred upon them they proposed "to appoint yearly and perpetual obsequies to be performed for him, which would be celebrated by all graduates with the greatest solemnity, and with every proper mark of honor, piety or religion . . ."[2] His own university doubled the deference Cambridge paid. It decreed in June 1515 that "all public preachers should pray openly for the good estate of the Archbishop of York, and after his death for his soul."[3]

Three years later Oxford University solemnly turned over to him its statutes and gave him a free hand in revising them. The surrender of the statutes into the hands of the Cardinal followed a state visit to Oxford in May 1518, when he accompanied the King and Queen on their progress to Abingdon. The Cardinal made a speech in which he declared how much he had the interests of the university at heart. He announced at the time that he proposed to found certain lectures, and out of the largeness of his heart he offered to "be intrusted with the care of reducing their statutes to some better form and order."[4]

The task of working some order out of the chaos of the statutes— "which were not only in much confusion, but in certain cases evidently repugnant to one another"—had been committed to other persons. However, the Cardinal said he would be glad to take the job in hand himself. His proposal met with solemn glee among the assembled officials, and word was at once dispatched to Archbishop Warham, who was chancellor of the university, to acquaint him with the beneficence of the Cardinal's mind and heart.

Warham was decidedly less enthusiastic than the officials. He made bold to say that if the authority of such statutes should devolve upon any persons besides those who were vested with it, "the University, considered as a society, would be dissolved: a mere empty name or shadow of power would only remain to it, and the authority which it formerly exercised wholly terminate in the person to whom you may desire it may be transferred." Such was his judgment of the Cardinal's brash proposal and its placid acceptance by the university. He went on to say that it would be well to have the Cardinal's sentiments on the statutes and find out in what respects he would have them altered. These views could in due course be considered by, and decided by, the university.

Active administrators of the university took a different view, and Warham was "at last prevailed upon by their repeated instances and representations to depart from his former opinion." It came about shortly after that the university in full convocation passed "an ample and solemn decree" that the statutes be put into the hands of the Cardinal "to be corrected, reformed, changed, or expunged, as he in his discretion should think proper." All the rights, liberties, and privileges of the university—the rights and privileges of the separate colleges being sternly excepted, of course—were turned over wholly to Wolsey;

"and he had full power of methodizing the public discipline, or of alter-
ing it, after what manner he judged most convenient."[5]

After the excitement of the decree was over, the Cardinal had in
his lap another burdensome duty. This he accepted with his customary
blithe disregard for the fact that he might never get around to the actual
work. He was more interested in the corporate confidence conveyed than
he was in the messy details of shaking down a wild mass of regulations
designed to pull together an institution whose very genius lay in the
fact that it was informal, casual, and amorphous. There is no sign that
he ever reformed Oxford any more than he reformed the Church, but he
added the honor of the request to his varied assortment of honors. And,
on a practical basis, the request put him constantly in mind of the university, its corporate existence being now at his discretion, and he was
inclined to bestow upon it favors and benefits which might not have
crossed his thoughts if he had not been so officially cast into the role of its
benefactor and proctor-at-large.

These favors were many and consistent and, seeing the sad state of
Oxford and of education in that day, not without some sharp value on
the whole course of education in England. Wolsey's strategy was to
secure the university against the town of Oxford and to gain for it exemption from taxes which the King visited upon his realm. He had
gained for the university an exemption from the general tax levied for
the support of the war against France in 1513. The custom of exempting
the university from contributing to public wars the Cardinal had insisted upon to the King "as a matter of academical right."[6] The immunity was granted, and it was again granted when revenues were
sought for a further war against France in 1522. The town of Oxford
paid a subsidy but the university did not, and Wolsey was the instrument of the immunity.

If the university was exempt from the support of public wars, it
was greatly aided in its unending private war with the town. The ar-

senal provided was a royal decree of unusual privileges. Wood, historian of early Oxford, reports that in 1523 "the King, at the influence of the noble cardinal, granted a large charter of liberties to the University."[7] It was part of the Cardinal's attempt to make the university "the most glorious in the learned universe." Wolsey caused the charter to be carried to the university by a special deputation. The deputation might well have been accompanied by the King's guard, for when the charter was promulgated, the townsmen were so incensed that they refused to submit to it. "Upon which account it was remitted to the King and proposed to be considered in Council."

In due course the charter was put in force. The mayor was obliged to take an oath at St. Mary's Church "to maintain the privileges and customs of the university." The charter did more, as Boase describes it, "than merely extend the powers of the chancellor and scholars, for it virtually placed the greater part of the city under their mercy."[8]

Despite its ample provisions, the charter did not cover all contingencies, and there was a spirited correspondence between the university and the Cardinal over details, quite as if he had nothing to bother about but the practical problems of Oxford. One letter touches on a matter full serious, for it tells of a pestilential distemper which had raged for months. The same distemper broke out again the next year and was so severe that many students had to retire from the university. The officials represent the colleges as reduced to a "most deplorable and disconsolate condition." There were various causes assigned to the pestilence. Wood notes that the contagion might have come from the fact that a vast concourse of students in a place "wanting both wholesome and convenient apartments" made the colleges like a city under siege. But the officials attributed the disease and its recurrence to the stagnation of waters in the adjacent fens, "and the noisome smells arising from them, occasioned by the want of a free current of water in the Thames, which their jurisdiction did not extend to open."[9] Wood claims that through the negligence of the citizens, the channel of the Cherwell and other currents near the university were choked with filth and dirt, which "occasioned a putrid and malignant air, replete with noxious vapors." More, the frequent floods overflowed the neighboring plains and "spread a slimy and vicious matter upon them, which, there being nothing to carry it off, did necessarily putrify and corrupt." The officials of the university prayed Wolsey, in this case as Lord Chancellor and an arm of the King, to help with some speedy remedy.

It was well that the higher learning had a friend at court, for the problems of both universities at this time were acute. Unsavory weather and noxious vapors had long been a feature of Oxford and its environs, and pestilence a tiger at the gates. Now there was another and more disturbing kind of distemper, and its symptoms were a falling off in the number of students who entered the colleges and a marked decline in public esteem. There was a crisis in education, and the nation, with its increased need of leadership and skills in government and commerce, might suffer if the crisis were not met. In 1523 the University of Oxford sent a jeremiad to Sir Thomas More to the effect that abbots had ceased to send their monks to the schools, nobles their sons, and clergy their parishioners. The halls were falling into ruin, the complaint ran, and only the endowed colleges showed any sign of prosperity.

The Oxford figures must be considered in the light of similarly pathetic conditions at Cambridge. Some years before, St. John Fisher as chancellor there had said: "Somehow, I know not how, whether it were continual strifes with the townsmen . . . or the long abiding of the fever . . . that carried off many of our learned men—or that there were few or no helpers and patrons of letters—whatever were the true causes, doubtless there had stolen over well-nigh all of us a weariness of learning and of study, so that not a few did take counsel in their own minds how they might get away from the university."[10]

In such a time and as matters stood, the universities needed staunch patrons of letters, advocates in high places who could by their influence help dispel the general contempt for education that had descended upon the public mind. Part of this contempt was traditional and of long standing. Richard Pace records a dinner incident that reveals the lingering attitude toward education among a certain segment of the population:

> There happened to be present one of those whom we call gentlemen . . . and who always carry some horn hanging at their backs as though they would hunt during dinner. He, hearing letters praised, roused with sudden anger, burst out furiously with these words: "Why do you talk nonsense, friend?" he said. "A curse on those stupid letters! All learned men are beggars: even Erasmus, the most learned of all, is a beggar (as I hear) and in a certain letter of his complains that he cannot shake poverty off his shoulders . . . I swear by God's body I'd rather that my son should hang than study letters. For it becomes the sons of gentlemen to blow the horn nicely . . . to hunt skillfully, and elegantly carry and train a hawk. But the study of letters should be left to the sons of rustics."[11]

Changes wrought by such new forces as the spread of the printed word affected public attitudes and made the old monkish learning of schools and universities seem irrelevant to modern needs. "It was," says Abram, "an epoch of commercial and industrial expansion, and a passion for trade seized upon the nation."[12] Among the middle and lower classes, from whose ranks most of the students seem to have come, the desire was for "knowledge which would help them in their business life." The curricula of the universities did not meet the changing needs of the day, and the most eloquent statement of this fact and the most clear cut criticism of the universities lay in the fact of public neglect.

Another suspicion loomed, too, at this time; a suspicion that the universities were changing and not necessarily for the better. Idea were gathered for the convenience of public gossip into a bundle called the New Learning. The term was, and is, an abstraction, the meaning of which has changed with each use of it, but in general it then designated views and impressions gained from Greek writers rather than Roman. These views were perforce less influenced by the Church and more concerned with the development of the individual and society through human energy than through divine guidance. Those who held or even entertained these views came to believe, unless watched and corrected, that man might advance his station and improve his society without the aid of priests or the instruments of the Christian religion as organized in the Church.

There had been for a long time some dalliance with the materials of the New Learning, but interest came during this period more definitely into the open. In 1516 Bishop Fisher of Rochester arranged for Erasmus to deliver a series of lectures on Greek at Cambridge. These seem to have excited nothing approaching tumult, for Erasmus grumbled not only about the low fees he got but also about "the poor attendance and inattention of the students, and the general lack of appreciation of his merits." In the same year, the statutes of Corpus Christi at Oxford provided that a public lecturer in Greek be among its principal officers.

To this overt change in the classics of education, in the way education had been formally and officially conducted, instant opposition arose, especially since the New Learning as taught at Corpus Christi found friends and enthusiasts among the students and spread a contagion of ideas as marked and noticeable as the pestilence that beset the university. Fox stood before the public as a man of pious bent and not to be blamed for self-seeking, having retired from the court to give the last years of his life to godliness and learning. He had spoken of "souls whereof I never see the bodies," and he had resolved that he would minister to individuals as well as preside over a vast diocese. There could be no suspicion, then, of Corpus Christi as arising out of alien or subversive sources. It was a sound place as far as auspices went. Yet there was no doubt that the establishment of a college with a body of teaching that revolved around Greek influence would stir men to questions.

In the midst of these doubts, and seeing the low estate to which education had fallen in the realm, Wolsey turned aside from his duties as Lord Chancellor and Legate and came forward as a patron of letters. His motives may have differed from act to act in the several moves he made, and no doubt these motives were at all times mixed. But at any rate he threw the weight of his public dignity and influence on the side of education and the New Learning. He provided at no expense to the university a foundation which should carry seven new lectureships. One was in Greek. And while he intended that these lectureships should in due time become the basis of a college he proposed to establish at Oxford, he instructed that they be read meanwhile in the halls of Corpus Christi College.

The continued attention to Greek was a signal for further commotion, which it took the weight of both the Cardinal and the King to still. Scholars at the university, "either in contempt of the literature of the Greeks . . . or out of idleness and a false taste for vain and trifling amusements," had formed a body known as the Trojans. The captain of the Trojans assumed the name of Priam, the second in command the name of Hector, the third Paris. The purpose was to "outbrave and ridicule those who addicted themselves to the study of Greek." It came about that one who knew Greek or employed his time in learning it "was not free at home or abroad from the insults and raillery of the adverse party, but was marked out, by one appointed signal or other, for the subject of their diversion."

Nor had the students been content with "wordy warfare." They had come "to open and public insult." The Trojans not only treated the Greeks "with opprobrious language but assaulted them in their persons."[13] Such incidents showed the way things might drift at Oxford and made it all the more important that the Cardinal continue his intervention on the side of enlightenment.

This he did in his usual way—by the use of authority from a high place. The King sent down a message to suggest that the students "would do well to devote themselves with energy and spirit to the study of Greek literature." In this way, as Erasmus puts it, "silence was imposed on these brawlers." By the open encouragement of Greek and by discountenancing the opposition, Wolsey had done much to promote the progress of the Greek tongue throughout the university. Soon after these events Greek was much encouraged in Cambridge, and the whole tapestry of the New Learning began gradually to be hung before the people.

In all his blandishments up to now, even to the founding of seven lectureships, the Cardinal had dealt with Oxford University as a unit. Yet he knew from his own experience at Magdalen that the university was at best a loose confederacy and that the real power lay in the several colleges. Each college was a separate entity with immutable prerogatives. A college owned its own property, managed its own affairs, set up its own program of instruction, and in general asserted itself as independent of the machinations of any higher body, such as the university, that might attempt control. To those who could read the map of learning, Oxford in essence meant *college* and not *university*. And if my lord Cardinal was to have an essential part in that center of enlightenment, he must add to the cluster of colleges one of his own. In this way he could have some substantial say in what was taught, selecting the subjects and the teachers and modulating the emphases the way he chose—at least, at the outset, and before the Fellows fiercely took control in the way of Oxford Fellows.

In a word, when Wolsey moved to found a college at Oxford he began to step out of the role of a contented patron of learning acting at a distance and signified that he wanted to have some direct part in the processes of education. Wolsey had seen Magdalen completed, seen the fruits of a founder's beneficence ripen into tangible beauty and useful substance. In a college ideas and stones could be joined, each rendering homage to the other. He could house learning, give it a better residence than it had ever had before because he knew, among many other matters, how to build. And seeing that my lord Cardinal was in other particulars not without envy, it must be said that the recent example of Bishop Fox, his early benefactor and discoverer, in building so successfully the College of Corpus Christi had a plausible bearing on his motives. For if a bishop could found and build a college that excited the whole university with sparks of new learning, what might not an archbishop and cardinal do?

Convenient to the Cardinal's purpose, there lay near the town of Oxford an ancient monastery of Austin Canons known roundabout as St. Frideswide's. Venerable in the countryside for services once rendered, it was now in a fortunate state of decay. It would make an excellent site for a college, for, while it was withdrawn from the other colleges which stood for the most part along the High Street of the town, it commanded a clear view of those colleges, and from the pinched windows of its cells the monks could look out across the meadows to the Tower of Magdalen. Its church might make an acceptable college chapel, and to the north lay enough solid land to afford a gracious spot for a stately dining hall and a magnificent quadrangle in thoughtful stone.

Early in 1524 Wolsey's agent in Rome wrote that he was "almost at a point with the pope about Wolsey's matters." Clement VII was "contented to confirm the legateship with all faculties for life, which was never heard before."[14] More to the point of the Cardinal's activities as educator, the agent wrote good news about the monastery which he would make into a college. Wolsey had sought its dissolution, and with the right to apply to his proposed college not only the property but any tangible proceeds that might result from the appropriation of its lands. Rome had been informed that the need for increased facilities for study was most pressing in England and that Oxford University "seemed likely to come to an end by reason of its slender revenues." The Pope had been persuaded to this effect, and the same letter which conveyed the intelligence that Clement would grant the legateship for life stated that "the ordering of Frideswide's in Oxford is also at Wolsey's pleasure."[15]

With the proceeds of St. Frideswide's and other monasteries which he had dissolved or had brought within the reach of his legatine arm, Wolsey was ready to set up his college at Oxford and to lay elaborate plans for the school to be founded at Ipswich. In attending the details of the dissolutions allowed, Wolsey showed his usual vigor and acted with a characteristically personal touch: instead of establishing a foundation or corporation for the receipt of the lands of the suppressed religious houses, he had instructed that the deeds be drawn to himself. These deeds "granted the lands to him and his heirs in fee simple forever, and no 'trust' or 'use' was expressed therein."[16] Wolsey would see to it that he owned every stick and stone of his colleges, just as much as he owned Hampton Court, York Place, and The More. These places would be residences for his person; his colleges would be residences for his ideas.

The Cardinal could do nothing, not even build a house of ideas, without trumpets. There were so many preliminaries and orations in connection with the beginning of the college that the marvel is he ever got beyond the stage of public talk. He sent the Bishop of London to Oxford in the quality of the Cardinal's orator to announce that he was ready to go ahead with the building of his college and to state that he hoped it would make Oxford "the most celebrated and flourishing seminary of learning in the whole world." The orator was further instructed to say that Wolsey promised to bring the King and Queen to Oxford about the beginning of Lent and at that time there would be further orations and entertainments fitting to the occasion and the founding of the college.

Preparations for the royal visit were busily set in motion, and it was considered what orations should be spoken and what exercises should be performed. But after all the arrangements had been made, and at not a little expense, and after particular attention had been paid to acts which might venerate the Cardinal, another pestilence struck, "which occasioned both the Court and the Members of the University to withdraw."[17] It was a frustrating experience, for no detail of preparation had been spared. To make a good appearance for the royal and legatine visit, orders had been issued for all the students who were absent in the country to hasten back and take up residence.

The vast ceremonies postponed by the pestilence never took place. Not long afterwards, however, the Bishop of London returned to Oxford. This time he came not as an orator but as an executioner, for he was empowered to eject the monks of St. Frideswide's, "that room might be made for introducing the scholars and lecturers of the Cardinal's Foundation, so that they might form a regular and independent body, whereas they had lived dispersed before in several halls and colleges." The foundation stone for the Cardinal's college was laid July 15, 1525. For one fortnight the Cardinal's accounts show that the numbers employed on construction included 122 freemasons, 25 handhewers, 47 roughlayers, 32 carpenters, 12 sawyers, and 228 laborers.[18]

In the bull granting the Legate powers to dissolve the Priory of St. Frideswide's and in the King's patent confirming to the Cardinal the powers of that bull, the new foundation was to be called The College of Secular Priests. Indeed this name was one expressed condition of the grant of the lands and properties of the priory. But in some way not clear to historians and easily speculated on in the light of Wolsey's general tendency to draw all things around him like his robes, the name was authorized "by other powers from the king" to be changed from The College of Secular Priests to Cardinal College.

The new name had the advantage of being an honest description. Nearly every stone of the handsome halls Wolsey caused to be emblazoned with his Cardinal's arms. The design showed his grandeur as a builder. The spacious dining hall revealed his interest in talk as a method of education. The statutes which he sent down to Oxford under his hand and seal described with minute foresight how the scheme was to be worked out. There were to be two hundred scholars, and there must also be an elaborate superstructure of functionaries to give the college a magnificence others did not have. There were to be a dean and sub-dean, threescore canons of the first rank and forty of the second. There were to be no fewer than thirteen chaplains, twelve clerks, and sixteen choristers. Lecturers were happily not overlooked in the design, but the statutes go on to specify that there be four "censors of manners and examiners of the proficiency of the students." There were to be three treasurers—a stipulation indicating Wolsey's own background as well as his views of money and its importance—four stewards, and twenty "inferior servants." Out of the funds there was also provision made "for the entertainment of strangers, the relief of the poor, and the keeping of horses for college business."[19]

No wonder the officials of the university wrote Wolsey to say that they rejoiced that "your lordship's erudition is equal to your great dignities" and to add: "We no longer consider your new society as an additional college to other colleges but as a University super-added to a University." It is, they add, "as if Oxford, by such an extraordinary accession to it, were really founded anew . . ."

Such prose in praise of the founder's beneficence—a founder to whom letters began "To the Right Reverend Father in God, and my very singular good Lord my Lord Cardinal of York, and Legate a Latere" and ended "at your Grace's Commandment"—might well have lulled Wolsey into complacency; and the dazzling deference paid him by Oxford and Cambridge could well have blinded him to the genuine concerns of education. Yet the record shows that his interests went beyond staff and real estate. Bishop Fox said of him that he "gathered together into that college whatsoever thing there was in the whole realm

—all such men as were found to excel in any kind of learning and knowledge."

In his search for teaching talent Wolsey turned even to "the other University." Some of his best men came from Cambridge, bringing with them ideas deeply tinged with Lutheranism. The results in some cases were not happy and confirmed the public suspicion of the dangers inherent in education. Unmindful of the criticism engendered by his choices, the Cardinal continued to search for scholars who would promote the spread of enlightenment. "On native scholars he heaped preferment, and the most eminent foreigners were invited by him to teach in the universities."[20]

His interest in teaching materials was no less personal or persistent. His agents posted at foreign courts were instructed to keep their unofficial eyes open for valuable manuscripts that could be borrowed for purposes of transcription. The same agent in Rome who was busy enlisting the necessary bulls for the suppression of the monasteries which would pay for Cardinal College was told to order copies made of Greek manuscripts in Italian libraries. Wolsey asked a Venetian envoy to ask the head of the Venetian Republic for "transcripts, for the college library, of the Greek manuscripts which had belonged to Cardinals Grimani and Bessarion."[21] One of his plans was to furnish the library of his college with the learning and curiosities of the Vatican, "and to have the Pope's manuscripts transcribed for that purpose." The Cardinal was never too busy in his official duties to use his position for the advancement of his project at Oxford or to beg from any source fresh materials that would fill the place with the spirit of the New Learning. To make sure of his purpose, "the great writers of antiquity were to be expounded daily and all conversation conducted in either Latin or Greek." Erasmus wrote: "Whoever was distinguished by any art or science paid court to the Cardinal and none paid court in vain."[22]

The best glimpses of the man beneath the red hat are to be seen, not in connection with Cardinal College at Oxford, but in the founding and attention Wolsey gave to his preparatory school, named the College of St. Mary, at Ipswich. Here boys would be properly started on the road to learning. The spirit of inquiry might be touched and the inner life quickened early so that time would not be lost but could be improved when the young scholar reached Cardinal College. And in his plans for arrangements for the educational care of tender youth, Wolsey showed his perception of education at its best.

The emphasis brought by the Ipswich school was sorely needed. The new quests which had begun to animate university education had not yet touched the lower schools. In these dismal places instruction often went forward by brutal rote and routine, the aim being to beat into the boy as many rules of grammar and as many submissive attitudes as possible in a given time. And the time given was often long. One boy at Winchester College wrote that he rose at five, "and after prayers at six, devoted himself to writing Latin verses with his fellow pupils, each one of them 'chained as closely to his desk as Prometheus to the crag on Caucasus.'"[23]

The headmasters of some of the schools were of course occasionally men of learning and of a sincere bent toward learning. But the status of the teacher was low and he enjoyed little esteem, as one Cambridge student revealed when he said to Erasmus: "Who would be a schoolmaster that could live in any other way?" The approach to lower education was, it appears, strictly in terms of conveying a given body of facts and rules to unreceptive minds. This approach made for dullness on the part of both the teacher and the pupil. Learning in school held a kind of physical terror, no doubt in part due to the fact that the dullness had to be relieved somehow. Thus the "best schoolmaster was held to be 'the greatest beater.'"

The observer from abroad saw the system with more sensitiveness and wrote of it sharply. Erasmus looked upon the schoolmasters he had seen as "a race of men most miserable, who grow old in penury and filth in their schools—schools, did I say? prisons, dungeons, I should have said—among their boys, deafened with din, poisoned by a foetid atmosphere, but, thanks to their folly, fully self-satisfied, so long as they can bawl and shout to their terrified boys, and box, and beat, and flog them, and so indulge in all kinds of ways their cruel disposition."[24] He tells of one cleric in charge of a school who would have nothing but flogging masters. Once when Erasmus was present at a meal the master called out a lad of about ten who had just come to the school from his mother, who had especially commended the boy to the master. "But he at once began to charge the boy with unruliness, since he could think of nothing else, and must find something to flog him for, and made signs to the proper official to flog him. Whereupon the poor boy was forthwith floored then and there, flogged as though he had committed sacrilege. The divine again and again interposed 'That will do—that will do'; but the inexorable executioner continued his cruelty till the boy almost fainted. By and by the divine turned round to me and said, 'He did nothing to deserve it, but the boys' spirits must be subdued!'"[25]

The degree of brutality exercised varied with the temperament of those who wielded the rod and doubtless with the circumstance and provocation. But the point to note is that flogging grew normally out of the dreary practices of the schools and the attitudes of the officials. It might or might not take place in the extreme degree which Erasmus describes, but it was always implicit in an approach to education which was essentially punitive. The child was severely threatened with learning and at the same time threatened with the consequences of not learning.

In beneficent contrast, Wolsey set forth the postulates and principles he wanted observed in his school at Ipswich. These he embodied in his only book. Vocal above his contemporaries, a man of many remarks, who met every crisis with a spate of words, nonetheless he had found no occasion to form his ideas into a system, this being the function of a book. His words were mortgaged to his business. But when it came to his views on education, only a book would suffice. Entitled *Rudimenta Grammatices*, it was published with the usual trumpets to herald the

Cardinal's greatness. Its title page bore his hat and arms and his motto, *Dominus mihi adjutor,* which, being interpreted, means, "God my helper"; or being interpreted by some could mean, "God my assistant." There is a blubbering and fulsome Latin poem which extols the virtues of Thomas, the Cardinal, Our President, and voices the sempiternal gratitude of the scholars in terms of almost Oxonian deference. The preface is itself a brew of sentiments calculated for the palate of public esteem: "None, I apprehend, can be ignorant how earnestly, how zealously, and how assiduously we have directed our labours to the point of the good of our country, and of our countrymen, and not to that of our private concerns. In this single respect, we shall think ourselves to have reaped the fairest harvest of piety, if, through the blessing of God we shall have improved the minds of our fellow citizens . . ."[26]

Once the turgid front matter of the book is overpassed, however, the content reveals the other Wolsey, known to few and scarcely known to himself. He has the grace to see and to say that the school he has founded at Ipswich and around which the whole book centers is "the highest and noblest testimony of our love to our country." He is willing to rest his case on this act and not on all his other assorted dignities. Then he gets down to the heart of the book, which is to provide a series of inspirational instructions to those who are to teach. He observes: "It avails little to have built a school, however magnificent it might be, unless it be furnished with skilful masters." It is upon the masters of the College of St. Mary that he lays the burden of his argument.

"We admonish particularly," he stresses, "that tender youth be not effected by severe stripes or threatening countenance or by any species of tyranny." Wolsey warns the master against overworking the pupil. "It will be best if the boy is led to regard the school as a place of pleasure, a literary playground." In all studies pleasure "should be so intermingled that the lad may think them a sport, not a labor." The pupils should not be "wearied by too long reading, nor exhausted by immoderate competition." Most remarkable of all is the allowance Wolsey makes for play, which he recognizes as important and not merely frivolous, seeing in it a way to relax the mind.

Wolsey laid down in delightful detail how the masters should undertake each of the subjects in the eight forms. They were to encourage in one form a "pleasing elocution," little attention having been paid to that matter in the schools. For another form the books, "if any," are specified. A further form is to read "Aesop, who is wittier? Terence, who is more useful?" The cardinal idea of the Cardinal all the way through his plans and instructions is to make reading a pleasure and to encourage intelligent training through contact with good authors. The master should use only those devices which arouse the student's interest in the writer.

Both the emphasis on the sharing of knowledge and the usefulness of learning indicate the fatherly interest Wolsey took in his school at Ipswich. He felt free to express and reveal his mind without validating his views to an academic hierarchy. The College of St. Mary was even more of a personal affair, as seems appropriate, to the man from Ipswich than Cardinal College was to the Cardinal of York. Here he would be a teacher, an intimate in the whole mysterious process of learning. Here he would not have to pose as a chancellor or legate while actually being a schoolmaster; he could be a schoolmaster forthrightly. There need be no role, no masquerade, no mumming. It was a comforting and sincere return to his first love, a love of learning, from which the whole journey of success had been a costly detour. His interests postponed and thwarted by a meddlesome destiny, he had at last come back to Ipswich with a mind aware of riches beyond the world of wealth and pomp.

Directions to parents were clear and simple. They were to provide the scholars with clothes for winter wear; ". . . also ye shall find him convenient books to his learning." Admission was based on ability and willingness to learn and not on social status: "If your child can read and write Latin and English sufficiently so that he be able to read and write

his own lessons then shall he be admitted into the school for a scholar."
If the child, after a reasonable season, "be found here unapt and unable
to learning, then ye, warned thereof, shall take him away."[27]

Rules and regulations, no matter how minute, were prepared by the
moving hand of Wolsey. No detail was too small to escape him, either in
building or operation of the school: "If your child be absent six days
and show not a reasonable cause such as sickness then his room is to be
void without he be admitted again and pay four pence. Also if he fall
thrice into absence he shall be admitted no more."

Wolsey had large plans and hopes as well as personal pride wrapped
up in his Ipswich project. His aim was to demonstrate the values of public education. He looked forward to "a great extension of local second-
ary schools, educating boys free of charge throughout an eight-year
classical course." He would see to it "that the very best in school and
university education, in the finest structural surroundings, should be
provided free of all charge for the sons of the people."[28] He would, with
the consent of the Holy See, convert the wealth and property of languish-
ing monasteries, which had served another day, into schools where
young men might be taught. It were better, as he had written to Warham, that children be brought up in learning than that a monastery be
maintained for doddering canons.

First, he had to dissolve the necessary number of monasteries—
eleven in all—to provide the money for a school which, of course, must
be grander than Eton. In particular he needed to take over a religious house
that would provide a proper site, as he had done at Oxford. Conveniently the Priory of St. Peter and St. Paul, hard by the parish Church of
St. Nicholas, where Thomas went to Mass as a boy, had sadly neglected
its educational obligations. There had been no schoolmaster at this
house of Augustinian canons in 1514 and again in 1526. The grounds
were surrounded by a substantial wall of red brick, not unlike the wall
that surrounded his beloved Hampton Court, and there was a priory
church, St. Peter's, which would serve handsomely as the chapel of the

new college. The Priory was surrendered March 6, 1527, and the parishioners of the adjoining church were left to seek their religious instruction elsewhere.

My lord Cardinal was now ready to build. He must consult with divers and sundry about materials and call upon any who might aid him, be they friend or foe. Even the Duke of Norfolk, who bore him no good will, wrote in March of 1528 to depose that he can save the Cardinal large sums of money on the building. Vast quantities of stone and oak would be needed to accomplish the ambitious designs. Wolsey had hoped to build with stone from Harwich Cliff. This meant negotiations with the Dowager Countess of Oxford to the end that he be allowed to take as much stone from her cliff at Harwich as he should need. The Countess demurred, and this consumed time and called for blandishments of charm and arguments. In the end the Countess reluctantly granted his wish, saying: "Be it hurtful or otherwise, Your Grace do your pleasure." Which he did. But the stone of Harwich was not enough, and the Cardinal had to turn next to the French King, with whom Henry was fortunately on good terms at the moment, and ask for stone from the quarries of Caen.

The gateways, one of them a miniature of his gate at York Place, could be of brick, but the college itself must have massive timbers as well as massive stone. And this requirement in turn called for giant oaks. Suffolk was at this time a place of oaks. Trees could be had right readily, but specifications had to be drawn and orders placed. How much detail this phase of the task alone required may be seen from a study of a paper that survives in the Record Office, giving the number of oaks to be felled, the location of the woods and their distance from Ipswich, as well as the names of the owners to whom payment should be made.

All phases of the undertaking had to be driven forward smoothly like six white horses. For speed was of the essence. There was something frantic about the way Wolsey rushed his school to completion. The foundation stone was laid June 15, 1528, but a letter dated January 26 of that year said that Wolsey had been building "some time since." Workmen labored night and day to get it ready for the opening in September 1528.

The man named dean of St. Mary's College was William Capon, a Cambridge man, who had founded a grammar school at Southampton. Whatever his other qualifications, he knew the founder's interests and kept in unceasing touch with the affairs of the college, both great and small, reporting them with due fidelity to Wolsey. He assures the Cardinal that he has received from Mr. Dawndy 171 tons of stone and that "within a fortnight next after Michelmas . . . we shall have 100 tons more," so that "your workmen will not be unoccupied for want of stone." The same reliable Mr. Dawndy also promised that before Easter next "we shall have here ready 1000 tons more of the said stone. And thus the holy trinity preserve your grace . . ."

He is no less meticulous in acknowledging gifts, including the receipt of nine bucks, one from His Grace's servant. And at the same time the Prior of Butley gave the dean a "fatte crane." Upon the advice of Wolsey's agents, one of them being Thomas Cromwell, who were visiting at Ipswich to see how the work progressed, ten shillings was given to the town fathers "to make merry"; and money was also conveyed to the bailiffs' wives and portmen's wives that they too might make merry.

There is no reliable evidence that the busy and preoccupied Cardinal ever visited the college he caused to be built in Ipswich, though he once spoke with modest satisfaction of the college as "not inelegant." There is much to show, however, that had the native returned, he would have been received on bended knee. In January of 1529 the master of the school wrote Wolsey a flowery letter to express the gratitude of the local people for the munificence of His Grace. An official letter signed by the bailiffs and the portmen put their sentiments firmly on record: ". . . we therefore shall daily humbly pray to God to send unto your Grace in this world Life, Honour, Prosperity and Health in Body, with the accomplishment of all your noble Acts, and in the Life to come the joys of Heaven . . ." The elder Wolsey, now dead these thirty-three years, must have smiled and turned over comfortably in his grave when these words were written.

Capon writes respectfully to say that it has been necessary to add a sexton to the staff and he hopes the Cardinal will approve, pointing out that the move was sanctioned by Mr. Cromwell when he looked the situation over. The Cardinal is given to understand that one man is not able to keep the church clean, ring the bells, prepare the altar lights, see all the ornaments well and sufficiently repaired, and "set forth every day all such things as is to be occupied about God's service." Hence the selection of the new sexton, who has been named "unto the time I know farther your Grace's pleasure." Capon further says that the number of priests needed to maintain the Masses specified in Wolsey's statutes to be said every day will also need to be increased.

The father's benediction and decision are sought on all matters both great and small. Wolsey must by his nature keep in such close touch with his colleges that he requires to be consulted on the addition of a new sexton. And he welcomes news that will give him a knowledge of how the enterprise is going as well as some picture of how it appears to operate. Capon tells him of plans to hold a procession on the eighth of September, which was Our Lady's Day. But the day "brought very foul weather and it rained sore continually, so that we could not go in procession through the town to Our Lady's Chapel according to our statute by your grace made, but we made as solemn a procession in your Grace's College Church as could be devised." He tells him also that the new copes, vestments, and altar cloths which Cromwell and his companions brought had been used on the occasion, and the whole spectacle had been seen by as many people as could stand in the churchyard.[29]

The hunger of the Cardinal for these details, snug though he was in his robes and palaces, shows the unaffected character of his interest. He who could manage the King's wars and browbeat the Pope must know down to the last detail, including the gift of a fat crane, what was going on in his colleges. And the hope for these colleges, based perhaps on a touching faith in their purpose, was to endure long after other hopes had vanished.

CHAPTER XII When Wolsey assembled workmen to build at Hampton Court Manor a habitation befitting his dignity, he caused fresh water for the palace to be brought from springs three miles distant in heavy conduits laid underneath the bodies of two rivers. And the system so fashioned continued to supply the needs of the palace for over three hundred and twenty-five years after his death.

The Cardinal had taken a page from the monks' books. Not uncommonly water was brought into towns from catchment areas by open channels called leats; not often by pipes. Wolsey would not, as many people did, drink the "diluted sewage" of the Thames. Spring water was collected in standpipes on Coombe Hill, then conveyed "in a double set of strong leaden pipes from Coombe to Surbiton, under the Hogsmill River (a small tributary of the Thames), and then under the Thames above Kingston Bridge, and so through the Home Park to the palace."[1] The leaden pipes, which were among the first molded in the north of England, were laid in lengths of twenty-five feet, joined with a heavy coating of lead at the joints. The diameter of each pipe was about two and a half inches, and the pipe itself was half an inch thick. How much labor must have been involved in laying the pipes can be seen from the fact that the weight ran fifteen pounds to the lineal foot; it is reckoned that over two hundred and fifty tons were used.

One cannot discern in the Cardinal's background or schooling any factor which might account for such remarkable ability as a builder. Wolsey seems to have been a stonemason at heart, an artist who employed bricks and timbers on a lavish scale to achieve an effect. It was a natural and incurable tendency in him, and he could not pause long in any house without seeing how it could be improved, or if the opportunity allowed, without making it over.

His inner uncertainty might explain his unceasing urge to build something solid on the good earth, but it could not explain the rare and enviable talent with which he wrought his effects. This talent expressed itself not merely in design and beauty but also in attention to the householder's basic concerns. Hampton Court had great veins for carrying rain water and other refuse into the Thames. The Cardinal's foresight had seen the importance of drainage, and it was arranged that rainfall from every part of the building should be gathered in sewers three feet wide and five feet deep, made snugly of brick. He could not escape the inevitable English damp, but he would not encourage it. Although the ground floor of the building is scarcely ten feet above the average level of the river, as Law remarks, it remains wonderfully free from damp.

Proper arrangements for sewage were a part of the Cardinal's struggle for convenience. In several parts of the palace were baths and toilet facilities, all of the principal apartments having private accommodations. The area of glass in Wolsey's palace "was more than doubled . . . The windows were glazed, and no longer closed only with a shutter."[2]

In spite of the moat that surrounded it—almost for decorative purposes, one might imagine—the palace was designed primarily for residence, not for defense. Another feature was the gallery, by means of which one could move from one part of the great house to another without crossing open courts or stumbling through other rooms. Wolsey's galleries "set a fashion that was followed by nearly every great house of Tudor or Jacobean times."[3] His ambulatory spaces were long porticoes, or halls with windows on each side, looking on gardens or the rivers. They afforded him a place for exercise indoors, protected from the unscrupulous English weather.

His health, which was wondrously indifferent, occasioned much anxiety and caused him to seek, if in vain, all the means by which the ills that flesh is heir to might be held off or subdued. There is a tradition, confirmed by subsequent details, that Wolsey chose the site of Hampton Court because the physicians of the realm, aided by learned doctors from Padua, looked over the countryside at his behest and assured him that this manor was by all odds "the most healthy spot within twenty miles of London." It was declared to be a place of "extraordinary salubrity." Report has it that he suffered from a kidney stone, which may account for the colic of which he often complained. Springs in the vicinity were said to provide waters free from substances which would irritate or increase the stone. There were also recurrent attacks of ague and of quinsy, the latter being a particular hazard to orators and talkative persons. In the course of it tonsils swell to the point of bursting; the term derives from two Greek words that picture the victim as a choking dog.

Wolsey wanted Hampton Court chiefly as a suburban home. He had built York Place in London, hard by Westminster, as a kind of official residence; he had come also to own a palace known as The More near Harrow; and as one who got in his grasp the revenues of the Abbey of St. Albans he occupied occasionally the official palace of the Abbot, this being called Tittenhanger. Hampton Court, however, was to be a haven of withdrawal, a convenient seat close enough to London to give him the feeling of keeping in touch with the affairs of Church and State, yet far enough away that he might escape importunate business suitors. In the English manner his home was his castle, complete with moat; the moat that no longer served any military purpose might now serve as a defense of privacy, a protest against invasion.

Beneath the layers that made up the public Wolsey was a householder, a person who showed a daily and painstaking interest in terracing, gardening, drainage, the color of brick, the choice of woods, and pleasing architectural effects. Even while he considered the lease of the original manor house and the demesne lands on which it stood, he invited the King and Queen to join him in an inspection of the property. He had to have the approval of friends, the nods of acceptance, as well as the sanction of his royal master. The royal couple visited the place on March 20, 1514, and on January 11, 1515, a ninety-nine-year lease was signed at a rental of fifty pounds per annum between the Knights of the Hospital of St. John of Jerusalem and "the Most Reverend Father in God Thomas Wolsey, Archbishop of York."[4]

Wolsey had his property, desirable in every respect, with a path of water that led to London. Nearby to the royal palace at Richmond, Hampton was already tinged with history. Elizabeth of York, the eighth Henry's mother, had gone there to make a retreat and pray for a happy delivery, Law declares, just a month before she died in childbirth. Henry VII had used the place as a subsidiary to his palace at Richmond. Hampton Court had, in other words, a record as a place of escape and withdrawal.

The first moves Wolsey made indicated that he hoped to keep its character private. Along with the manor house were some two thousand acres of pasture land. These he proceeded at once "to convert into two parks, fencing them partly with paling, and partly enclosing them with a stout red-brick buttressed wall." Into this wall he caused to be inserted black bricks so arranged as to form crosses at intervals and thus herald to the passerby the ecclesiastical dignity of the owner. The moat, one of the last to be dug in England, in itself announced the intended privacy. And as a further means of withdrawal the Cardinal gave immediate attention to extensive gardens and mazes. Early bills still exist in the Record Office for spades, barrows, seeds, and plants. One bill is for twigs to bind the arbor. Another is for "four days weeding in my lord's garden and orchard at 3d the day." Another is for "a tub to water th'erbs."[5]

The Cardinal's primary work at Hampton Court, whatever turn toward public display it inevitably took later, was guided and sweetened by sentiment. He kept in touch with his former wife, Joan, and the man she married, George Legh. This couple had "issue one son and three daughters," the son named Thomas and the daughters Isabell, Margarett, and Marye. When George Legh fell into dispute over property with Sir John Stanley, natural son of the Bishop of Ely, the Cardinal right earnestly championed the cause of the Leghs, keeping Stanley in prison twelve months before he was induced to give up a contested lease.[6]

All of these sustained family loyalties and interlocking relationships furnished grist for gossip and indignation. At the same time they were signs to show a side of his nature which was balked by convention but which sought in Hampton Court to express itself all the same. Wolsey was a family man without a family. What privacy and home life he managed to eke out of his histrionic existence came to him at Hampton Court. The sharpest instances of what one writer calls his "calculated inaccessibility" are to be found in his life at Hampton Court. There is significance in the statement of the Venetian ambassador who had occasion to visit him frequently at his country residence: "One traverses eight rooms before reaching his audience chamber."[7] The rooms were in a sense inner moats. Brewer tells us that the Cardinal would slip away from London when the press of official duties became too burdensome there, have eight stout oarsmen take him to Hampton Court, and leave word that he was not to be troubled with business until he returned to town.

The importunity of one Sir T. Alen, a confidential agent of the Earl of Shrewsbury and Lord Steward of the royal household, shows the problem that both the Cardinal and those who dealt with him faced. Alen once tried vainly to get an audience with the Cardinal in London. Failing, he followed Wolsey to Hampton Court "and besought his Grace that he might know his pleasure." Wolsey refused to grant him an audience. Undismayed, Alen persisted, and the next day he sought to interview the Cardinal while he was walking in one of his gardens. This caused the Cardinal displeasure and Alen despair. Later he wrote of Wolsey: "When he walks in the Park he will suffer no suitor to come nigh unto him; but commands him away as far as a man will shoot an arrow." Alen ends his lamentation, having violated all the principles of privacy, by saying to the Earl who had sent him on his mission: "I had rather your lordship had commanded me to Rome than to deliver him letters and bring answers to the same."[8]

Such complaints were not confined to those who hounded him to his lair. Members of his own household, his agents abroad, as well as officers of the court on the King's business, found him hard to engage. Likewise dignitaries of the Church and diplomats on errands of state. For all his efforts to maneuver the world and the Pope, he longed for some semblance of solitude; he could not hope to get it anywhere save in Hampton Court and then, busy with household as well as official duties, only occasionally. And when he failed to find it there his resentment of intrusion led to rudeness of Olympian proportions.

Not even the Cardinal, who was a master of pretense, could pretend that Hampton Court was merely his home. Being but a feature of his conspicuous existence, it had to be multi-purpose—a setting for affairs of state as well as for the affairs of his own heart. He took a lively and personal interest in supervising its construction, floating back and forth in his stoutly rowed barge between the manor and Westminster on the genial waters of the Thames. It was the interest of any man who watches the building of his house day after day, winces at the delays, notes with pleasure the fulfilment of line, swears at the gaucheries of the builders, solaces his mind with imagination of the completed project.

Wolsey's concerns grew more complicated as his edifice developed before his eyes. His palace must excel. It must demonstrate, as did his offices, the rise of an Ipswich lad. Hampton Court had to be spaciously conceived and executed with some proper sense of hospitality as well as comfort. He built with a vengeance, as if to vindicate at one and the same time the class and the loins from which he had sprung and the kingdom in which he dwelt. For if this residence of the King's chief minister could dazzle the eyes of foreign ambassages accredited to it, it would argue eloquently for the state of the nation. As with men, so with nations: grandeur and magnificence, not merely military might, were becoming signs of self-esteem. The ability to build served as a token by which the rising power and selfhood of small and competitive England could assert itself. Hampton Court must stand as a tower to tell the world what tiny England, bringing men and materials together from many parts and artists from afar, could accomplish practically overnight.

The result of all this English energy directed by the Cardinal had the appearance rather of a city than a palace. The edifice being destined by its design and appeal to be tampered with and expanded by Henry VIII and successive monarchs who fancied themselves Wolseys, the size of the original structure cannot be determined. Law reckons the palace to have covered no fewer than eight acres and to have had in its vastness a thousand rooms. It was the largest building that had been erected in England since the Romans left. This was important, size being in English eyes a part of magnificence. Bigness could be seen at a glance; it afforded a canvas for the imagination.

Significant to the purpose of impressing visitors and the laying on of hospitality, the entire first court was made up entirely of rooms for guests. One French ambassador reported that there "were two hundred and four score beds, the furniture to most of them being silk, and all for the entertainment of strangers only."[9] He observes also that "the very bed chambers had hangings of wonderful value, and every place did glitter with innumerable vessels of gold and silver." The Cardinal's prodigal sense of color showed itself on every hand. His own colors were byse and gold. Byse has been described as a fierce light blue. He liked his colors strong. The inventory of his effects occupies forty folio pages, and it shows "scores upon scores of beds of red, green and russet velvet, satin and silk, with rich curtains and fringes of the same materials, and all with magnificent . . . canopies and backs."

Sheets were made of silk of Rennes. "Blankets were soft and white and furred with lamb's wool." Hundreds of counterpanes are listed, some of "tawny damask, lined with blue buckram." Others were of blue, green, and red satin; of blue and yellow silk. One was of "red satin with a great rose in the midst, wrought with needlework, and with garters." Still another had a tree in the middle "and beasts with scriptures, all wrought with needlework."

In his endeavor to beguile foreign visitors with the quality of English goods, the Cardinal had not neglected his own comfort. The inventory lists one bed, acquired not too long before his fall from the King's grace, which was "for my Lord's own lying." It had eight mattresses, each of them "stuffed with 13 pounds of carded wool." There were four pillowcases to go along with the deep mattresses, "two of them seamed with black silk and fleurs-de-lys of gold; and the other two with white silk and fleurs-de-lys of red silk."[10]

The speed with which the whole establishment of Hampton Court was brought into being, if not actually finished, was not less impressive than its size and munificence. The lease of the manor was not formalized until the early part of 1515, and by May of the following year, crews having been busy night and day, the palace was far enough along that Wolsey felt that he could appropriately entertain the King and Queen at a banquet there. Work went on steadily afterwards, of course, and it was not until four years later that Wolsey lived there for long periods of time. No record has been found of master plans for the building; and there is no record of an architect. It is not unlikely that the Cardinal laid out the plans which appeared simple but were actually a departure from prevailing modes and foreshadowed a symmetrical treatment of buildings that were to follow. There was a succession of large courts "built on an axial line . . . through the archways between them." The gatehouses were "embellished with turrets and bay-windows, but the rest of the work, including the sides of the courts," was very plain.

There were many details which, although not novel, were relatively untried and called for close attention in construction. Bay windows had been introduced in the fifteenth century, but then they were small. Wolsey gave them a new distinction by making them more than one story high. Also the heads were squared in a firm English fashion instead of pointed after the manner of the Continent. Mullions and transoms "were much increased in number."[11] The chimneys, lofty and irregularly grouped where they were needed, were of cut and molded brick. Here English workmanship was shown at its best. Each chimney was a piece of useful art. Italians were given more decorative assignments in the courts. There was for some odd reason "a series of terra-cotta busts of four Roman emperors done in relief by the Italian artist Gian da Maiano. Still surviving, they look strange against the flat, undecorated Tudor brickwork."

Merely to build, staff, equip, and furnish such a far-flung establishment as Hampton Court might well have engaged all the faculties of a man of Wolsey's stature. He "employed some two thousand five hundred artisans and laborers, all of whom were treated in a liberal and kindly manner."[12] How many of these artisans, used on his various building enterprises, were put to work at any one time on Hampton Court it is impossible to say, but we do know the undertaking was well organized. One report has it that workmen sang while they built Hampton Court Palace, music being a ready part of the common life in those days, what with lutes being kept in barbershops to accompany any sudden outburst of song. Chalk was carried from Taplow and Windsor; timber came from Reigate. Brick kilns were kept in service at Battersea, from which bricks were bought at four shillings per thousand—the effect was all the more striking because the bricks varied in color from light red to purple-brown. A fast pace in construction was possible in part because the site was on water. Lime came from Limehouse.

Wolsey did not scruple to let diplomats know how close such matters as the furnishings of the palace lay to his bounding heart. He had an unashamed weakness for Damascene carpets, as the Venetian ambassador easily discovered. Venice, being a land of shrewd merchants who competed with the English, never stood in great favor with Wolsey, and he managed always to keep her ambassador in a position where the Venetian might feel constrained to grant a favor. Once when some Venetian merchants had incurred his momentous displeasure, they sought to reconcile the Cardinal by the gift of carpets.

This proposal Wolsey haughtily refused, making it clear that he would have no traffic with merchants. He was by no means as coy or hard to persuade, however, if a gift to his establishment could be made to look official. When the ambassador returned to Venice, he reported that the Cardinal wanted Venice to send him a hundred Damascene carpets. These, the ambassador made clear, the Cardinal had asked for several times, and he had "expected to receive them by the last galleys." The ambassador strongly recommended the gift, adding that if the Venetian Signory itself should not choose to incur the expense, "the slightest hint to the London factory would induce that body to take it on themselves." If the gift were made, the ambassador felt sure it might lead the English to reduce the duties on Venetian wines. "But to discuss the matter further," he said, "until the Cardinal receives his 100 carpets would be idle."[13] The Cardinal's inventory notes the receipt of sixty carpets from Venice not long after.

Wolsey might thus, without troubling his roomy conscience, obtain certain perquisites that came from his privileged position. But the task of managing the enormous household which he created was a task on which foreign ambassadors could not help. The duties of this management devolved upon him and taxed any energies that remained from his other assignments. Merely to select, recruit, and look to the welfare of a staff of five hundred household servants in various stations called for an energetic mind and rare insight. Some of these were lords and some were gentlemen, all pledged to service in the Cardinal's household, according to the custom of the day, for such political advantage or training in manners and graces as this association might afford.

In the great hall of the palace, where there was food to be had at all hours, there were three officers: the steward, who was a priest; the treasurer, who was a knight; and the comptroller, who was a squire. While some of the servants thus had dignity by virtue of birth or connection, others had it by virtue of the knowledge and skills they brought to their jobs. And they all had business with my lord Cardinal and could not be ignored like so many sticks. The master cook presided over one of the two principal kitchens, the privy kitchen for the Cardinal's own table. He was a man dressed in velvet and satin, and he wore a gold chain around his neck. In the hall kitchen there were two clerks of the kitchen and a comptroller, a clerk of the spicery. Besides these valuable aides who looked after the intake and outgo of food, there were two master cooks and twelve assistant cooks "and laborers and children of the kitchen."[14] Responsibility in this division of labor was minute.

The harried master of Hampton Court had in his pay and care hundreds of other servants at lower levels of duty, all of them now and then, and often daily, on his mind. There were eighty who labored in the bakehouse, buttery, scullery, wafery, and other places connected with the preparation of food. Nearly a hundred more were employed in such places as the woodyard, laundry, and wardrobe. The Cardinal's stud and stable had sixteen grooms besides a master of the horse and various officers, together with helpers enough to attend to something like one hundred horses and mules for general use, six special horses for occasions of state, and six gray and white mules "for my Lord's own saddle." The rest of the staff included one hundred and sixty personal attendants, among them twelve gentlemen-ushers and various waiters for his privy chamber. There were sixteen doctors, or leeches, in the Cardinal's employ, two secretaries, three clerks, and four counselors learned in the law. All served the Cardinal, and in serving him were available to the household he entailed. And there had to be running footmen, messengers, and heralds to take word of my lord's bidding and to keep England and Europe at his beck.

As if this host of attendants would not suffice, there were others of a more delicate sort that required special care in selection and handling. These included sixty priests in copes, "who attended the services on great festivals and walked before the Cardinal in procession round the cloisters of Hampton Court." Every great house in those days had its choir, both for the entertainment and beguiling of visitors and members of the families and servants and for singing at other lords' manors. Even in the savage north this was so. These choirs were a matter of personal rivalry among the lords. Traill tells us that the Earl of Northumberland "was concerned to strengthen the voices of his basses, counter-tenors, standing tenors and 'tribles.' His taberett, lute and rebeck visited the houses of lords at the great feasts, as theirs visited his, and each household's minstrels received on these visits their fixed rewards."[15]

Wolsey's choir was his pride and joy, and his rivalry was spurred by King Harry's boisterous love of music. Nothing would satisfy Wolsey but to recruit a choir that would catch the King's ear and perhaps excite his envy. In both particulars he succeeded. He had twelve singing priests, twelve singing children, and sixteen singing laymen, as well as soloists for singing parts of the Mass.

It was one of the mistakes Wolsey made, as if by compulsion, that he surpassed the King. The King told Cornish, the master of the Chapel Royal, and the judgment was duly reported to Wolsey by Richard Pace, that "your Grace's chapel is better than his, and proved the same by this reason, that if any manner of new song be brought unto both the said chapels to be sung ex proviso, the said song should be better and more surely handled by your chapel than by his Grace's."

Henry took a fancy to one of the singing boys in the Cardinal's choir and had Pace, royal secretary at the time, write and say that the King admired the boy's voice greatly and would like to have him for his own chapel. Wolsey took the hint and delivered the boy, and in acknowledgment thereof the King's secretary wrote: "My Lord, if it were not for the personal love that the King's Highness doth bear unto your Grace, surely he would have out of your chapel not children only but also men . . ." The boy was a great success, and Wolsey got the satisfaction at least of hearing the master of Henry's choir extol Mr. Pigot, Wolsey's choirmaster, for the excellent way in which the boy had been trained.[16]

All of which is to show that my lord Cardinal could not preside over a manor of the dimensions of Hampton Court, touching as it did the immediate destinies of five hundred distinct and often temperamental individuals, without involving himself in detail which he could not anticipate and complexities that would have wrecked a lesser man. Even if he had not been concerned with people, he still had the tangible and removable property to worry about. Two Venetian ambassadors at separate times independently estimated the worth of his gold and silver plate to be £150,000—all of this under the roof of a man whose father had bought a house for £8 and some land. Giustiniani said that wherever he turned there was a sideboard of plate. And the plate on public display was not all. Cavendish tells us that every chamber had "a bason and ewer of silver, some gilt and some parcel gilt, and some two great pots of silver in like manner, and one pot at the least with wine and beer, a bowl or goblet, and a silver pot to drink beer in; a silver candlestick or two, with both white lights and yellow lights of three sizes of wax . . ."

With the growth of Wolsey's power and the multiplication of his duties, Hampton Court became more and more of a hostel and less and less of a home. Always there was the need of impressing visitors. In the total picture the outside as well as the inside had to have fastidious care. The cult of the garden had begun in England. As the houses were marked by symmetry, "so were the gardens neat and formal, the broad gravelled paths carrying on the lines of the building and flower-beds." The beds were filled with flowers "for the delectation sake unto the eye and the odoriferous savors unto the nose." These features had increasing importance as Wolsey made Hampton Court the center of the kingdom.

Henry was wont to repair to the Cardinal's house divers times in a year for his recreation. When he did, "banquets were set forth, masks and mummeries, in so gorgeous a sort and costly manner, that it was heaven to behold. There wanted no dames, nor damsels, meet or apt to dance with the maskers or to garnish the place for that time, with other goodly disports." Cavendish tells of one occasion when the King suddenly appeared in a mask, accompanied by a dozen others in masks, all dressed as shepherds. The hair and beards of the masks were made of gold wire or silver "or else of good black silk." The group was accompanied by sixteen torchbearers.

The affair had been prearranged to look spontaneous. A banquet was in progress when, outside, cannon announced the arrival of unexpected guests. My lord Cardinal was sitting alone under the cloth of state and, at the sound of the guns, he sent a lord and a knight to see whatever it was that so disturbed their peace. They returned, after looking out upon the Thames, and reported that it must be a foreign ambassage.

At this point my lord Cardinal instructed the lord and the knight to go and greet the guests in French, finding their mission, and "desiring them to sit down with us, and to take part of our fare." The welcoming committee "went incontinent down into the hall, where they received them with twenty new torches, and conveyed them up into the chamber, with such a number of drums and fifes as I have seldom seen in one place and time." When the newcomers arrived in the chamber they went to the Cardinal, two and two together, and the Lord Chamberlain said: "Sir, forasmuch as they be strangers, and cannot speak English, they have desired me to declare unto you that they, having understanding of this your triumphant banquet, where was assembled such a number of excellent fair dames, could do no less, under the supportation of your Grace,

it to repair hither to view as well their incomparable beauty . . . to
ince with them and to have their acquaintance."

So the mummery went, ending right happily of course. The lord
ardinal, after further ado, bethought and said to the Lord Chamberlain
at he detected "a noble man amongst them, who is more meet to occu-
 this seat and place than am I; to whom I would most gladly surrender
e same, according to my duty, if I knew him."

This intelligence in English the Lord Chamberlain relayed to the
ests in whispered French and then duly reported that the lord Cardinal
id been right all along: there was such a man; and if his Grace were
le to pick him out, he would be "content to disclose himself, and to
ke and accept your place, most worthily."

Then the Cardinal looked over the shepherds in disguise and said:
Meseemeth the gentleman with the black beard should be even he." To
e rollicking delight of the assembled multitude, my lord Cardinal
issed. He had fixed upon Sir Edward Neville. The King was as amused
 the guests at the mistake "and could not forbear laughing." He then
illed down his own visor and showed "such a pleasant countenance and
eer" that all rejoiced. The Cardinal offered the King his seat of honor
neath the cloth of state, but the King said he would first go and change
s attire. When he and his maskers had returned, "every man new ap-
reled . . . in came a new banquet before the King's Majesty." It was
ade up, Cavendish estimates, of full two hundred dishes.[17]

Of such elaborate and costly nonsense and fantastic party-crashing
ere the King's and the Cardinal's lighter moments compounded. It was
 if the whole palace with its sturdiness and its careful plan had been
rned into a doll's house. No doubt these pastimes did cheer the sover-
gn and keep between him and his minister some camaraderie; they af-
rded the King the pleasure of being aggressively incognito, and there
as doubtless something healthy in having both Wolsey and Henry pre-
nd that Henry was only a rustic. It was an escape from fact—a pleas-
t conceit with overtones of irony.

CHAPTER XIII

Now you understand that my lord of York used the premises of Hampton Court as a spacious stage where he could play the role in which he fancied himself cast: arbiter of the destinies of Europe Agape with admiration, his gentleman-usher records: "All ambassadors of foreign potentates were despatched by his wisdom, to whom they had continual access for their despatch. His house was always resorted to like a king's house, with noblemen and gentlemen, with coming and going in and out, feasting and banqueting these ambassadors divers times, and all other right nobly."[1]

From the moment of his rise to power, Europe held a perennial and fatal fascination for Wolsey. Its chicanery was strong drink, and he could not leave it alone or get enough of it. Its affairs had the character of mummings and disguisings, not unlike the games and pastimes with which he was wont to beguile his jaded guests. He played Europe like a game.

In this respect he was not alone, but he had to a remarkable degree that enthusiastic simplicity of mind which leads men to believe that complex problems can be settled at the summit. He saw nations in the guise of kings. It was his bent and his genius to deal with persons, not with problems, with heads of state or their pliant spokesmen, not with the clamant voice of peoples. The concern he showed in his own country for the welfare of farmers and for the administration of justice among commoners seems never to have been transferred into perception of the aspirations that might lie behind the façade of royalty abroad. Rather he behaved as if Europe were populated entirely by kings and queens and bishops especially the Bishop of Rome, and assorted wily ambassadors. Hence my lord Cardinal's conduct of foreign affairs had the clean lines of a great epic and the poignant failure of a great drama. It was played out to its bitter end because he pitted himself blindly against crowned heads and reckoned not with forces that were more than kings and cardinals.

In what he ignored and neglected, as well as in what he did, one must assess Wolsey as the King's minister for foreign affairs. He interested himself primarily in the known, organized, tangible world, the world readily at hand and accredited, the countries more or less like England, a proper club of countries. This meant a small part of the known world.

The unspeakable Turk, while he surged ever closer to the heart of Europe, never got beyond the edge of Wolsey's calculations. The Turk was outside the rim of civilized society. His strenuous advances, of course, served as a strident warning, sounded the alarum for Europe. The threat of the Turk afforded the ever-ready means by which Christian princes could be urged to unite—in a way that Wolsey wanted them to unite. The infidel furnished the excuse for peace in Christendom; yet even after he had overthrown Hungary and stormed the very gates of Vienna, the excuse was never quite sufficient.

A sultan who came to be known as Soliman the Magnificent ascended the throne of the Turk in 1520, moving his forces all the way to the banks of the Danube, throwing the shadow of the fez across all the council tables of Europe. But with Soliman the Magnificent the magnificent Cardinal had no diplomatic intercourse. Incurable negotiator though he was, Wolsey sought to drive no bargains with Soliman. Francis I, one of the kings Wolsey used in his games of chess and charades, was later to arrange an alliance with Soliman. Francis dealt with Soliman as a fellow king with fellow interests. The Cardinal treated him as a heathen afar. Such a sultan, enlightened in the noble arts of war and given to fits of versemaking under a nom de plume, could not be ignored by any man who looked upon Europe. But he could be kept snobbishly beyond the English pale. He was but the tocsin by which my lord of York called the kings of his day to peace and to war.

Likewise Moscow remained remote and inert in the diplomatic fancies of the Cardinal. Russ was not even a threat and consequently did not penetrate the solemnities in which England, France, and the Empire performed the ritual of diplomacy. The Kremlin kept cautiously to itself, suspicious of the rest of Europe, and it required stern initiative to enter into negotiations with those who guarded its secrets. Some fitful attempts were made, but not by Wolsey. In 1516 the Emperor Maximilian sent forward an ambassador to Moscow. His name was Sigismund von Herberstein. He had been sent on various missions in Europe, and his aim in this case was to try to fashion a peace between Russ and Poland-Lithuania.

Herberstein was received on his approach to Moscow with a combination of hospitality and suspicion. "First a courtier met him on the road with a gift of two horses, then an interpreter appeared . . . He was escorted into the Moscow gate by 15 nobles and 30 grooms, who cleared a way through the staring crowd. But when he asked questions about the Kremlin and its people out of frank curiosity, he aroused the suspicion of the guides; thereafter he got information in roundabout ways, without asking questions."[2]

If Russ was coming gradually to be a part of the outside world, it was not a part of Wolsey's world. One could not expect Wolsey to establish intercourse with a country where the Pope was held in low esteem. Indeed Herberstein in speaking of Vasily, the reigning prince, notes that "there is no one to whom he is more obnoxious than to the Pope, whom he does not condescend to designate by any title but that of Doctor."

Nor did my lord of York pay any more heed to the lands across the turbulent Atlantic than he did to the city across the plains and rivers of Russ. Columbus died without knowing that he had discovered a new continent. Wolsey seems to have lived and died in ignorance of the significance of what Columbus discovered and of the significance of other voyages being made in distant waters. During 1519, when Henry and Wolsey were zealously occupied with the election of a new emperor of that decadent vestige of medievalism known as the Holy Roman Empire, a Portuguese sailor in the hire of Spain drifted to the south of

South America, sailed through "dark and forbidding" straits there and "so came into the Pacific Ocean."

A new continent, even a new nation, engaged the mind of Wolsey less than a new intrigue. There were no kings or queens or bishops or castles in the world beyond the wide seas. "His outlook was that of a man oblivious of the marvelous opening-up of the world which was going on around him and of the part which his country might play therein. Until quite the end of his ascendancy there is no authenticated voyage of discovery or attempt to penetrate new markets with the produce of industry."[3] Interest in exploration had sagged after the death of the seventh Henry, and the few projects for exploration put forward in the reign of Henry VIII died for lack of venturesome support. The City Companies in London were asked "at Wolsey's instance in 1521 to furnish ships for an expedition to the north-west, with a promise of very substantial privileges in the new trade to be opened up."[4] But Wolsey had other fish to fry, and not the expendable energy to follow through. The reply of the City Companies showed that "they were unable to envisage the meaning of the proposal and saw in it only a wanton hazarding of men's lives."[5] It was better to hazard English lives in France, where such hazarding had become a habit. What was the appeal of a land peopled with naked savages when one could play at wits with richly robed princes?

Apart from his addiction to drama and pageantry, there was another reason why Wolsey ignored the world outside his immediate ken and kept his eye on Francis instead. It was his sense of indebtedness to Pope Leo X. The red hat which Wolsey had so diligently tried to wrest from the hand of Leo had been held just beyond his grasp until Francis had routed the papal forces at Marignano. Only after events had italicized the Pope's need of Henry's help had the red hat been sent. It therefore became incumbent upon Wolsey, in exchange for the high honor conferred upon him, to acknowledge the Pope's plight and lay plans for his relief. The Turks could come later. After Marignano it was Francis who was the menace at the gates of Rome.

In this manner it came about that Wolsey was named in effect England's minister for foreign affairs by the same act that he was named Cardinal Ebor. His future course was set and determined by the circumstances in which he received the cardinalate. He was at the very beginning of the fullness of his power drawn inextricably into the dogfights of Europe, all the more so because the wishes of the papacy coincided with the wishes of the King of England. My lord of York expertly served two masters. He did it comfortably and with none of the spasms of conscience that usually come from divided loyalty. It was one of the buoyant forces in his destiny that the King of England sought the same ends as the Pope of Rome.

Certainly after Marignano Leo X did not wish Francis removed from the environs of Milan any more heartily than Henry VIII. The spectacular victory of Francis had humiliated Henry and had left him gasping. Henry's resentment of Francis was personal, the resentment of one cocky and bumptious youth for another. To make matters more acute, Francis seemed to compare favorably with the young English King in all respects and to excel him in many. Henry showed a lively and competitive curiosity about his opposite number in France. Of those who had seen the French King he asked close questions. Piero Pasqualigo, a Venetian who had accompanied Sebastian Giustiniani to London, had seen Francis in Paris. He tells of Henry's inquisitiveness: "His majesty came to me and said, 'Is the king of France as tall as I am?' I told him there was little difference. 'Is he as stout?' I told him he was not. 'What sort of legs has he?' I replied, 'Spare.' Whereupon he opened the front of his doublet, and placing his hand on his thigh, said, 'Look here: I have a good calf to my leg.' "[6] When Giustiniani told Henry that the French King was adored by his subjects, Henry ejaculated: "By God!

he gives them poor reason to love him, running thus at the very commencement of his reign into the toil and charges of war!"[7]

Henry's jealousy of Francis, sharp and uncomfortable even when the two stood eying each other through the reports of ambassadors, had been increased unbearably by the seven-league stride with which the Most Christian King had crossed the Alps where no military force had crossed before. And at Marignano there had been much letting of blood upon the field, the battle having lasted eighteen hours in all and having covered two days and part of a night. Francis had been in the thick of it and at the center of danger. There was a further triumph for the French, for the Switzers had called them, harking back to the Battle of the Spurs, "hares in armor." The fierce and manly combat of the French had avenged this derisive term. The same Frenchmen who under the reign of the gouty Louis had quailed and run at the sight of Henry's forces had under Francis defeated the best fighters in the whole of Europe, defeated them decisively and in a kind of gory combat that made Henry's first military venture seem but a summer outing.

The news of Marignano stunned the English. On October 11, 1515, almost a month after the battle, Wolsey still pretended not to believe the news. Henry showed even greater signs of dazed incredulity at the unwelcome intelligence. Both Francis and his mother Louise had written directly to Henry to notify him of the victory; Henry regarded the letters as forgeries confected by the French to suit some ultimate and imagined purpose.

To convince the King of England of the victory, the King of France at last sent into England an agent named de Bapaume, armed with letters and equipped with corroborative detail. De Bapaume's meticulous report of his delivery of the letters and the incidents that followed gives a picture of the English consternation. King Henry did not "take any great pleasure" in reading the letters; "for it seemed, to look at him, as if tears would have burst from his eyes, so red were they from the pain he suffered in hearing and understanding the good news and prosperity of my master, who had advertised him thereof by his letters."[8]

Thus at last the bloody fact of Marignano was admitted. De Bapaume went next "to my lord the Cardinal of York, being at Westminster, whom likewise I informed of the good news of the king and his prosperity. He told me he rejoiced at it, and that he esteemed the victory of the king and his success as much as if they had been the king's his master, by reason of the alliance and friendship between them."

Immediately after these resounding assurances of ingenuous friendship, Henry and Wolsey launched a project designed to circumvent Francis by cunning stealth. By some testimony, the scheme was Wolsey's "own work." It is so testified by the papal chamberlain Paris de Grassis. In October of 1515 Richard Pace, a man of letters and a diplomatist of proven skill, was dispatched to Zurich to hire Swiss troops to attack Francis in Italy. It was agreed that the English would put up 120,000 crowns for the hire of 20,000 Swiss soldiers.

The scheme was known to Venice as early as December of 1515 and, as Fisher points out, once known to Venice it became the open talk of Europe. Venice being still an ally of France, its ambassador Giustiniani came hastily to Wolsey to protest the transfer of money. Wolsey denied the report with unctuous eloquence. Giustiniani reported the scene in some detail to his home government. On January 2, 1516, he wrote from London that the King had returned to Greenwich and that he had immediately gone to see the Cardinal, "who, for authority, may in point of fact be styled ipse rex." He went on to say that, having paid the Cardinal the usual compliments, he commenced discussing the "affair of the moneys." The Cardinal listened to him "most attentively and patiently for the space of a quarter of an hour"—the longest recorded attention Wolsey ever gave anyone. Then he immediately set about correcting Giustiniani's misapprehensions, saying: "I will speak to you with all sincerity and truth, and will tell you what becomes a

Cardinal on the honour of the Cardinalate." He went on to say: "It is true that the most serene King has remitted moneys to Flanders which will reach Germany, and perhaps Italy, for two purposes: in the first place, for the purchase of inlaid armour and other costly furniture; then again we are aware that a number of princes, whom I will not particularize to you, either in France, in Germany, in Italy, have pledged a quantity of very fine jewels, and of great value, which we hope to obtain at no great cost, and therefore thought fit to avail ourselves of this opportunity for purchasing similar things, which in other times could not be obtained at a much greater outlay . . ."

On and on went my lord of York, covering himself with a cloud of words. "No man in this kingdom," he said, "has so much as thought of waging war on the King of France, or of opposing any of his undertakings." "By the honour of the Cardinalate," he added, "what we tell you is the truth." And as for those who had told tales of England's military intent to the Venetian ambassador: "They lied in their teeth."[9]

Meanwhile Wolsey's agent in Zurich, Richard Pace, was having the devil's own time with his negotiations. The chief problem was to keep the control of the huge sum advanced out of the grasping hands of the Emperor Maximilian. The thought of so much gold all around him but not under his extravagant control almost crazed the aging Emperor, who had been too busy hunting the chamois and paying his attentions to the Princess of Hungary, a girl not yet in her teens, to halt the march of Francis when he first crossed the Alps. Now at the sight of money he became warlike and offered to lead the Swiss against the French. "He is always dunning for money," the Pope said of him.[10] And Machiavelli remarked that if the leaves on all the trees of Italy had been converted into ducats for his use, they would not have been sufficient for his need.[11] Maximilian went so far as to write his daughter Margaret in the Netherlands, asking her to seize the gold he heard the English had consigned to Antwerp and deposit it to his treasury.

It is not remarkable that the English scheme, carried out furtively and at a great distance, with many grasping hands along the route and with Maximilian a necessary party to it, should have ended in a joke that shook the sides of Europe. Pace did a masterful job in planning the expedition against the French, handicapped by many trammels though he was. Wolsey's instructions to Pace were that he appear to be only a private citizen with no official mission and that he carry out the negotiations without reference to the ambassador regularly accredited to Maximilian. In spite of all the hazards, Pace arranged the attack, leading one column himself while Maximilian in charge of the twenty thousand Swiss led the other on the march to Milan. Revenge would be sweet.

The reasons for what happened will long remain among the abominable mysteries of history. The wily and impecunious Maximilian led his troops within nine miles of Milan and came to a stubborn halt. Pace, in an ague of bewilderment, upbraided him and laid before him in his tent all the reasons why he should leap to the attack of Milan. Pace later wrote to Wolsey of the affair: "The said Emperor could not deny that these our reasons were evident, and made this answer only, viz., that he trusted that the king's grace would not desert him. For all this yet that day he would not move, but did sit still in pensiveness, and was angry with every man that did move him to set forthward."

Not only did he sit still in pensiveness and not move forthward; he moved backward, returning to his dominions without allowing any of the troops in his command so much as to scratch a Frenchman. In the commotion and disorder that followed, the Swiss plundered and murdered, sacked villages in the route of the retreat, and their leaders fell to quarreling among themselves. All of which did not disturb the Emperor; indeed he made use of Pace's embarrassment to press for more money. Pace reported the demand to Wolsey, for the Emperor threatened that if Pace refused he would "make terms with France, and write over to England that Pace had been the cause of his defection." Pace further warns Wolsey that the Emperor is sending an agent to England

and reminds Wolsey "that all money put into the Emperor's hands, or committed to any of his, shall be, in great part thereof, evil expended, as this present bearer can at large show unto the same, and declare what business and trouble I have only in resisting against this."[12]

The large ears of diplomacy caught every detail of the news quickly. These disastrous and ridiculous events in the spring of 1516 marked the first official meddling of Wolsey in his new and supreme position as Lord Chancellor of England and chief adviser to the English King. There had been nothing like it since Ferdinand, scarce four years before, had left an English force stranded and unsupplied on the shores of Spain in what was to have been a concerted attack on France. In the present case no English troops had been involved, but English honor and dignity had suffered quite as much of a defeat as in 1512. Then Wolsey had been only the King's energetic Almoner carrying out what could be construed as his Majesty's orders. In this case he was Lord Chancellor of England and generally esteemed to be responsible for the farce in which Maximilian played the doughty lead.

Nor did England's disgrace end with the fleecing by Maximilian. Other events were to increase her isolation and weaken her position in the courts of Europe despite the exertions of the Cardinal. In these events Ferdinand was to play as his last earthly act a contributing part. On January 23, 1516, "hunting and hawking to the last in fair weather and foul, and following more the counsel of his friends than his physicians," Ferdinand died. When he did, the throne of Spain passed to a solemn, spindle-legged youth of eighteen, Charles the grandson of Ferdinand. But the succession lacked the cleanness necessary to prevent trouble, and it was necessary at every turn to assure it and protect it. For Charles was master of the Netherlands and a resident there; he had never been to Spain, and there was no positive assurance that his rulership would be accepted. In fact, there was no positive assurance that he would even be able to reach Spain. Yet he must try. This child of ancient

Burgundy must move on to meet his destiny, and there was suspense and a sense of that destiny in the air when in the Netherlands Charles was proclaimed King of Spain.

This solemn and dramatic moment brought into the drama of Europe one who would ultimately prove the ruin of Thomas Wolsey. But at the moment Charles was a lisping and ineffectual young man, of worth only by descent, merely a further embarrassment to be reckoned with in the threatened isolation of England. As such, he afforded bother enough. His advisers were all Flemings and inclined sentimentally and practically to France and not to England. Immediately they began maneuvers by which Charles would be encouraged to cuddle up to Francis, and by August 13, 1516, the alliance of the two had been solemnized in a pact called the Treaty of Noyon.

Again Wolsey turned with incurable hope, if not naïveté, to Maximilian. Perhaps he could be persuaded to undermine the Treaty of Noyon. He agreed to go to the Netherlands and entreat Charles to dismiss the councilors who had been responsible for the Treaty of Noyon. England advanced the money and Maximilian spent it, but instead of undermining the Treaty of Noyon he joined it himself, saying to Charles as he did: *"Mon fils, vouz alles tromper les Français et moi je vais tromper les Anglis."*[13] All of Wolsey's attempts to circumvent the union of princes had failed; indeed Wolsey and his agents were not even consulted, for in March of 1517 Charles, Maximilian, and Francis made a fresh League of Cambrai for the partition of Italy. From this arrangement too England was excluded.

It was not a happy position for an English king and his minister who a few years before had been the talk and toast of Europe. The English had paid more than a million and a half crowns to help Maximilian rid Italy of the French, and the French were still there. England had sought to prevent the union of Charles and Francis, and the two not only were now fast in a treaty but they had extended their alliance to include Maximilian, the very man who had disgraced the English.

Having failed ingloriously through the mercurial Maximilian in an act of covert war to rescue the Pope from the Most Christian King, Wolsey now undertook to construct the kind of peace the Pope had been plaintively pleading for. Wolsey suddenly became conscious of the terrible Turk and lent his lordly ear to the solicitations of Leo that an expedition against the Sultan be organized.

Earlier both the King and Wolsey had shown a dull indifference to Leo's pleading. Wolsey himself had glibly consented to the enterprise, but Warham as Archbishop of Canterbury and head of Convocation opposed it, and Henry took the position that the prattle about the Turk was simply designed to distract him from his task of cutting Francis down to size. Henry had gone so far as to say to Giustiniani that the true Turk was the King of France. England's indifference to the danger continued through the summer and fall of 1515. Meanwhile the Turks, who had gained Syria and Egypt and were now threatening Rhodes, began actually to molest Italy. "Turkish corsairs swarmed in the Mediterranean, and swept the coast from Terracina to Pisa. On one occasion they plundered the church of Loretto; on another they sailed up the Tiber, and nearly made a prisoner of the Pope whilst he was hunting at Pali."[14] These forays were carried out by Turkish brigands and were not official; but they were painful just the same, and they served as harbingers to show what might well occur when the Sultan chose to set his face against the West.

Still the princes of Europe, busy with the excitement and dash of their own rivalries, held back. But with the shameful and at last undeniable failure of Maximilian's expedition and the drawing up of the Treaty of Noyon, England being ceremoniously ignored in the talk among Christian princes, Wolsey began to change his tune and to sing in rich tones his praises of the Pope's scheme for the union of Christendom and the repulse of the Turk. In December of 1516 Giustiniani reports that the Cardinal was much exercised. He assured the Venetian that, once other matters were settled, his King would go against the Turk.

He "would perform memorable feats, and excel all others, adding *'and perhaps I myself will go in person.'*" The emphasis indicated by italics is Giustiniani's in his report of the interview to his own government. The ambassador reports also that he urged Wolsey to the cause by pointing out a number of practical considerations. "I exhorted him to the utmost, telling him that it was not merely a question of the Christian faith, and of preserving the rest of Christ's patrimony, but of obtaining two empires, five kingdoms, and so many provinces and cities now held by the Turk, but which of yore belonged to Christians."[15] He was also at pains to lay before the Cardinal the fact "that said conquests might be made with less money than would be expended for the waging of war in Italy."

This last thrust could hardly have pleased my lord Cardinal, his memory rankled as it was by Maximilian's costly perfidy. Nor is there any sign that he wanted to join in the recovery of Christian ground. It was clear to him now, however, that the time had come to unite Christendom against the infidel, obedient to the fervent and prayerful wishes of the Pope. The Pope would be the architect of the peace; the Cardinal would be the master builder who carried out the plans.

In two energetic years after the Treaty of Noyon, which was formalized in August of 1516, Thomas Wolsey changed the alignments of Europe and made England the acknowledged leader of European affairs. He did it by invoking the image of the Turk as a threat and the image of the Pope as a solution. But the deals and negotiations necessary to the accomplishment were infinite.

The arrangements which were consummated in a remarkable document known as the Treaty of London and accepted by the great powers in October of 1518 came about through Wolsey's sedulous cultivation of France. To this cultivation France yielded not unwillingly, Francis knowing that Maximilian was not long for this world and that Charles would probably succeed the old beggar. It would be as well to be on good terms with England. Hence parleying began.

One subject concerned in these talks was the return of Tournai to France for a consideration: Francis was to buy back what Louis had lost, and the Cardinal was to have from the French King a pension to replace the fees he had been supposed to receive from the diocese as its bishop. Tournai had fallen to Henry in 1513. At that time Louis Gaillart, the bishop-elect, had not been permitted by Henry to possess the temporalities of the bishopric, and the proceeds of it had been given to Wolsey. Still Gaillart had refused to budge from his claim, and Wolsey had tried in vain to get Francis to appoint him to some other position. Francis dallied and delayed. Meanwhile Gaillart secured a bull from the Pope for his settlement in the diocese.

All this had created an evil temper in my lord Cardinal, and it was at the time of his temper, whether because of it or not, that he had dispatched Pace to Zurich with gold to be spent upon ousting the French from Milan. In negotiating the Treaty of London, however, the whole moot matter of Tournai was genially disposed of. Francis agreed to pay Henry 600,000 crowns in twelve annual installments for the repossession of the city, and the Cardinal's grievous disappointment and lordly umbrage over not getting the revenues of the see had been nicely taken care of by the promise of yearly pension from Francis of 12,000 livres.

The question of Tournai having been settled, in August of 1518 a splendid French mission came to London and amid banquets, masques, processions, mummeries, and devisings the final details of an intimate alliance between England and France were sorted out and agreed upon.

But Wolsey's Peace was to be more than an alliance between England and France. It was to be a universal and permanent peace. The Treaty of London exceeded any hopes and pleas the Pope had dared express. The Pope, as Giustiniani pointed out, had labored to impose a truce of five years upon Christian princes, "whereas his lordship had made a perpetual peace."[16] The lines of the document were remarkable and new, for they were drawn to bind England and France together and yet the provisions were flexible enough to reach out and embrace all Christian countries in a great concert of powers, each country pledged to join the others in resisting an attack made upon any one of them.

It was solemnly agreed that "if the Dominions respectively then belonging to the said Confederates should be in a hostile Manner invaded by any of them, or by any other Power whatever, the Party invaded should admonish the Aggressor to desist, and to make Reparation; which if he refuse to do (within the Space of a Month) the rest of the Confederacy might declare themselves his Enemies, and in two Months after, at an equal Expence, make War upon him both by Sea and Land; That they should to this End, allow the troops of each other free Passage through their several Dominions . . ." It was further provided and consented to that "none of the Confederates should permit their Subjects to bear Arms against the Other, or should retain any Force of Strangers, to serve against the said Confederates, on Pain of being interpreted to violate the League, which yet should continue in full force among the Rest . . ."[17]

Matters that troubled practical princes, such as the use of mercenaries, were thus taken care of, but a new and imaginative feature had been added: the powers that subscribed to the Treaty of London agreed to band together in force against any power that broke the peace. Far more than an alliance of great powers, Wolsey had fashioned a league of nations designed to organize peace as well as preserve it. The league was to embrace not only England and France but Spain, Denmark, Portugal, Scotland, all the Italian states, the Swiss confederation and the towns of the Hansa. It was at least universal locally, and it projected, to the astonishment of the diplomatic world, a confederacy on a vaster scale and with more adherents than the Pope or any other arbiter had dreamed of.

And the author and finisher of the league was the Cardinal of York, he who had been ignored by Charles and Francis two years before and cheated by Ferdinand and Maximilian. His name now invoked respect wherever intrigue was talked or contemplated. Men and princes must reckon with him anew. Giustiniani noted that "whereas such a union of Christian powers was usually concluded at Rome, this confederacy had been concluded in England, although the Pope was its head."[18] Fox declared that the Treaty "was the best deed ever done for England; and next to the king the praise was due to Wolsey."[19]

CHAPTER XIV

Permanent and universal peace having been achieved, Christian princes could now turn their energies to other matters—such as the election, for example, of a successor to the Emperor Maximilian. On January 19, 1519, the gay old pauper died; probably laughed himself to death at the kings and diplomats he had made fools of. His death left vacant the throne of the Holy Roman Empire and provided the signal for a scramble to see who might seat himself on that throne. The contest, which lay between Charles and Francis, was in essence a popularity contest with Europe as its picturesque setting. Being Emperor was in some respects like being Maypole Queen: the honor carried with it a great deal of ceremonial adulation but not much function. The title was mixed with faded glories and old lace, and one needed a good memory to appreciate the true dignity of the position. But it carried with it, by virtue of earlier associations and the idea for which the term Holy Roman Empire had once stood, a higher degree of prestige than any other royal position in Europe.

The only immediate function the Emperor would serve was that of trying to rule Germany, whatever else he might claim or attempt, and the choice of Emperor would be made by the Electors of that country, a sturdy and vigorous group of princes in whom tradition and practice had vested the right of determining who would occupy the throne.

Charles of Spain was the grandson of Maximilian and on that ground might lay special claim to preference; but actually he knew no German, had no knowledge of the country or its special problems, and was as much a foreigner there as the King of France. The King of France, being of much renown and superior in years and experience, enjoying acclaim for his victory at Marignano, believed firmly that he had a chance to be chosen king of the Germans and gave evidence of this belief by pouring unlimited funds into the contest: three million crowns, according to his testimony. His efforts and expenditures protracted and delayed the deliberations into May of 1519 and brought reports of a deadlock in the electoral college. At this point Henry sent Richard Pace forward to offer with proper blandishments the candidacy of the King of England. But Pace found that all of the Electors had made their pledges to one side or other.

The decisive factor proved to be the alliance of the Pope with Francis. Leo openly declared against Charles, and this, as Brandi puts it, "proved to be the surest means of securing the votes of the Electors for the Hapsburg dynasty."[1] The Germans had begun "to grow restive at the ostentation of French power." The marvel is that Francis ever got such serious consideration as he did. On the evening of June 27 the Electors appointed the following day as the day of decision. "At the sound of the bell every man must pray God to send down his grace on the Electors 'that they might choose a king who would be useful to God Almighty the Holy Roman Empire and us all.' "[2] The man who in their unanimous judgment filled these requirements was Charles, who assumed the role of Emperor under the title of Charles V.

The net effect of the election, beyond its immediate result, was to embitter the spirit of Francis irreparably and to bring him into open hostility with his rival. At the beginning of the contest for the crown of Emperor the two kings had continued their spirit of outward amiability. Francis had declared that "his brother Charles and he were, fairly and openly, suitors to the same mistress: the more fortunate, added he, will carry her; the other must rest contented."[3]

Now that the election was over, he was anything but contented. It was natural that, his hopes drawn taut by the long delay, he should be indignantly disappointed. Yet his personal disappointment afforded less concern to him and the rest of Europe than the military encirclement which his country now faced. By adding the domains of his grandfather to his own possessions, Charles now had dominions which stretched from the Netherlands through Aragon and Castile and their Italian dependencies—Naples, Sicily, and Sardinia—around France to include Germany. Moreover, Charles was lord of dominions across the sea—dominions as yet of unproven wealth, but fabulous and calculated all the more because of the uncertainty of their worth to add dimensions to his dignity. Here was an overlordship which Francis and France could not regard with equanimity. It was an empire greater and more extensive than any known in Europe since that of the Romans.

In spite of appearances on the map, Francis had of course certain advantages. His country was "compact, united, rich, populous." Further, France "being interposed between the provinces of the emperor's dominions," the French King enjoyed a strategic position which might overbalance the outward advantage given by the superior territories of Charles.[4]

Especially might this be so if Francis could stay in the good graces of the English King and the Cardinal. He had long expressed a wish to meet and discourse with Henry, and Henry himself had been pleasantly disposed to the prospect. He had not only shown a lively curiosity about the French King's appearance and qualities of build, but upon hearing that Francis had a beard he had resolved not to cut off his own beard until he should meet his brother of France. The gesture was taken in good faith by Francis. When the intelligence of King Henry's beard and resolution was conveyed to Francis by Sir Thomas Boleyn, the English ambassador, he likewise made a solemn oath that he would devote his beard to the promised meeting.

The growth of the beards was looked upon as a ratification of the agreement of the two kings. It was looked upon by the French as a solemn and religious token. But, alas, a Frenchman of repute returned to France during these days of tremulous waiting and reported that Henry had cut off his beard. This act the French regarded as breach of faith and a declaration that Henry had no real design to have the interview take place. Sir Thomas Boleyn explained the disappearance of the beard as best he could, not having firm instructions from the home government. He doubted not that the beard had been cut at the insistence of the Queen, who had "formerly made pressing instances to His Majesty, when his beard grew long and incommodious, that, to oblige her, he would cut it off." He added assurances that it "was not done with any design of frustrating the interview and that the King's mind and affection were still the same."[5]

In spite of hesitations and misgivings, plans for the majestic interview went forward. On January 10, 1520, Francis named my lord of York as his proctor for the occasion. Hall records that both kings "committed the order and manner of their meeting unto the Cardinal of York."[6] The meeting was to take place not far from Calais in a valley known as Val Doré, halfway between the towns of Guines and Ardres. In April Sir Robert Wingfield was at the Parisian court and from there wrote to Wolsey: "Sir, the king here would gladly know whether the king his brother would be content to forbear the making of rich tents and pavilions; which thing he would be well contented to forbear on his part."[7] This suggestion, so modestly and diplomatically put, must have afforded my lord of York as much amusement as it did those who later looked upon and reflected upon the magnificently tinseled meeting. For the Cardinal was not one to put a small mouth on anything, and all his preparations suggested that the occasion would be a display of English mercantile might, as the invasion of France had been eight years before.

He summoned his artificers and set them to work on plans and structures no less elaborate than those required for an invasion, so that France had no choice but to compete in the display if she was not to be hopelessly outshone.

The scene of the meeting came to be known as the Field of Cloth of Gold, which Pollard says is a mistranslation of the French, *Le Camp du Drap d'Or*. At any rate, the name seemed to suit the richness and elegance of the pretensions made on both parts, and particularly by the English. Godwin says that eleven thousand artificers labored over the necessary buildings. Two Italians who later visited the lavish scene when it was complete testify that three thousand artificers were required to construct the features of the English scene alone.

Still, with all the preparations for a kind of world fair and with all the growing beards, the projected meeting was delayed. And the fault lay with the English. In the shadows beyond the council fires of all of Henry's deliberations stood the gaunt, grave figure of the new boy Emperor. If Francis needed the aid of England, Charles would need it too. It would be foolish, an act lacking in diplomatic guile, to talk with Francis until England could determine what Charles had to offer. Henry and Charles must meet privately before Henry and Francis met publicly.

In reaching this decision it was not my lord of York but Catherine of Aragon who played the winning role. Wolsey himself was firm for the French interview, being proctor to the occasion and heavy with responsibility for the arrangements and being of course drawn toward peace with France by his pensions there. Friendship with France had been a fixed point in his scheme of things, unnatural though it was to the hatred which the English had long borne their Christian brothers beyond the Channel. His first treaty, even before he became Lord Chancellor, had been arranged through the marriage of Louis XII of France to Mary the King's sister. It lay within the logic of circumstances, seeing the Emperor's wide dominions and overweening power, that England and France should be united for everlasting peace and that the Kings of the two countries should meet and cement this union of purpose by the right hand of fellowship. To this lofty end, and with his French pensions ever on the horizon, he sought to hasten the interview.

But in his clever calculations my lord Cardinal had reckoned without the power that still resided in the Queen. He had underestimated the power of a woman, a woman of great and stern abilities in affairs of state and of great tenderness and devotion in affairs of family. Charles V was Emperor; he was also her nephew, the son of her tragic and beloved and distrait sister Joanna. And the Emperor was by her marriage nephew to the King of England her husband. It would not be amiss that Charles pay a visit to his aunt and uncle in England. Henry could not be averse to a meeting which combined the features of a family reunion with an act of homage from an Emperor to a King.

Catherine set about busily to bring Charles to England before Henry should set off for France. She moved first on the diplomatic plane and then resorted to womanhood. She let it be known in Spain that it would be well for Charles to come by way of England on a trip he planned to make to Germany. A Spanish ambassador in the person of de Mesa brought the suggestion to the English court. He elaborated it into a proposal that the Emperor and the two Kings should meet and settle all the problems of Christendom at once, with my lord of York as Cardinal and Legate *a latere* of course presiding over the conference of the princes.

The suggestion had merit, its chief merit being that it flattered the vanity of Wolsey, exalting him for at least a season above the three great rulers of the acknowledged world. But Wolsey rejected the proposal and hewed to his line that Henry and Francis should meet as he had planned. Wolsey likewise stood stubbornly in the way of the more modest suggestion that Charles visit Henry. Catherine made clear and reasoned arguments against the French alliance among the King's councilors. One of her statements, carefully prepared in advance, was heard by the King and was reported later to Wolsey, who, according to de Mesa, was much shaken by it. Her ability had been demonstrated when as regent she commanded the defense of the country against the Scots at the time of Flodden; and if she had lost caste as Ferdinand's daughter and ambassador in the early days of her marriage, she had retained respect of the court and the people for her piety and her devotion to England in a moment of crisis.

The subject of the meeting now became an open contest between the Queen and the Cardinal, but it was never quite played in the open. Circumstances were on the side of the Cardinal, who had only to encourage delay until it was too late to make the proper arrangements for the entertainment of the Emperor before Henry must set off for the French interview. The Emperor himself raised many difficulties. He could not promise to reach England save at some indefinite time in the spring of 1520.

Meanwhile Wolsey went steadily forward with the plans for the Field of Cloth of Gold. And meanwhile the court and the imperial ambassadors watched Henry's beard as a sign of his wavering resolution. When it disappeared, the French looked gloomy and construed it as a sign that the Queen had won her tussle with the Cardinal. When it reappeared, the Imperialists around the court said it was because the Queen had found she liked it after all; the Venetians, being friends of the French, retorted that it was because the French had won. And the gradually increasing luxury of the King's whiskers sent the French hopes soaring.[8]

In the spring of 1520 Catherine's hopes sank very low. It was then that the strong sense of womanhood which marked all her doings came to the fore. Mattingly tells us that "in the presence of the imperial ambassadors and a number of nobles and counselors, she fell on her knees before her husband and declared that the greatest wish of her heart was to see her nephew, the successor to her father's kingdom." Henry assured her, as he raised her from her knees, that he would do everything he could to satisfy her wish. But the delay lay with Charles and not with Henry. The English King had written Charles to say that he must cross to Calais on May 31 and that unless Charles reached England by the middle of May the interview would have to be canceled. The Emperor did everything he could to hasten his passage, but the weather was against him. The middle of May came and went, and the Spanish ships had not appeared off the white cliffs of Dover.

Wolsey could now vigorously oppose further delay, and with good grace. The deadline of the visit had passed. The Channel ports were busy shipping all the paraphernalia designed to impress the French. A thousand and one details about tents and huts and palaces had to be attended to. Still the King delayed, held in check by the entreaties of his Queen. Time was running out. Mattingly believes that it was only the efforts of the Queen that made the meeting possible, and de Mesa thought that only last-minute solicitations by Catherine had kept the two from missing each other by a few hours. For it was not until the evening of May 26, 1520, that the Emperor's fleet arrived.

Meanwhile, the court had moved to Canterbury and Wolsey had gone on to Dover. When word came of the Emperor's arrival, Wolsey, whatever his views, was now the King's welcomer, and he put out in a small boat to meet the Emperor and conducted him to Dover Castle, where lodging for the night had been provided. Word of the Emperor's arrival had been conveyed to the King at Canterbury, and the King, as Godwin records it, "although it were midnight, takes horse and a little more than an hour later comes by torchlight to Dover Castle where the Emperor lay; who, sea-weary, was then asleep but being certified of the King's arrival he suddenly apparelled himself and met the King at the top of the stairs."[9]

What happened during the remaining days and nights before the English royal party left in state for Calais, no one, not even Wolsey, fully knew. Henry rode the next morning with Charles to Canterbury, where Charles met his aunt for the first time, showing her a shy and becoming deference, only to be embraced warmly and welcomed by her with unabashed tears. Henry and Catherine and Charles had breakfast together; Wolsey was not invited to the family board, nor was he bidden to be present at two long talks the three had during the remainder of the Emperor's stay. But it was plain to any observer that the family conference had worked out as Catherine had fondly hoped and fervently prayed it might. The visit of the Emperor of the Holy Roman Empire to England was unprecedented. Henry's pride had been touched as Catherine expected, and his vanity was all the more pleased and touched by the fact that this Emperor was a diffident and retiring young man of twenty-one who listened attentively to the advice and counsel he sought from the man he treated as a father. Later Charles was to complete the picture of filial fidelity by writing to thank Henry for "the advice you gave me like a good father when we were at Cantoberi."[10]

Whatever else he did at Canterbury, Charles paid Henry during his stay in England the highest compliment that can be paid even to a king: he made Henry feel needed. He came as a suppliant and a son, one who had scarcely known his own father and mother and who now at a high stage of responsibility needed the help Henry could give in the midst of all his imperial perplexities. In this role his attitude of pious deference was greatly assisted by his physical equipment and appearance. Nature had made him up for the part and left him free to operate behind a permanent mask of simple-mindedness that concealed a cunning mind. He spoke with a stammer and a pronounced lisp. His underjaw protruded so much that his teeth did not meet, and the portraits painted of him even by obsequious artists present his face and gaping mouth and vacuous eyes in a manner that suggests an overdressed dimwit, the degenerate end of a long line of illustrious sires. The impression left upon his bluff and hearty uncle, oversupplied with glandular vitality, must have been one of pathos and helpless need. Here was the Emperor of the greater part of Christendom who asked and wanted only the protection and assistance of the English King against any hostile forces that might be thrown against him.

How well Charles captured Henry's solicitude is to be noted in the fact that before his ships set sail from Dover he and the English King had arranged to meet quietly at Gravelines after the formalities of the Field of Cloth of Gold had been overpassed. And the pact of filial friendship he had established with Henry of England turned the meeting between Henry and Francis, so agreeably sought by Francis and so elaborately planned by my lord of York, into a pompous and costly farce. Even so, it must at whatever cost be carried through. Henry's bushy beard testified to that.

Henry and Francis met at last—on June 7, 1520, in the awed presence of thousands of their followers and in the sight of thousands of the common people of France who watched from the hills that created the Val Doré. They met as Wolsey had planned, despite all the delays and difficulties; they met and embraced in the presence of the multitude; and with their rich retinues they remained together for sixteen days.

Yet, oddly, they did not meet at all. Their minds remained at home or dwelt on things extraneous or afar. Henry and Francis were young and stately princes so evenly matched and endowed by nature and fortune that they spent the time preening themselves before admirers, each taking the measure of the other. There were fits and starts of friendliness, some scenes in which the two young men dropped their royal masks. But there was one occasion when the taut rivalry between them snapped in a split second of near conflict, and only the babbling intervention of their courtiers and the timely attention of their queens rescued them from the undignified spectacle of a fist fight.

It was but a moment in human history, this extravagant meeting of the two Kings, but it was one of those illumined moments when even the casual eye could see plainly at work forces usually lost in the shadows of culture or in the cushions of diplomacy. Here in the valley between Guines and Ardres these forces were not only visible but attired for their parts. History was being planned and rehearsed—demonstrated, as it were, and as it was, and evermore would be. Here were the anointed elite of two great nations, bound by a solemn treaty of friendship, meeting to sanction the future peace of the world. The author and director of the scene was a Cardinal and Legate of His Holiness. He gave the scene a religious setting and did all he could to clothe realities in magnificence; the realities were there just the same. The elite were there, with fixed schemes and purposes and a convenient sense of their own destinies. The common people were not, save those who came to serve their betters or to gape from distant hills.

The whole affair was staged and produced by my lord of York, and a study of it affords an instructive picture of the duality of his mind, part of which lingered romantically in the age of chivalry and the other part attempted, however unsuccessfully, to deal with the basic problems of government and justice. The Field of Cloth of Gold afforded the last great canvas of the Middle Ages. Such a panoplied event as he now superintended could have taken place without anomaly two hundred years before; such an event did not take place again. It marked the end of the age of chivalry and somehow prophetically dramatized the end of the age of churchmen. Particularly it adumbrated the end of an age in which a Cardinal could cloak the intrigue of princes in the vestments of his office.

From the standpoint of its effect upon witnesses, both English and French, the setting of the Field proved to be as rich and impressive as one would expect under Wolsey's diligent management. He spared no pains to make that setting colossal. Nor did he spare the nobility pains either. With the royal approval he gave them instructions, at whatever cost, to see that the wealth of England was appropriately represented there.

Plans in such an enterprise were subject constantly to change and often to elaboration. At first it was planned to house the English King and Queen in Guines Castle, with Francis and his queen settled in the castle at Ardres across the valley. But the castle at Guines was found to be in hopeless disrepair, its weedy moat and its keep "too ruinous to mend." So in the course of a few weeks the busy English artificers erected and decorated a summer palace, being an exact square of 328 feet, on the castle green. It was a task that called for incredibly careful workmanship and the shipping of costly materials over great distances. According to the astonished testimony of two Italian observers, the palace was "made of boards painted to look like brick, a round tower being placed at each corner. The gatehouse in the center of one quadrant had loopholes and battlements defended by statues of armed men in the act of discharging stones and iron balls from cannons and culverins." The great hall in the palace, they said, was "as lofty as that of the Pasaro palace at San Benetto, but longer, with a ceiling of green sarcenet and gold roses, decorated with hangings of silk and gold, woven with figures and horses represented to the life."[11]

Outside this transient palace, English ingenuity and foresight had contrived a gilt fountain, said to be of antique workmanship, with a statue of Bacchus "birlying the wine." The fountain sported "three runlets, fed by secret conduits hid beneath the earth." These "spouted claret, hypocras, and water into as many silver cups, to quench the thirst of all comers." Thus the new age of inventiveness mingled with the perishing age of chivalry. Within the palace the old world held sway, as if in a citadel. Chairs were covered with "cushions of Turkey work, cloths of estate . . . overlaid with tissue and rich embroidery." The palace was "pierced on every side with oriel windows"—windows glazed in a day when glass was still a luxury—and the trimmings overlaid with gold. A French dignitary, de Fleuranges, looked upon the palace flung up with such artistry and declared that "every quarter of it, even the least, was a habitation fit for a prince."

As befitted a palace planned by my lord Cardinal, it had attached to it a spacious chapel more adorned than the palace, served by thirty-five priests and a covey of singing boys. The copes and vestments of the "officiating clergy were cloth of tissue powdered with red roses, brought from the looms of Florence, and woven in one piece, thickly studded with gold and jewelry." In the chapel stood "a beautiful silver organ with gold ornaments." And to lend further wealth and piety stood also twelve golden images of the Apostles, "as large as children of four years old." Henry must move in an atmosphere of unction, and he could not visit France without the Twelve Apostles, whether they be as before in the form of cannons or now in the form of golden images.

The chapel was for the meditation and religious solace of the English royal household. For the chapel in which he would sing high Mass before the two kings and their attendants, Wolsey had brought to the Field of Cloth of Gold a chapel fabricated ahead of the sailing from England and capable of being assembled overnight. He had thought of everything.

The details were as the sands of the sea. Assembling the vast concourse of knights and nobles from all over the kingdom, scheduling their embarkation at Dover and other Channel ports, transporting them across quarrelsome waters, landing them at Calais, moving them on and lodging them in and around Guines—such an operation required at each step the precision and foresight of a military leader. The dimensions of the English party were those of an army. In the King's retinue, including dukes, earls, marquises, bishops, barons, knights, and their attendants and servants, marched 4544 persons. The Queen's contingent was smaller, but respectable, numbering 1260 persons. The Rutland Papers solemnly record that the total number of persons who came with the King and Queen was 5804. Nor was this the end. The King and his attendants had 2406 horses and the Queen and her attendants 817, making a total of 3223 horses.[12]

Orders of precedence, both in the line of march and in lodging arrangements, had to be handled with due delicacy, for there was an aristocracy among servants as rigid as among nobles. The Lord Chamberlain, the Lord Steward, the Lord Treasurer of the King's household, the comptroller, "with their numerous staffs, had to be lodged in apartments adapted to their rank and services." Lesser officers and servants formed a colony apart from the royal household but integral to the scene: 2800 tents were spread out on the barren plain that marked the English pale at Guines, each marked with a pennon or badge to show the rank or service of the occupant.

Merely to provision such a host for the duration of the meeting meant that Wolsey had to plan as shrewdly as he had in the days of 1513. It was necessary to supply and transport to the spot 340 beeves, 2200 sheep, 800 calves, 560 tuns of beer, and to provide 4000 pounds of wax for lights. Always beyond the sound of trumpets in fanfare, the ceremonial boom of cannon, the thud of hooves, and the breaking of lances in the lists could be heard the bleating of sheep and the bawling of beeves. It was a sound familiar to a man who had spent his boyhood near the market place in Ipswich.

In his creative management of tangibles Wolsey's genius shone as bright as the scene he had fashioned. And if there were muttered complaints against him for the cost and inconvenience he had caused the nobles, there was ample recognition of his services by both the Kings. The vast contemporary painting depicting the arrival of the English cavalcade shows Wolsey riding at the side of Henry, the Marquis of Dorset going on before with the sword of state. And before the first meeting of the two Kings it was my lord of York who paid a ceremonial visit to the French King. The Cardinal's procession was led by a hundred archers of the guard, followed by fifty gentlemen of his household, "clothed in crimson velvet with chains of gold, bareheaded, bonnet in hand, and mounted on magnificent horses richly caparisoned. After them came 50 gentlemen ushers, also bareheaded, carrying gold maces with knobs as big as a man's head; next a cross-bearer in scarlet, supporting a crucifix adorned with precious stones." After all of these came the Cardinal Legate, in mock humility mounted on a mule "trapped in crimson velvet, with gold front-stalls, studs, buckles, and stirrups."[13]

When Wolsey with all his fancywork reached the town of Ardres and came before the French King's house, he was greeted as became his velvet virtues with the roar of cannon, the sound of drums, trumpets, and fifes. Here was a personage indeed. For the French King received him as an equal, and showed toward him the signs of greatest affection. It was Wolsey's magic hour, the height of his splendor. The great commoner had become a ruler among rulers, riding forth in conspicuous equality with his own King, being saluted bonnet in hand by another. As the indefatigable and Argus-eyed master of arrangements, he had made himself indispensable. The very eating of Kings and Queens depended on his managerial skill. And in addition to being Lord Chamberlain to the two royal households, he was, by virtue of his ecclesiastical offices, a person who could stand with kings and seem of no lesser rank. Both his ability and his dignity found their finest opportunity in the meeting of chiefs of two great nations on the Field of Cloth of Gold.

All the extravagance could not mask the suspicions and politely repressed hostility the governing classes of England and France brought with them to the Field. It was, in fact, this hostility which made the elaborate arrangements and safeguards necessary. In effect and outcome the heralded interview of the Kings and the mingling of their selected subjects was a failure, a gross and costly formality that accomplished nothing; it was as if the witnesses had been called to prove what everyone knew already: that Henry and Francis were rivals and that the daring victor of Marignano who had made Henry ridiculous by his exploits would not at this stage of the game, when he was still flushed with a sense of his own prowess, make any bid for Henry's favor. Or if the matter be put on a more diplomatic plane, Francis regarded Charles, with his encircling empire, as the real enemy he could not brook. His intent in the interview had been to woo Henry to his own support, but the futility of that purpose became plain when the interview was postponed continually in order that Henry might meet first with Charles. And the unhappy turn of events—against the wishes of Wolsey and the hopes of Francis—doomed the meeting to irrelevancy.

The meeting had been held because Wolsey's industrious preparations had made it inescapable. All the nobles and calves and beeves and knights and sheep he had set in motion could not be turned back without grave embarrassment to both countries. But these properties made the meeting all the more of a fiasco and made my lord of York, when it was clear that the meeting of Henry and Francis was but an interlude between another meeting of Henry and the Emperor, look ridiculous. In the strenuous pursuit of a thousand and one details dealing with physical comforts and rampant display, he had missed the point entirely. The same foresight which enabled him to see that there was wax for lights—four thousand pounds of it—deserted him when he looked upon the probable course of events. He had failed to calculate Catherine and the strength of family ties and the impression an Emperor in the form of a gauche and retarded youth would make on a King who had never had a son.

Of course careful efforts were made, both ahead of the event and during the course of the meeting, to insure success. Wolsey had arranged that no French ships should put out to sea until all the English party had returned. It was a daring and hazardous venture to trust the French with the cream of England, and every precaution had to be taken. The air had been poisoned by rumors. One of these, to the effect that the French were fitting out ships ready to strike England, had stopped preparations for the interview. And on the very eve of the meeting Henry is said to have "discovered that three or four thousand French troops were concealed in the neighboring country."

Further precautions had been taken in a schedule of protocol, so that each King did simultaneously what the other King did. When Henry set sail for Calais, Francis left Montreuil for Ardres. And when on June 7 the actual meeting was to take place, it was announced by a shot fired from the castle at Guines which was answered by a shot fired from the castle at Ardres.

Henry had directed Edward Hall, recorder of London, to keep a diary of the incidents, and the result is inserted in Hall's *Chronicle;* also he caused a painting to be made, which may be seen in Hampton Court. Francis ordered Monsieur Peyresc to compose a journal of the meeting and Maréchal de Fleuranges wrote an account of it in his memoirs. The photographers were present in force.

Henry, who by the testimony of both biased chroniclers and French observers was the comeliest and most commanding prince of his age, was dressed in cloth of silver damask, thickly ribbed with cloth of gold. He rode a charger arrayed in trappings overlaid with fine gold, all topped with a red beard and ruddy countenance. Attending close upon the King was Sir Henry Guilford, who with English profligacy led a spare charger splendidly caparisoned.

On the surrounding hills was a vast cloud of witnesses—the uninvited, drawn from their dingy homes by curiosity, clinging to their bleacher seats in spite of the severity of provost-marshal and threats of chastisement. They had come from the French frontier or the populous cities of Flanders; they had come for the show and to hell with politics. When Francis set out from Montreuil, the procession drew to it a multitude of vagrants and idle followers. Accounts say that no less than ten thousand of these had been forced to turn back by "a proclamation ordering that no person, without special permission, should approach within two leagues of the King's train, 'on pain of the halter.'" Still thousands of others had gathered round to look at the Kings—among them beggars, itinerant minstrels, vendors of provisions and small luxuries to those who had been negligent in their packing, wagoners, plowmen, laborers, all proving that a cat can look at a King. Now they gazed down upon knights and ladies and Kings and Queens dressed in their finest and on parade and as if they had no higher purpose than to amuse the common people. What a setting for an opera!

They saw now the two royal parties approaching each other. Then there was a momentary pause—"a breathless silence, followed by a slight stir on both sides." Then amid the shouts of the spectators on the surrounding hills "and the shrill burst of pipes, trumpets, and clarions, two horsemen were seen to emerge, and, in the sight of both nations, slowly descend into the valley from opposite sides. These were the two sovereigns. As they approached nearer they spurred their horses to a gallop." As they reined up, they embraced first on horseback and then, dismounting, embraced again. Then in the friendliest of spirits they walked together to a pavilion that had been provided at the place of meeting and entered it to talk. No one else was allowed to enter, except Wolsey, of course, and the Admiral of France. As they entered the pavilion, the two parties attending the Kings began to intermingle awkwardly, making good cheer and toasting "each other in broken French and English: 'Bons amys, French and English!' "[14]

Inside the pavilion the French and English Kings were apparently "bons amys" too. De Fleuranges in his memoirs records a touching incident as they sat together there. Henry proposed to make some amendments to their former articles of alliance. As he began to read the draft of the new treaty, the first words he encountered were: *I Henry King.* He stopped for a moment, significantly, and then added *of England,* not adding the words *and France,* as was the usual style of English monarchs with their long and agitated pretensions to the throne of France. Francis remarked this delicacy, as Hume puts it, "and expressed by a smile his approbation of it."[15]

It was a good beginning, showing a spirit of concession that augured well. Thereafter both Henry and Francis feinted at friendship, but the days were tightly scheduled with ceremonies, and reciprocity was so minutely ordered that it was difficult for them to meet as man meets man. On the Sunday that the French King dined at Guines with the Queen of England, the English King dined with the French Queen. Catherine was gracious to Francis, having the assurance of Henry's prior meeting with Charles to comfort her. Henry on his part was treated to a bevy of French femininity; the prospect of his being entertained by the beauties of France had been one of the lures Francis had insinuated into the early negotiations for the meeting, and Henry now made the most of the fare offered. In the ruddy manner of the English, he kissed the French Queen, then kissed Louise of Savoy (the King's mother), then the Duchess of Alençon, and finally all the ladies of the company. After this example of collaboration the King sat at a great banquet until five in the evening. By the time the banquet was over, both the King and his horse were feeling their oats. "To display his skill before the ladies, he set spurs to his horse, making it bound and curvet 'as valiantly as any man could do.' "

All very pleasant, these pastimes. Still they did little to advance the purpose for which the meeting was called. The Kings were kept apart by the very ceremonies designed to bring them together. In Wolsey's Book of Ordinances the arrangements to be observed on every occasion, whether of gaiety or piety, had been meticulously set forth. Everyone, including the Kings, had his part written in the script, and he must play it accordingly. Regulation was imperative in the eyes of my lord Cardinal and Legate; his regulation and planning went far beyond the sheep and beeves; it kept the richly dressed puppets of England and the marionettes of France obedient to his strings.

The protection provided by excessive scheduling may have pleased Henry; at least he seemed content to accept it. Francis was not. He made a magnificent gesture to break through the stultifying ordinances. Being of a gallant and generous turn and given to spontaneity and trust, he grew restive under the confinement of precautions.

One morning Francis arose early and, slipping past his own guards, rode straight to Guines, accompanied only by two of his gentlemen attendants and a page. When he reached the English King's apartments there, the guards were astonied to see him and not less to hear him say, 'You are all my prisoners: carry me to your master." Which they did. Henry, who had not yet risen from his couch, rubbed his eyes at the sight of the beaming French King who had come to pay him homage without benefit of protocol so early in the morning. Then he arose and threw his arms around Francis and said: "My brother, you have played me the most agreeable trick in the world and have showed me the full confidence I may place in you: I surrender myself your prisoner from this moment." He then took a collar of pearls of great price and placed it around Francis's neck, begging him to wear it for the sake of his prisoner. To this suggestion Francis assented, but only on the condition that Henry "should wear a bracelet, of which he made him a present, and which was double in value to the collar."[16]

Francis had penetrated the *cordon sanitaire* by his premeditated spontaneity. From then on there was a certain camaraderie between the two Kings; both had escaped from the governess of propriety. The next day Henry, not one to be outdone, rode to Ardres without guards or attendants. Henry and Francis were now acknowledged as individuals, not merely monarchs, and given some freedom from the abominable ordinances. Both had taken prudent steps toward each other but not enough to bring them together.

Then one day in the midst of festivities and in the presence of the two Queens, Henry, feeling jovial and playful after beating Francis at archery, seized the long-legged Frenchman by the collar, shouting, "Come, you shall wrestle with me!" It was a touch of informality Francis had not expected and he was, for a moment, caught off his guard. But he recovered quickly, and in the unpredicted struggle which followed, Francis, being released by surprise from his polite obligations as a host, threw Henry with a thud on his royal rump. If Francis had been surprised, Henry was dumfounded. This was no way to treat a pampered king. No one, certainly not since childhood, had ever laid a controlling hand on him or clipped his will or thwarted so much as one of his whims. Accounts say that he rose to his feet in a rage, squared away and muttered, "Again!"[17]

The moment was as breathless as Henry. Fortunately the Queens came forward promptly, and courtiers flocked around and smothered the crisis with a blanket of jolly palaver, all making very light of what they had beheld. They thus prevented further rounds of the wrestling match, but they could not rub out the effect of what had happened. It was not according to protocol, not in the meticulous script of ordinances my lord Cardinal had written for the occasion.

The outward relations between the two sovereigns and their attendants continued cordial to the end of the prescribed festivities. Politeness had been ordered and delivered. The royal parties behaved in a resolutely civilized way. And to smooth anything amiss, my lord Cardinal and Legate gave the great assemblage his religious benediction as the two Kings prepared to part. In a showy chapel of wood built on the Field in one night and furnished with twenty-four enormous gold candlesticks and with the golden images of the Twelve Apostles, Wolsey sang himself a high and solemn Mass before the two Kings and their Queens and pronounced sacerdotal indulgences on them and their followers. In attendance upon him were two cardinals, two legates, four archbishops and ten bishops, not to mention assorted members of the French and English nobility. The air was "perfumed with incense and flowers," and the altars were hung with cloth-of-gold tissue.

It was an inspiring moment, and the religious atmosphere brought forth the most gallant impulses of those who took part. When the Cardinal of Bourbon, "according to the usages of the time, presented the Gospel to the French King to kiss, Francis, declining, commanded it to be offered to the King of England, who was too well bred to accept the honour." Later the two Queens were equally ceremonious. After a friendly dispute as to who should kiss the Pax first, they ended by kissing each other instead.

Behind the French Queen on this vast occasion knelt a young Englishwoman, as small as a footnote on the great page of history being written there. The sister of one who had been a mistress to Henry, she was a woman of inconspicuous charm, with nothing in particular to draw sudden attention. It was said later that she had a bosom not much raised, but of her eyes men remarked that they "are black and beautiful, and take great effect."[18]

Her name was Anne Boleyn.

NOTES

NOTES

The following book will be of particular value to the reader whose interest may be stirred to a point where he will want to read further in the period covered:

Conyers Read, ed., *Bibliography of British History, Tudor Period, 1485-1603* (Oxford, 1933). Issued under the direction of the American Historical Association and the Royal Historical Society of Great Britain.

Certain abbreviations of titles will be found in the Notes as follows:

L. & P.

Letters and Papers, Foreign and Domestic, of the Reign of Henry VIII, Preserved in the Public Record Office, the British Museum, and Elsewhere in England . . . arranged and catalogued by J. S. Brewer (London, 1876). The Roman numeral designates the volume, and the numbers following, unless specified as pages, designate the documents in the volume.

STATE PAPERS

State Papers published under the authority of His Majesty's Commission, King Henry VIII, Volumes I and II (London, 1830-1852). Of this collection the historian Read says: "Contains only material in the P. R. O. Correspondence printed *in extenso*. Superseded by *Letters and Papers* except where full text of letter is needed."

SPANISH CALENDAR

Calendar of State Papers, Spanish. Vols. I, II, and Supplementary Volume, 1485-1525, by G. A. Bergenroth; Vols. III-VII, 1524-1544, by Pascual de Gayangos y Arce.

VENETIAN CALENDAR

Calendar of State Papers, Venetian. Vols. I-IX, 1202-1603. By Rowdon Brown, Cavendish Bentinck and Horatio Brown.

BOOK I

CHAPTER I

[1] Arthur Mee, ed., *The King's England: Suffolk* (London, 1941), p. 79; for details of early Ipswich, John Wodderspoon, *Memorials of the Ancient*

Town of Ipswich in the County of Suffolk (London, 1950) and G. R. Clarke, *The History and Description of the Town and Borough of Ipswich* (London, 1830).

2 J. Bohn, ed., *Chronicles of the White Rose of York* (London, 1945), "Warkworth's Chronicle." References in order of material quoted: pp. 109, 115, 132, 133, 38.

3 James Gairdner, ed., *The Paston Letters 1422-1509 A.D.* (London, 1872), Vol. III, p. 15.

4 Augustus Jessopp, *The Coming of the Friars and Other Historical Essays* (New York, 1895), p. 172, quoting Villani. Contains much valuable data on the Black Death, especially in East Anglia.

5 G. M. Trevelyan, *English Social History:* A Survey of Six Centuries—Chaucer to Queen Victoria (London, 1942), pp. 10, 11.

6 *Ibid.*, p. 23.

7 S. T. Bindoff, *Tudor England* (Harmondsworth, 1950), p. 12.

8 Edward P. Cheyney, *Social Changes in England in the 16th Century as Reflected in Contemporary Literature* (Boston, 1895), pp. 27, 28.

9 S. H. Burke, *Historical Portraits of the Tudor Dynasty* (London, 1893), Vol. I, pp. 102, 103.

10 Cheyney, *op. cit.*, p. 36.

11 L. F. Salzman, *England in Tudor Times* (London, 1926), p. 8.

12 Eileen Power, *Medieval People* (Boston, 1935), p. 131.

13 Sir Walter Besant, *London in the Time of the Tudors* (London, 1904), Vol. I, p. 275.

14 Trevelyan, *op. cit.*, p. 71.

15 Frederick Chamberlin, *The Private Character of Henry the Eighth* (New York, 1931), p. 82.

16 Philip Lindsay, *The Tragic King, Richard III* (New York, 1934), pp. 50, 51.

17 *The Annalls of Ipswiche, The Lawes and Customes and Government of the Same.* By Nathaniel Bacon, Serving as Recorder and Town Clark in that Towne (Ipswich, 1654). Edited by W. H. Richardson (Ipswich, 1884), pp. 131, 134, 147.

18 *Ibid.*, pp. 137, 139.

19 Vincent R. Redstone, "Social Condition of England During the Wars of the Roses," *Transactions of the Royal Historical Society,* Vol. XVI (1902), Appendix, pp. 199, 200.

20 James Gairdner, *History of the Life and Reign of Richard the Third* (Cambridge, 1898), pp. 16, 17.

CHAPTER II

[1] Dorothy Hartley and Margaret M. Elliot, *Life and Work of the People of England* (New York, 1926), Vol. II, p. 35.

[2] Thomas Wright, *Homes of Other Days*, A History of Domestic Manners and Sentiments in England From the Earliest Known Period to Modern Times (London and New York, 1871), p. 425.

[3] Frederick J. Furnivall, ed., *Early English Meals and Manners* (Oxford, 1868), pp. 46, 47.

[4] Eileen Power, *Medieval People* (Boston, 1935), p. 163, quoting Thomas Deloney's works.

[5] James Gairdner, ed., *The Paston Letters 1422-1509 A.D.* (London, 1872), Vol. III, p. 481.

[6] Christina Hole, *English Home Life 1500-1800* (London, 1947), p. 41 ff.

[7] H. F. M. Prescott, *Mary Tudor* (New York, 1953), p. 26.

[8] G. Laurence and Alice Bertha Gomme, *The Traditional Games of England, Scotland and Ireland* (London, 1894-1898), Vol. I, p. 234.

[9] J. Brand, *Observations on the Popular Antiquities of Great Britain.* Chiefly Illustrating the Origin of Our Vulgar Customs, Ceremonies and Superstitions (London, 1900), p. 229.

[10] *The Annalls of Ipswiche, The Lawes and Customes and Government of the Same.* By Nathaniel Bacon. Edited by W. H. Richardson (Ipswich, 1884), pp. 140, 147.

[11] Alice Stopford Green, *Town Life in the Fifteenth Century* (London, 1907), Vol. II, pp. 22, 23, 16.

[12] Furnivall, *op. cit.*, pp. 18-20, 179, quoting John Russell's *Boke of Nurture*.

[13] *Ibid.*, pp. 201-202, quoting *The Boke of Curtsaye*.

[14] *Ibid.*, p. 66.

[15] *Ibid.*, p. 7.

[16] *Ibid.*, pp. 63, 64, 66.

[17] *Ibid.*, pp. 128, 129.

CHAPTER III

[1] Descriptions of early butchering practices are posted in modern Ipswich.

[2] Hastings Rashdall, *The Universities of Europe in the Middle Ages.* Edited by F. M. Powicke and A. B. Emden (Oxford, 1936), Vol. III, p. 362.

[3] *Ibid.*, p. 371.

[4] Charles Edward Mallet, *A History of the University of Oxford* (London, 1924), Vol. I, p. 389.

[5] Rashdall, *op. cit.*, p. 417.

[6] Rashdall, *op. cit.*, p. 432.

[7] Mallet, *op. cit.*, p. 389.

[8] H. C. Maxwell Lyte, *A History of the University of Oxford from the Earliest Times to the Year 1530* (New York, 1886), p. 208.

[9] *Ibid.*, p. 209.

[10] Gladys Temperly, *Henry VII* (Boston, 1914), p. 308, citing Wilkins' *Concilia*, iii, 618, 619, 620.

[11] Richard Henry Gretton, *The English Middle Class* (London, 1917), p. 78.

[12] James Gairdner, *Henry the Seventh* (London, 1899), p. 6.

[13] James Gairdner, *History of the Life and Reign of Richard the Third* (Cambridge, 1898), p. 185.

[14] *Ibid.*, p. 206, quoting Croyland's *Chronicle*.

[15] For an excellent account of the battle of Bosworth, see Alfred H. Burne, *The Battlefields of England* (London, 1950), p. 137 ff.

[16] H. A. L. Fisher, *The History of England from the Accession of Henry VII to the Death of Henry VIII (1485-1547)* (London, New York and Toronto, 1934), p. 10. (Vol. V in *The Political History of England,* edited by William Hunt and Reginald L. Poole.)

[17] Sharon F. S. A. Turner, *The History of England* (London, 1823-1826), Vol. III, p. 551, quoting Drake's *Ebor,* p. 121, note.

[18] Matthias A. Shaaber, *Some Forerunners of the Newspaper in England* (University of Pennsylvania, 1939), p. 39.

[19] James Gairdner, *Henry the Seventh,* p. 90.

[20] Details of the story of Lambert Simnel may be found in Fisher, *op. cit.,* and other standard reference works of the period.

[21] Fisher, *op. cit.,* pp. 1, 2.

CHAPTER IV

[1] G. M. Trevelyan, *English Social History* (London, 1942), p. 75.

[2] W. W. Copes, *The English Church in the Fourteenth and Fifteenth Centuries* (London, 1900), p. 363.

[3] Anthony Wood, *The History and Antiquities of the University of Oxford* (Oxford, 1792-1796), Vol. I, p. 648.

[4] H. D. Traill and J. S. Mann, eds., *Social England: A Record of the Progress of the People in Religion, Laws, Art, Industry, Commerce, Science, Literature and Manners from the Earliest Times to the Present Day* (London, 1903), Vol. III, p. 240.

[5] William Dunn Macray, *A Register of the Members of St. Mary Magdalen*

College Oxford from the Foundation of the College (London, 1894), New Series, Vol. I, pp. 14, 15.

6 Wood, *op. cit.,* p. 651.

7 Macray, *op. cit.,* p. 26.

8 S. T. Bindoff, *Tudor England* (Harmondsworth, 1950), p. 29.

9 Alice Stopford Green, *Town Life in the Fifteenth Century* (London, 1907), Vol. I, pp. 52, 53.

10 H. C. Maxwell Lyte, *A History of the University of Oxford from the Earliest Times to the Year 1530* (New York, 1886), p. 213.

11 *Ibid.,* pp. 214-215.

12 Charles Edward Mallet, *A History of the University of Oxford* (London, 1924), Vol. I, p. 392.

13 George Cavendish, *The Life of Cardinal Wolsey* (London and New York, 1885), p. 14.

14 Thomas Wright, *Homes of Other Days* (London and New York, 1871), pp. 373, 384.

15 Dorothy Hartley and Margaret M. Elliott, *Life and Work of the People of England* (New York, 1926), Vol. II, p. 51.

16 Hartley and Elliott, *op. cit.*

CHAPTER V

1 Ethelred L. Taunton, *Thomas Wolsey: Legate and Reformer* (London, 1902), p. 19.

2 A. F. Pollard, *Wolsey* (London, 1929), p. 13, note 5.

3 H. A. Wilson, *University of Oxford* (London, 1899), p. 56.

4 Taunton, *op. cit.,* p. 17.

5 George Cavendish, *The Life of Cardinal Wolsey* (London and New York, 1885), p. 14.

6 Taunton, *op. cit.,* p. 20.

7 George Baskerville, "The Secular Clergy," *Mediaeval England* (a new edition of Barnard, *Companion to English History*). Edited by H.W.C. Davis (London, 1924), p. 412.

8 *Ibid.,* p. 422.

9 Charles Earle Funk, *Thereby Hangs a Tale* (New York, 1950), p. 60.

10 *A Relation or Rather a True Account of the Island of England With Sundry Particulars of the Customes of These People, and of the Royal Revenues Under King Henry VII. About the Year 1500.* Translated from the Italian, with notes, by Charlotte Augusta Sneyd (London, Camden Society, 1847), p. 30.

[11] Arthur P. Stanley, *Historical Memorials of Canterbury* (London, 1885), p. 46.

[12] *Ibid.,* p. 48.

[13] *Ibid.,* p. 88 ff.

[14] *Dictionary of National Biography,* Vol. V, p. 704.

CHAPTER VI

[1] Robert Bell Calton, *Annals and Legends of Calais* (London, 1852), p. 56.

[2] *Ibid.,* p. 55.

[3] T. W. Cameron, "Wolsey's Early Life," *English Historical Review,* Vol. III (1886), p. 469.

[4] S. H. Burke, *Historical Portraits of the Tudor Dynasty* (London, 1893), Vol. I, p. 45.

[5] Garrett Mattingly, *Catherine of Aragon* (Boston, 1941), p. 25.

[6] Frank Arthur Mumby, *The Youth of Henry VIII, A Narrative in Contemporary Letters* (Boston, 1913), p. 9.

[7] *Ibid.*

[8] George G. Coulton, ed., *Life in the Middle Ages* (New York, 1930), Vol. III, pp. 155-164.

[9] Wilhelm Busch, *England Under the Tudors.* Translated under the supervision of the Rev. A. H. Johnson and Alice M. Todd (London, 1895), Vol. I, pp. 236-237.

[10] George Cavendish, *The Life of Cardinal Wolsey* (London and New York, 1885), p. 20 ff.

[11] Ethelred L. Taunton, *Thomas Wolsey: Legate and Reformer* (London, 1902), p. 32, referring to Weaver's *Somerset Incumbents.*

[12] Busch, *op. cit.,* p. 311.

[13] Arthur D. Innes, *England Under the Tudors* (New York, 1926), p. 19.

BOOK II

CHAPTER I

[1] Sebastian Giustiniani, *Four Years at the Court of Henry VIII. Selection of Despatches Written by the Venetian Ambassador, July 12th, 1515, to*

July 26th, 1519. Translated by Rawdon Brown (London, 1854), Vol. I, p. 27.

2 A. F. Pollard, *Henry VIII* (London, 1951), p. 19.

3 *Leviticus* 20:21.

4 S. H. Burke, *Historical Portraits of the Tudor Dynasty* (London, 1893), Vol. I, p. 67.

5 Garrett Mattingly, *Catherine of Aragon* (Boston, 1941), p. 125.

6 Iris Brooke, "Dress," *Life Under the Tudors.* Edited by J. E. Morpurgo (London, 1950), pp. 201-202.

7 A. Hartshorne, "Costume Civil," *Mediaeval England.* Edited by H.W.C. Davis (London, 1924), p. 166.

8 H.A.L. Fisher, *The History of England from the Accession of Henry VII to the Death of Henry VIII* (London, New York and Toronto, 1934), p. 167.

9 Rose Graham, "Monasteries," *Mediaeval England.* Edited by H.W.C. Davis (London, 1924), pp. 373-374.

10 E. L. Cutts, *Parish Priests and Their People in the Middle Ages in England* (London, 1898), p. 268.

11 Edward Geoffrey O'Donoghue, *Bridewell Hospital, Palace, Prison, Schools from the Earliest Times to the Reign of Elizabeth* (London, 1923), p. 37.

12 George Ormerod, *The History of the County Palatine and the City of Cheshire* (London, 1819), Vol. III, p. 332.

13 A. F. Pollard, *Wolsey* (London, 1929), p. 14.

14 *Ibid.,* p. 15.

15 *Ibid.,* p. 16.

16 Fisher, *op. cit.,* p. 164, quoting *Discorsi,* iii, 31.

17 J. D. Mackie, *The Earlier Tudors 1485-1558* (Oxford, 1952), p. 271.

CHAPTER II

1 Francis Godwin, *Annales of England* (London, 1630), p. 29.

2 George Cavendish, *The Life of Cardinal Wolsey* (London and New York, 1885), pp. 24, 25.

3 J. D. Mackie, *The Earlier Tudors 1485-1558* (Oxford, 1952), p. 270.

4 H.A.L. Fisher, *The History of England from the Accession of Henry VII to the Death of Henry VIII* (London, New York and Toronto, 1934), p. 168. See note same page, citing Vergil's *History,* lib. xxvii, 623.

5 A. F. Pollard, *Henry VIII* (London, 1951), p. 140.

334

[6] Garrett Mattingly, *Catherine of Aragon* (Boston, 1941), p. 143.

[7] *Ibid.*

[8] A. F. Pollard, *Wolsey* (London, 1929), p. 17.

[9] Fisher, *op. cit.*, p. 173.

[10] *Ibid.*, p. 174.

[11] *L. & P.*, I, 3355.

[12] Ernest Law, *England's First Great War Minister* (London, 1916), p. 9.

[13] Mattingly, *op. cit.*, p. 151.

[14] *L. & P.*, I, 3555.

[15] *Ibid.*, 3469.

[16] Law, *op. cit.*, p. 19.

[17] *Ibid.*, p. 28.

[18] *Ibid.*, p. 69, citing de Favri, attaché of the Venetian Embassy.

[19] *Ibid.*, p. 68.

[20] *L. & P.*, I, 3820.

[21] *Ibid.*, 3877.

[22] *Ibid.*, 4005.

CHAPTER III

[1] H.A.L. Fisher, *The History of England from the Accession of Henry VII to the Death of Henry VIII* (London, New York and Toronto, 1934), p. 181, citing *Archaeologia*, Vol. XXVI, p. 395.

[2] *Ibid.*

[3] C.W.C. Oman, "The Art of War," *Social England.* Edited by H. D. Traill and J. S. Mann (London, 1903), Vol. III, Section I, p. 94.

[4] Ernest Law, *England's First Great War Minister* (London, 1916), p. 99.

[5] *Ibid.*, pp. 97, 98.

[6] *Ibid.*, p. 207.

[7] Fisher, *op. cit.*, p. 182.

[8] Sir Charles Oman, *The Sixteenth Century* (London, 1936), p. 106.

[9] Law, *op. cit.*, p. 218.

[10] Garrett Mattingly, *Catherine of Aragon* (Boston, 1941), p. 160.

[11] S. H. Burke, *Historical Portraits of the Tudor Dynasty* (London, 1893), Vol. I, p. 119.

[12] Law, *op. cit.*, p. 221.

[13] J. D. Mackie, *The Earlier Tudors 1485-1558* (Oxford, 1952), p. 281.

[14] Mattingly, *op. cit.*, pp. 157-158.

[15] *Original Letters Illustrative of English History, Including Numerous Royal Letters from Autographs in the British Museum.* Edited by Henry

Ellis, Keeper of the Manuscripts in the British Museum (London, 1825), Series I, Vol. I, Letter XXVIII, pp. 78-81.

[16] *Ibid.*, Letter XXIX, pp. 82-84.

[17] *Ibid.*, Letter XXX, pp. 84-85.

[18] *Ibid.*, Letter XXIX, p. 83.

[19] J. S. Brewer, *The Reign of Henry VIII From His Accession to the Death of Wolsey* (London, 1884), Vol. I, p. 30.

[20] James Gairdner, *Henry the Seventh* (London, 1899), p. 165.

[21] For a vivid account of the battle, see Alfred H. Burne, *The Battlefields of England* (London, 1950), p. 156 ff.

[22] Francis Godwin, *Annales of England* (London, 1630), p. 12.

[23] Mackie, *op. cit.*, p. 282.

[24] Frank Arthur Mumby, *The Youth of Henry VIII, A Narrative in Contemporary Letters* (Boston, 1913), p. 219.

CHAPTER IV

[1] Ethelred L. Taunton, *Thomas Wolsey: Legate and Reformer* (London, 1902), p. 38, citing *L. & P.*, I, 4747.

[2] Richard Fiddes, *The Life of Cardinal Wolsey* (London, 1726), p. 40.

[3] *Ibid.*

[4] A. F. Pollard, *Wolsey* (London, 1929), p. 22.

[5] Taunton, *op. cit.*, p. 37, quoting Matthew Paris, *Chronica Majora* (Roll Series), IV, pp. 546-547.

[6] Pollard, *op. cit.*

[7] *Ibid.*, p. 23.

[8] Taunton, *op. cit.*, p. 42, quoting Creighton's *Wolsey*, pp. 34-40.

[9] George Cavendish, *The Life of Cardinal Wolsey* (London and New York, 1885), p. 87.

[10] A. F. Pollard, *Henry VIII* (London, 1951), p. 121.

[11] Garrett Mattingly, *Catherine of Aragon* (Boston, 1941), p. 167.

[12] Pollard, *Wolsey*, p. 32, note 3.

[13] H.A.L. Fisher, *The History of England from the Accession of Henry VII to the Death of Henry VIII* (London, New York and Toronto, 1934), p. 209.

[14] Pollard, *Wolsey*, pp. 34-35.

[15] Fisher, *op. cit.*, p. 209.

[16] Pollard, *Wolsey*, p. 37.

[17] *L. & P.*, II, 2.

[18] Edward Hall, *Hall's Chronicle; Containing the History of England, Dur-*

336

ing the Reign of Henry the Fourth, And the Succeeding Monarchs, To the End of the Reign of Henry the Eighth. In Which are Particularly Described the Manners and Customs of Those Periods. Carefully Collated with the Editions of 1548 and 1550 (London, 1809), p. 579.

[19] Pollard, *Wolsey*, p. 30.
[20] *Ibid.*, pp. 44-45.
[21] *Ibid.*, p. 42.
[22] Fisher, *op. cit.*, p. 195.
[23] David Hume, *The History of England from the Invasion of Julius Caesar to the Revolution of 1688* (London, 1810), p. 494.
[24] S. H. Burke, *Historical Portraits of the Tudor Dynasty* (London, 1893), Vol. I, p. 130.
[25] J. S. Brewer, *The Reign of Henry VIII from His Accession to the Death of Wolsey* (London, 1884), Vol. I, p. 40.
[26] *L. & P.*, II, 209.
[27] *Ibid.*, 224; Brewer, *op. cit.*, p. 90.
[28] *L. & P.*, IV, 227, 229.

CHAPTER V

[1] Sebastian Giustiniani, *Four Years at the Court of Henry VIII* (London, 1854), Vol. I, p. 100 ff.; J. S. Brewer, *The Reign of Henry VIII from His Accession to the Death of Wolsey* (London, 1884), Vol. I, p. 99.
[2] Brewer, *op. cit.*, p. 100.
[3] A. F. Pollard, *Wolsey* (London, 1929), p. 55.
[4] *Ibid.*
[5] Giustiniani, *op. cit.*, p. 128.
[6] Ernest Law, *England's First Great War Minister* (London, 1916), p. 100.
[7] E. L. Cutts, *Scenes and Characters of the Middle Ages* (London, 1930), p. 234.
[8] Pollard, *op. cit.*, p. 56; *L. & P.*, I, 1153; Edward Hall, *Hall's Chronicle* (London, 1809), p. 583.
[9] J. H. Lupton, *Colet* (London, 1887), p. 194.
[10] Frederic Seebohm, *The Oxford Reformers, John Colet, Erasmus and Thomas More* (London, 1887), p. 84.
[11] Lupton, *op. cit.*, p. 197.
[12] *L. & P.*, II, 1315.
[13] H.A.L. Fisher, *The History of England from the Accession of Henry VII to the Death of Henry VIII* (London, New York and Toronto, 1934), p. 213.

[14] Pollard, *op. cit.*, p. 48.
[15] Fisher, *op. cit.*, p. 215.

CHAPTER VI

[1] G. M. Trevelyan, *English Social History* (London, 1942), p. 37.
[2] A. F. Pollard, *Wolsey* (London, 1929), p. 71.
[3] Lucy Toulmin Smith, "Town Life," *Mediaeval England*. Edited by H.W.C. Davis (London, 1924), p. 314.
[4] L. M. Larson, *History of England and the British Commonwealth* (New York, 1924), p. 247.
[5] Pollard, *op. cit.*, p. 96.
[6] George Cavendish, *The Life of Cardinal Wolsey* (London and New York, 1885), p. 39.
[7] J. D. Mackie, *The Earlier Tudors 1485-1558* (Oxford, 1952), p. 296.
[8] Sebastian Giustiniani, *Four Years at the Court of Henry VIII* (London, 1854), Vol. II, p. 315.
[9] *L. & P.*, II, 1552, 1814.
[10] Pollard, *op. cit.*, p. 74.
[11] *Ibid.*, p. 60.
[12] Alice Stopford Green, *Town Life in the Fifteenth Century* (London, 1907), Vol. I, p. 212 ff.
[13] Pollard, *op. cit.*, citing Pollock and Maitland, ii, 436.
[14] *L. & P.*, III, 608.
[15] L. F. Salzman, *England in Tudor Times* (London, 1926), p. 89.
[16] *L. & P.*, III, 1070.
[17] Mackie, *op. cit.*, p. 297, quoting Edward Hall, *Hall's Chronicle* (London, 1809), Vol. I, pp. 227, 585.
[18] Pollard, *op. cit.*, p. 78.
[19] *Ibid.*, p. 77.
[20] A. F. Pollard, *Henry VIII* (London, 1951), p. 88.

CHAPTER VII

[1] Garrett Mattingly, *Catherine of Aragon* (Boston, 1941), pp. 38-39.
[2] A. T. Thomson, *Memoirs of the Court of Henry the Eighth* (London, 1826), Vol. I, p. 312. Various accounts are given of this incident.
[3] J. S. Brewer, *The Reign of Henry VIII from His Accession to the Death of Wolsey* (London, 1884), Vol. I, p. 385.
[4] *Ibid.*

338

⁵ H.A.L. Fisher, *The History of England from the Accession of Henry VII to the Death of Henry VIII* (London, New York and Toronto, 1934), p. 237.

⁶ Thomson, *op. cit.*, p. 316.

⁷ *Ibid.*, pp. 316-317.

⁸ George Lyman Kittredge, *Witchcraft in Old and New England* (Cambridge, 1929), p. 109.

⁹ Brewer, *op. cit.*, p. 238, quoting "A Boke or Counseill Against the Sweate," note 9.

¹⁰ *Ibid.*

¹¹ Francis Bacon, *History of the Reign of King Henry VII.* Edited by J. Rawson Lumby (Cambridge University Press, 1902), pp. 12-13.

¹² David Riseman, *The Story of Medicine in the Middle Ages* (New York, 1935), p. 241.

¹³ Brewer, *op. cit.*, p. 241, citing *L. & P.*, II, 3645.

¹⁴ *Ibid.*, pp. 240-241, citing *L. & P.*, II, 4125.

¹⁵ *Ibid.*, p. 243.

¹⁶ *A Relation or Rather a True Account of the Island of England With Sundry Particulars of the Customes of These People, and of the Royal Revenues Under King Henry VII. About the Year 1500.* Translated from the Italian, with notes, by Charlotte Augusta Sneyd (London, Camden Society, 1847), pp. 20-21.

¹⁷ *Ibid.*, p. 20.

¹⁸ Edward Hall, *Hall's Chronicle* (London, 1809), p. 586 ff. This gives a full account of the riots.

CHAPTER VIII

¹ Ernest Law, *England's First Great War Minister* (London, 1916), p. 33.

² W. C. Richardson, *Tudor Chamber Administration* (Baton Rouge, 1952), pp. 236, 237.

³ Frederick J. Furnivall, ed., *Early English Meals and Manners* (Oxford, 1868), p. 46.

⁴ A. F. Pollard, *Evolution of Parliament* (London, 1926), p. 264.

⁵ Richard Henry Gretton, *The English Middle Class* (London, 1917), p. 112.

⁶ Sir Walter Besant, *London in the Time of the Tudors* (London, 1904), Vol. I, pp. 36, 37.

⁷ G. M. Trevelyan, *English Social History* (London, 1942), p. 117.

⁸ George Ralston, "Country Life," *Mediaeval England.* Edited by H.W.C.

Davis (London, 1924), p. 334.

[9] W. J. Corbett, "Agriculture," *Social England.* Edited by H. D. Traill and J. S. Mann (London, 1903), Vol. III, p. 152.

[10] A. F. Pollard, *Wolsey* (London, 1929), p. 86.

[11] Lord Ernle, *English Farming, Past and Present* (London, 1927), p. 60.

CHAPTER IX

[1] John H. Harvey, "The Building Works and Architects of Cardinal Wolsey," *British Archaeological Association Journal,* Series 3, Vol. VIII (1943), pp. 50-59.

[2] John Heneage Jessee, *London: Its Celebrated Characters and Remarkable Places* (London, 1871), p. 2.

[3] *A Relation or Rather a True Account of the Island of England With Sundry Particulars of the Customes of These People, and of the Royal Revenues Under King Henry VII. About the Year 1500.* Translated from the Italian, with notes, by Charlotte Augusta Sneyd (London, Camden Society, 1847), p. 78, note 41.

[4] Gladys Temperly, *Henry VII* (Boston, 1914), p. 309.

[5] G. M. Trevelyan, *English Social History* (London, 1942), p. 46.

[6] A. F. Pollard, *Henry VIII* (London, 1951), p. 271, citing *L. & P.,* II, 1733.

[7] Paul Van Dyke, *Renascence Portraits* (New York, 1905), pp. 208-209.

[8] *Ibid.,* p. 209.

[9] G. M. Trevelyan, *England in the Age of Wycliffe* (London, 1920), pp. 328-329.

[10] H. S. Bennett, *The Pastons and Their England—Studies in an Age of Transition* (Cambridge, 1932), p. 144.

[11] J. J. Jusserand, *England Wayfaring Life in the Middle Ages (XIVth Century)* (New York, 1925), p. 312.

[12] Trevelyan, *English Social History,* p. 44.

[13] A. Abram, *Social England in the Fifteenth Century* (London, 1909), p. 50.

[14] *L. & P.,* II, 2492.

[15] Sharon F. S. A. Turner, *The History of England* (London, 1823-1826), Vol. IV, p. 571.

[16] James Gairdner, *History of the Life and Reign of Richard the Third* (Cambridge, 1898), p. 163.

[17] Francis Aidan Gasquet, *Henry VIII and the English Monasteries* (London, 1889), p 13.

[18] *Ibid.,* p. 14.

[19] Edward Hall, *Hall's Chronicle* (London, 1809), p. 593.

[20] A. F. Pollard, *Wolsey* (London, 1929), p. 179.

[21] Gasquet, *op. cit.*, p. 15.

[22] Ethelred L. Taunton, *Thomas Wolsey: Legate and Reformer* (London, 1902), p. 73.

[23] *Ibid.*, p. 77.

[24] *Ibid.*, p. 90.

[25] *Ibid.*, p. 91.

[26] Hall, *op. cit.*, p. 657.

[27] Pollard, *op. cit.*, p. 192.

CHAPTER X

[1] E. L. Cutts, *Parish Priests and Their People in the Middle Ages in England* (London, 1898), p. 371.

[2] Edward Hall, *Hall's Chronicle* (London, 1809), p. 691.

[3] Ethelred L. Taunton, *Thomas Wolsey: Legate and Reformer* (London, 1902), p. 87, citing *L. & P.*, IV, 478.

[4] Cutts, *op. cit.*, p. 374.

[5] A. L. Rowse, *Tudor Cornwall, Portrait of a Society* (London, 1941), p. 165.

[6] *Ibid.*, p. 166.

[7] *A Relation or Rather a True Account of the Island of England With Sundry Particulars of the Customes of These People, and of the Royal Revenues Under King Henry VII. About the Year 1500.* Translated from the Italian, with notes, by Charlotte Augusta Sneyd (London, Camden Society, 1847), p. 51.

[8] Rose Graham, "Monasticism," *Mediaeval England*. Edited by H. W. C. Davis (London, 1924), p. 373.

[9] *Italian Relation* (see note 7 above), p. 79, note 41.

[10] Graham, *op. cit.*

[11] Paul Van Dyke, *Renascence Portraits* (New York, 1905), p. 210.

[12] G. M. Trevelyan, *English Social History* (London, 1942), p. 72.

[13] Philip Hughes, *The Reformation in England* (London, 1954), Vol. I, p. 67.

[14] Francis Aidan Gasquet, *Henry VIII and the English Monasteries* (London, 1889), p. 19.

[15] *Ibid.*, p. 20, quoting Hall, *op. cit.*

[16] Hall, *op. cit.*, p. 694.

[17] Richard Fiddes, *The Life of Cardinal Wolsey* (London, 1726), p. 351.

[18] J. S. Brewer, *The Reign of Henry VIII from His Accession to the Death of Wolsey* (London, 1884), Vol. II, p. 394, as quoted in Gasquet, *op. cit.*, p. 22.

[19] A. Abram, *Social England in the Fifteenth Century* (London, 1909), p. 58.

[20] Brewer, *op. cit.*, Vol. I, p. 443.

[21] Ralph Roeder, *The Man of the Renaissance. Four Lawgivers: Savonarola, Machiavelli, Castiglione, Aretino* (New York, 1933), p. 418.

[22] Brewer, *op. cit.*, p. 576.

[23] Taunton, *op. cit.*, p. 144, quoting Bergenroth, *Spanish Calendar*, Vol. II, No. 370.

[24] A. F. Pollard, *Wolsey* (London, 1929), p. 169, and note 3, same page.

CHAPTER XI

[1] Richard Fiddes, *The Life of Cardinal Wolsey* (London, 1726), p. 177.

[2] *Ibid.*, p. 175.

[3] Ethelred L. Taunton, *Thomas Wolsey: Legate and Reformer* (London, 1902), p. 103.

[4] Fiddes, *op. cit.*, p. 168.

[5] *Ibid.*

[6] *Ibid.*, p. 292.

[7] *Ibid.*

[8] Charles W. Boase, *Oxford* (London, 1890), p. 102.

[9] Fiddes, *op. cit.*, p. 172.

[10] George G. Coulton, ed., *Medieval Panorama* (New York, 1944), p. 662.

[11] Frederick J. Furnivall, ed., *Early English Meals and Manners* (Oxford, 1868), p. 13.

[12] A. Abram, *Social England in the Fifteenth Century* (London, 1909), p. 219.

[13] Fiddes, *op. cit.*, p. 202.

[14] Taunton, *op. cit.*, p. 85; *L. & P.*, IV, 15.

[15] Francis Aidan Gasquet, *Henry VIII and the English Monasteries* (London, 1889), p. 17.

[16] A. F. Pollard, *Wolsey* (London, 1929), p. 326.

[17] Fiddes, *op. cit.*, p. 293.

[18] John H. Harvey, "The Building Works and Architects of Cardinal Wolsey," *British Archaeological Association Journal*, Series 3, Vol. VIII (1943), p. 55.

[19] Fiddes, *op. cit.*, p. 287.

[20] John J. Lingard, *The History of England from the First Invasion by the Romans to the Accession of William and Mary in 1688* (London, 1883), Vol. IV, p. 395.

[21] Lewis Einstein, *The Italian Renaissance in England* (New York, 1902), p. 55.

[22] S. H. Burke, *Historical Portraits of the Tudor Dynasty* (London, 1893), Vol. I, p. 231.

[23] T. L. Jarman, "Education," *Life Under the Tudors*. Edited by J. E. Morpurgo (London, 1950), p. 79.

[24] Frederic Seebohm, *The Oxford Reformers, John Colet, Erasmus and Thomas More* (London, 1887), p. 120.

[25] *Ibid.*, p. 130.

[26] Caesar Caine, "Cardinal Wolsey's College, Ipswich," *British Archaeological Association Journal,* New Series 20 (1914), pp. 91-106 and 225-241.

[27] *Ibid.*, p. 231; Foster Watson, *The English Grammar Schools to 1660* (Cambridge, 1906), p. 16 ff.

[28] T. Corcoran, "Thomas Cardinal Wolsey, Educator," *Studies,* Vol. XX (1931), pp. 30-33.

[29] Fiddes, *op. cit.*, Collections, pp. 103-104.

CHAPTER XII

[1] Ernest Law, *The History of Hampton Court Palace in Tudor Times* (London, 1885), pp. 23-24.

[2] J. A. Gotch, "Domestic Architecture," *Mediaeval England*. Edited by H. W. C. Davis (London, 1924), p. 81.

[3] James Lees-Milne, *Tudor Renaissance* (London, 1951), p. 44.

[4] Law, *op. cit.*, p. 16.

[5] *Ibid.*, p. 22.

[6] Edward Geoffrey O'Donoghue, *Bridewell Hospital, Palace, Prison, Schools from the Earliest Times to the Reign of Elizabeth* (London, 1923), p. 38.

[7] Sebastian Giustiniani, *Four Years at the Court of Henry VIII* (London, 1854), Vol. II, p. 314.

[8] A. F. Pollard, *Wolsey* (London, 1929), note p. 318.

[9] Law, *op. cit.*, p. 72.

[10] *Ibid.*, p. 74.

[11] Gotch, *op. cit.*, pp. 80-81.

[12] S. H. Burke, *Historical Portraits of the Tudor Dynasty* (London, 1893), p. 230.

[13] Giustiniani, *op. cit.*, p. 315.

[14] Law, *op. cit.*, p. 84.

[15] H. D. Traill and J. S. Mann, eds., *Social England* (London, 1903), Vol. III, p. 147.

[16] *L. & P.*, II, 4024.
[17] George Cavendish, *The Life of Cardinal Wolsey* (London and New York, 1885), p. 41 ff.

CHAPTER XIII

[1] George Cavendish, *The Life of Cardinal Wolsey* (London and New York, 1885), p. 41.
[2] Harold Lamb, *The March of Muscovy* (New York, 1948), p. 96.
[3] James A. Williamson, *Maritime Enterprise 1485-1558* (Oxford, 1913), p. 21; *An Historical Geography of England Before A.D. 1800.* Edited by H. C. Darby (Cambridge, 1936).
[4] Williamson, *op. cit.*
[5] James A. Williamson, *Voyages of the Cabots* (London, 1929), p. 97.
[6] Sebastian Giustiniani, *Four Years at the Court of Henry VIII* (London, 1854), Vol. I, p. 90.
[7] J. S. Brewer, *The Reign of Henry VIII from His Accession to the Death of Wolsey* (London, 1884), Vol. II, p. 99.
[8] Brewer, *op. cit.*, Vol. I, p. 106 ff. Quoted in full.
[9] Giustiniani, *op. cit.*, pp. 156-157.
[10] *L. & P.*, II, 1877.
[11] Giustiniani, *op. cit.*, p. 160, note 1.
[12] Brewer, *op. cit.*, Vol. I, p. 124 ff.
[13] *L. & P.*, II, 2930.
[14] *Ibid.*, 2017.
[15] Giustiniani, *op. cit.*, Vol. II, p. 16.
[16] *Ibid.*, p. 219.
[17] Richard Fiddes, *The Life of Cardinal Wolsey* (London, 1726), p. 207.
[18] Giustiniani, *op. cit.*, p. 219.
[19] *L. & P.*, 4540.

CHAPTER XIV

[1] Karl Brandi, *The Emperor Charles V: The Growth and Destiny of a Man and a World-Empire.* Translated from the German by C. V. Wedgwood (New York, 1939), p. 60.
[2] *Ibid.*, p. 61.
[3] David Hume, *The History of England from the Invasion of Julius Caesar to the Revolution of 1688* (London, 1810), p. 500.

344

[4] *Ibid.*, p. 501.

[5] Richard Fiddes, *The Life of Cardinal Wolsey* (London, 1726), p. 218.

[6] Edward Hall, *Hall's Chronicle* (London, 1809), p. 601.

[7] Sharon F. S. A. Turner, *The History of England* (London, 1823-1826), Vol. IV, p. 174.

[8] Garrett Mattingly, *Catherine of Aragon* (Boston, 1941), p. 207.

[9] Francis Godwin, *Annales of England* (London, 1630), p. 39.

[10] Mattingly, *op. cit.*, p. 211.

[11] James Lees-Milne, *Tudor Renaissance* (London, 1951), p. 24.

[12] *Rutland Papers: Original Documents of the Courts and Times of Henry VII and Henry VIII Selected from the Archives of the Duke of Rutland*, edited by Will. Jordan (London, Camden Society, 1842), pp. 28-49.

[13] J. S. Brewer, *The Reign of Henry VIII from His Accession to the Death of Wolsey* (London, 1884), Vol. I, p. 351. For further details on the meeting of Henry and Francis and Wolsey's management of it, see Edward Hall, *Hall's Chronicle* (London, 1809), p. 601 ff.

[14] Brewer, *op. cit.*, p. 354.

[15] Hume, *op. cit.*, p. 502.

[16] *Ibid.*

[17] Mattingly, *op. cit.*, p. 213.

[18] S. H. Burke, *Historical Portraits of the Tudor Dynasty* (London, 1893), Vol. I, p. 113.